An Open Path

An Open Path

Christian Missionaries 1515–1914

JACK BEECHING

Hutchinson of London

"I go back to Africa to make an open path
for commerce and Christianity."

Dr David Livingstone, 1858.

Hutchinson & Co. (Publishers) Ltd
3 Fitzroy Square, London W1P 6JD

London Melbourne Sydney Auckland
Wellington Johannesburg and agencies
throughout the world

First published 1979

© Jack Beeching 1979

Set in Monotype Bembo

Printed in Great Britain by The Anchor Press Ltd
and bound by Wm Brendon & Son Ltd
both of Tiptree, Essex

British Library CIP data

Beeching, Jack
  An open path
  1. Missions – History
  I. Title
  266'.009'03   BV2120

ISBN 0 09 140080 5

Contents

Maps

Introduction

In the long stretch of time between 1492, when Columbus first set foot in the New World, and 1914, when war broke out among those European powers which had managed meanwhile to divide up most of the other continents between them, when merchant or colonizer went abroad a missionary almost always followed.

Earliest were the Roman Catholics. By keeping company first with the Spanish conquistadores, later with colonizers from France, the Catholic church managed to leave a rather large mark on the world. Most of Latin America is Catholic; some of Africa. But the Protestants soon made up for lost time: by 1910, at a world conference of Protestant missionary societies mainly from northern Europe and North America, they could number their converts in millions.

In 1910 the European empires which had given this missionary movement its great opportunity looked as if they were there to stay. But two successive world wars cracked them up. With new nation-states taking the place of old colonies, might not Christian missions, and the native churches they had fostered, soon fade away into insignificance?

What in fact has happened since, as we can see from our daily papers, is so complex as to be puzzling. In many parts of the world, the missionaries, or those they once converted, have become people to reckon with. Respectable Church of England clergymen have been deported from South Africa. In Uganda, not long ago, an Anglican archbishop was murdered. In Latin America, Jesuits peaceably at their pastoral work have been shot down by assassination squads. In Rhodesia, an Irish bishop was sent to prison for succouring black guerrillas and, not long after, in the same tract of country, other similar guerrillas hacked other missionaries and their families brutally to death. Though the missionaries themselves are occasionally expelled from the new states with new names which, the day before yesterday, were colonies, native Christian churches remain there, and often show great vitality. The old joke stereotype of a missionary as a fatuous man in a dog-collar, being boiled alive in a cannibal's cauldron, evidently needs a careful second look.

Though conquistador, trader and colonizer usually went overseas in each other's company – for how could the missionary travel, except in the merchant's ship? – yet their motives were never quite the same. Any particular merchant, soldier or emigrant might try conscientiously to live up to his religious belief, just as an individual missionary might well yield to the temptation to enrich himself. But, by and large, the purpose of their lives was contradictory.

The merchant had gone abroad to make his pile, and bring it safe home. His counterpart, the man who meant to settle, had first to get land into his possession, and then, in any way possible, find others than himself to do the hard work of raising a crop. Wind-power had blown along the sailing ship which landed him, but before the tractor arrived on the farm, almost the only source of energy was muscle-power. So colonizing led straight on to seizures of land, often to forced labour, sometimes to slave labour. Now the missionary would be hard-pressed to find in the Christian gospels any proposition sanctifying slave labour.

A colony soon became a market. The people hitherto living there would give up wearing their furs or their homespun. They would barter whatever they could lay their hands on for blankets or cotton goods. They learned to use metal tools, and to hunt with firearms. They soon enough discovered how to sozzle themselves with trade spirits. Thus their traditional society began to break up. They became by slow degrees immersed in a money economy. Against their will they entered a world market – an economic system which, at the end of the account, was dominated by far-off countries which were often bitter rivals – countries which had discovered how to set going an industrial system, and establish a world market based on free enterprise. By 1914, this market structure had absorbed and united almost the whole of our globe.

But all this time, the best of the missionaries – with the worst, in this book, we have not a great deal to do – had ideas and intentions quite distinct from those of making a pile or acquiring an estate. What they stood for may not have sounded very realistic, and they may not always have practised what they preached, but the religion they had come out to advocate was in many ways at odds with the economic and social changes happening around them.

If a missionary believed what he said, how could he help but come into collision with a man who traded on native ignorance, so as to buy cheap and sell dear, or who used fraud or violence to secure himself land and labour? Merchant and colonist might patronize the missionary, might find him useful at times and even pay lip-service to his creed, but, in the long run, they were competitors. The missionary gave expression – sometimes an imperfect and lopsided expression – to a system of thought which, having emerged from slave society and survived the collapse of feudalism, could never be totally identified with emergent capitalism or any other transitory economic system. Whatever new turn economic and political developments may take, it now seems probable that the Christian religion, modified perhaps but not essentially altered, is likely to withstand any foreseeable radical social change, and survive. The surprising persistence of churches in Communist countries is the proof.

Missionaries who took their vocation seriously had to begin by persuading their hearers of the truth of two propositions. The first was that any human being whatever, whether labourer, pauper, prostitute, savage or even slave, was a person of unique value, had a soul. The second was that any relationship based on sexual pleasure which degraded the less willing partner to the status of an object was inhuman. The purpose of sex (in their view) was the procreation of living creatures with uniquely valuable souls. Therefore, sexual relations should be based upon an unbreakable partnership, in which parenthood was responsible and sex sacramental.

Love in the missionary position – that is to say, in plain language, recommending to men brought up in other sexual habits that they should make love, as St Jerome indicated, on the prayer-bones, as a symbol that they accepted lifelong marriage and responsible fatherhood – this for a long time was an elbow-nudging, smoking-room joke, a snigger at the missionaries' expense. Few of us, nowadays, are likely to agree heart and soul with the missionaries' view of matrimony. Their ideas sound old-fashioned, even discredited – though some native peoples who heard them for the first time seem to have found them emancipating. And of course the missionaries taught much else – from ploughing and printing to philosophy, from first-aid to brotherly love. But the hard fact, soon recognized, was that no church could hope to strike root in a foreign land until the monogamous family – the old-fashioned Christian family – could be implanted there. Once that had been brought about, the church was virtually ineradicable. To change sexual behaviour was, in this sense, at the heart of the missionaries' problem.

Sometimes, as we shall see – on Tahiti, for example – a mission took grotesque forms, the missionaries corrupting happy, naked islanders, and imposing on them the repressiveness which the acquisitive middle class of their day took for granted, as a preliminary to covering their guilty nakedness with three yards of imported cotton goods. But even on Tahiti – and missionary behaviour was seldom worse anywhere – these spoilsports were also strenuous in putting down polygamy, ritual orgy, human sacrifice and ritual cannibalism – authentic pleasures, no doubt, all of them, so long as you were not the victim, the pleasure-object. Even at their worst, there was a strange ambiguity in what they did – they were never simply and solely the moral agents of the commercial country which had sent them out. At their best, they were good men by anybody's standards.

Except at the very beginning, a missionary landing in a foreign country usually found himself in a society which already was coming apart with guilt and anxiety, as the clay pot clashed with the iron pot – as a money economy continued to disintegrate the native peoples' own subsistence economy. And what could he do about it?

Sometimes the best missionaries tried to protect their flock inside an artificially created utopia with its own way of life. When this was not possible they looked for ways – sometimes imaginative ways – to resolve the torments of anxiety by organizing their listeners' consciousness anew, in terms of forgiveness, loving-kindness, and respect for the individual. That is to say, they tried to implant a consciousness which, whether they knew it or not, would be at odds with the profounder causes of their congregation's suffering, in the long run.

But, in the short run, does not the religious cast of mind which they encouraged also imply submission to established authority, passive acceptance of oppression? Did the missionaries really intend to do more than produce willing servants, happy slaves?

Here is the central paradox. A family in which children feel secure, so that they look on their parents as human equals, is as all observers well know a place where the passion for justice makes itself felt very soon – a passion which may have to be unlearnt later, in school, factory and barracks. The missionaries introduced into other lands a family structure of this type. They articulated the passion for justice to which it inevitably gives rise, by their gospel accounts of a man chaste, voluntarily poor, who drove the money-changers out of the temple, repudiated the sword, and chose for himself the death inflicted on a rebel slave. The missionaries at work in the great empires which expanded across the world from 1492 to 1914 may not usually have aimed at this outcome, but despite themselves they encouraged an attitude of mind which, as we can see from our newspapers, might in due course become a matrix for social as well as personal liberation.

The individual has a conscience; a state apparatus has not. Christian belief, as we can by now be sure, helps a man or woman patiently to resist the arbitrary and amoral policies of the centralized state. Technology provides the modern state – however small and new – with inordinate means of manipulating the people who have no choice but to live inside its frontiers. When the excesses of state authority become abhorrent – in Paraguay, in Lithuania, in Uganda – then everyday examples of Christian behaviour nourish a countervailing power.

Missionaries of course were men of their own time, as we are of ours, and imbued, therefore, almost unawares with contemporary notions which they never stopped to question. Often they accepted, not very critically, the midde-class commonsense of their day, with its money-worshipping overtones. The declared intention of their work may not have been to liberate, though the outcome, as we shall see, often went that way despite them. But they too had to face an excruciating conflict in their everyday lives – the contradiction between the gospel they preached, and the harsh facts of life, cheek by jowl with settler and trader.

That is what this book, as a narrative essay in human behaviour, tries to portray – the adventure, the heroism, the shame of their lives, and even the funny side.

I All the Peoples of the World

'We must now see if there is such a person as a slave by nature, and whether it is good and just for some people to be slaves or not.' *Aristotle*

'God did not intend that his rational creature, who was made in his image, should have dominion except over irrational creation, not man over man but man over beast.' *St Augustine*

'We desire to say that the Spanish custom is not to our liking, for everyone to take care of himself, instead of helping one another in their daily toil.' *Guaraní of the San Luis Reduction, to the governor of Buenos Aires, 1768, petitioning the return of the Jesuits*

August in the old Spanish city of Valladolid is oppressively hot. On this August day in 1550, fourteen dignified men sat sweltering in their robes, on a dais across a great hall. They were counsellors, appointed to advise the Emperor Charles V and come to hear evidence of great importance. It concerned America, and the arguments which echoed round that great hall still resonate in our minds today.

The enormous empire of Charles V stretched from Austria to Spain, from California to Patagonia. The Emperor himself, a man of tender conscience, was uneasy that when Spanish soldiers opened up unexplored tracts of the New World, the native peoples found living there might be abused. In certain ways, Charles V had the old-fashioned outlook of a crusader, and, as he saw it, the only moral justification of conquest was that a defeated people might thereby be led to adopt the religion of their conquerors.

But should they be first defeated, even enslaved, and then more

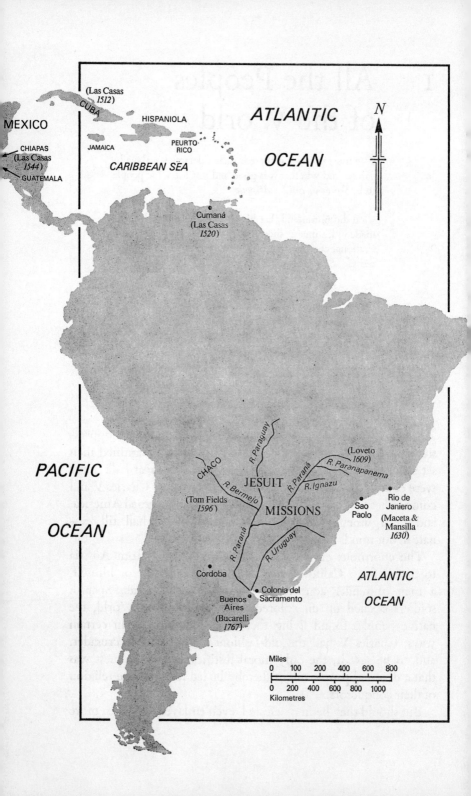

N

(Las Casas
1512)
CUBA

MEXICO

HISPANIOLA

ATLANTIC

CHIAPAS
(Las Casas
1544)

JAMAICA

PEURTO
RICO

OCEAN

GUATEMALA

CARIBBEAN SEA

Cumaná
(Las Casas
1520)

PACIFIC

CHACO

R. Paraguay

(Loveto
1609)

R. Paranapanema

R. Paraná

JESUIT

R. Bermejo

R. Ignazu

OCEAN

(Tom Fields
1596)

MISSIONS

Sao
Paolo

Rio de
Janiero
(Maceta &
Mansilla
1630)

R. Paraná

Cordoba

R. Uruguay

ATLANTIC

Colonia del
Sacramento

OCEAN

Buenos
Aires
(Bucarelli
1767)

Miles
0   100   200   400   600   800

0   200   400   600   800   1000
Kilometres

or less forcibly converted? Or should they be left in possession of their lives and property, and have Christian preachers come to convince them?

Charles V had come around to thinking that what Pope Paul III had laid down, thirteen years before, in his *Sublimis Deus*, might be politically wise as well as humane. American Indians, the papal bull had said, must never be treated as 'dumb brutes for our service' for they, too, were part of mankind, 'by no means to be deprived of their liberty, or the possession of their property, even though they should be outside the faith, nor should they in any way be enslaved'.

By 1550, the followers of Martin Luther and John Calvin were a growing threat to both Pope and Emperor. But the Protestants so far had hardly got a footing in the New World, except as cod fishermen off Newfoundland. Now suppose that because of enlightened missionary work a large new Catholic church, loyal to the Pope, could somehow be created among those millions of American Indians who were now subjects of the Emperor, as a counterpoise to the Protestant gains in Europe?

The problem before the Council of Fourteen was therefore not only one of moral principle, but of practical politics. The precise and subtle question put to them had been this: 'Is it lawful for the king of Spain to wage war on the Indians before preaching the faith to them, in order to subject them to his rule, so that afterwards they may more easily be instructed in the faith?' The question was not altogether religious or political, but arose also out of a harsh economic reality. Over there, in the virgin wilderness of America, enormous pioneering work was waiting to be done. Land must be ploughed and crops harvested before the roads and cities, the churches and universities of a new, transatlantic Spanish civilization could be implanted. And who was to do all this work, except the conquered Indians? It was no secret that in putting them to forced labour, the conquistadores had already worked thousands of Indians to death.

The Council of Fourteen, in their robes on their dais, must by this time have been almost out of their minds with boredom. They had been listening for the past five days to the voice of one speaker – a seventy-six-year-old Dominican in a shabby black gown. The old man was bishop of Chiapas, a diocese no one had ever heard of, in the wild country wedged between Mexico and Guatemala. He was a tough, bald-headed old man, with a big nose and a sensitive, friendly mouth, but furiously in earnest, nailing down each separate point in his endless speech with a long theological quotation. The Council of Fourteen knew his arguments already. They had been hearing them for years.

Aware their minds might have been wandering, the Council on the fifth day of the harangue asked one of their number, a jurist called Domingo de Soto, to oblige them by summing up briefly what the old man had been saying. 'More than was necessary,' answered de Soto. Yet the Council of Fourteen had treated this bald-headed, long-winded old bishop with every show of respect. He was a famous man and, what was more, he had the ear of the Emperor. He was called Bartolomé de las Casas, and few men living knew more about untamed America.

In the past thirty years, almost every legal protection that Spain had devised for the Indian could be traced back to Las Casas. As a young student from Salamanca University, he had crossed the Atlantic very early, probably in 1504, with Columbus. He was the first Christian priest ever to be ordained in America and, as a priest, he had taken part in Diego Velasquez's conquest of Cuba in 1512. For his services he was rewarded afterwards, like the other conquistadores, with a grant of land, and Indians to work it for him.

A few months had been enough to show Las Casas the horrors of this system. The Carib Indians on Cuba were literally worked to death. Those who resisted were tormented into the grave, in ingenious and spectacular ways ('branded with hot irons, roasted, dismembered, mangled, stabbed, whipped, racked, beheaded in sport, drowned, dashed against the rocks, famished, devoured by mastiffs'), and these evil memories haunted Las Casas for the rest of his life. By 1514 he had come to the firm conclusion that 'everything done to the Indians thus far was unjust and tyrannical'.

His first proposal for mending matters, offered in 1517, was a disaster. Las Casas suggested that settlers farming on Hispaniola might be able to free their Indians from forced labour if they were granted a royal licence to import a dozen black slaves apiece. The Genoese merchants who controlled much of Spain's trade with her new possessions were already becoming aware of the large profits to be made in the African slave trade. The idea was in the air, and here was a pioneer priest giving it sanction.

But it did not take Las Casas long to see – and eventually, in his *Historia de las Indias*, to admit in public – that he had made a fool of himself. Henceforth he opposed both black and Indian slavery, 'and for the same reason'. His next experiment, though better thought out, was not much of a practical success, either.

Spaniards reaching the New World had gone there to be gentlemen. 'Not even the rudest peasant', Las Casas declared, 'would lift his hand.' But suppose a group of Spanish farmers and craftsmen, of a different cast of mind, were to volunteer for a colony where, under the guidance of a priest, they would do all the necessary hard work themselves? What better way of demonstrating to the Indians the virtues of civilization than providing them with a good example? In 1520, Las Casas set up his community of hard-working pioneers at Cumaná, on the Venezuelan coast. But the Indians there had been provoked by the brutality of other Spaniards, raiding ashore from the Caribbean islands. They came down and massacred the settlers.

Baffled, Las Casas retreated for eight years to a monastery in Santo Domingo. Long reflection, and discussion with the Dominicans there, clinched his conviction that American Indians were like people anywhere else in the world, and therefore – as he declared at Valladolid – might be 'persuaded and brought to a good order and way of life, and made domestic, mild and tractable, provided the method that is proper and natural to men is used; namely, love, gentleness and kindness'.

Las Casas's next mission, to the still warlike Indians of Guatemala and Nicaragua, had worked out better. The Indians of Guatemala have both a poetic tradition and a national epic: the *Popul Vuh*. Las Casas mastered their difficult native tongues, and wrote couplets in verse to explain to them Christian doctrine;

he wedded their ancient rites and customs to church festivals. In 1539, he went back to Spain, and there helped draft the New Laws of the Indies.

As early as 1512, the Laws of Burgos had laid down that 'No one may beat or whip or call an Indian a dog, or any other name, unless it is his proper name'. In 1523, the Spanish Cortes ordered that all grants of Indian forced labour – *encomiendas* – so far made to Spanish settlers in the New World should be revoked, and no more such concessions granted. If properly enforced, the New Laws of the Indies, passed in 1542, would have extinguished Indian slavery entirely within one generation, and introduced work for wages. But when Blasco Nuñez de Vela tried applying the New Laws in Peru, the Spanish settlers there rose in armed insurrection. They killed the royal representative, and carried his head around dangling from a string; in 1547, some of the New Laws were revoked.

Of course, any law passed in Spain to put down forced labour would be evaded, thousands of miles away, in Spanish America: how could it be otherwise? As bishop in Chiapas, Bartolomé de las Casas had decided to refuse absolution to settlers who did not obey the New Laws. In his last six months there, he found himself excommunicating almost every member of his flock. But even if evil practices could not be ended by legislation, or by the authority over men's minds of the church, then at the very least, so this tough and obstinate old priest had decided, let it be made clear to the Council of Fourteen that the maltreatment of Indians was wrongful, even if it took five days.

The essential debate in that hot, ornate room in Valladolid in 1550 was about principle: how could conquests, discoveries and settlements be made to accord with justice and reason? There was scope for improvement. On 12 March 1550, only five months before the Council of Fourteen began to sit, Pedro de Valdivia, founder of the city of Santiago in Chile, had written to the Emperor to say he had taken two hundred prisoners. 'I had sent often to summon them and bid them come in peace,' he wrote, 'telling them to what end your Majesty had sent me to this land, and they had not done as I bade them.' So, said Valdivia ingenuously, he 'had their hands and noses cut off, for their contumacy'.

Las Casas had tried to hammer home the lesson he believed his life's work had taught him: 'The only justification for the presence of Spaniards in the New World is the Christianization of the Indians by patient, peaceful means alone.' Las Casas argued that when Indians were no real threat, only preachers, not soldiers, should be sent to win them over. In more dangerous places, he declared, build forts – and conquer the hearts of the untamed peoples on the far side of your frontier by peace, good example, and love.

The hard-headed man put up to argue against him at Valladolid was a scholar and humanist called Juan Ginés de Sepúlveda, a friend of Erasmus. Sepúlveda was sixty, but tried to look younger by wearing his hair down in a fringe over his bald forehead, and brushing a dandified parting into his square beard. Those who disliked Sepúlveda said that he was 'dominated by the desire to increase his own property' and that he 'did nothing in his life except sell, rent and accumulate ecclesiastical benefices'. Here, before the royal council, as everyone was well aware, he spoke on behalf of the great Mexican landowners. He was more adroit than the old bishop, and got all his points across in three hours. The arguments he intended to use for contradicting Las Casas he had already rehearsed in his *Demócrates*, a manuscript which had been circulating all that year, and from *Demócrates* we may reconstruct his speech.

In the dying days of the Roman Empire in the west, St Augustine had once pointed out that a slave, by the very circumstances of his everyday life, had chances denied to others for practising the virtues of obedience, forgiveness, humility, modesty and patience. There may have been Christian slaves here and there who were cheered up by this argument, but no one since has ever thought it more than the attempt of a theologian in a collapsing society to make the best of a bad job. Sepúlveda knew he would have difficulty changing the Council's mind either theologically or in any other way on the question of forced labour, especially since he knew that the Emperor detested it, so he went to work, instead, at trying to demolish Las Casas's central contention that 'all peoples of the world are men' – that, in God's view, all humans are equal.

Sepúlveda had made a name for himself, two years before, by the elegant Latin translation he published in Paris of Aristotle's *Politics*. Living at a time when all the hard work was done by slaves, the famous Greek philosopher had tried to justify an economic system which, in his own day, could not be done away with, by claiming that some men, of their very nature, are set aside as slaves, to be made use of by superior men, born to be their masters. On this useful philosophical assertion, rather than on Augustine's half-hearted excuse for slavery, Sepúlveda based his argument: the Spaniards were the natural superiors of the Indians, and entitled to act accordingly.

American Indians according to Sepúlveda, were born inferior, 'as children are to adults, as women are to men'. Inferior because sunk in sin; did not the Caribs practise sexual abominations – were they not sodomites? (So far as we know, they were not.) Against sinners and idolaters, a war would always be justified. They were precisely the creatures described by Aristotle – put into the world to work for other men better than themselves. What had the Indians known about iron, or horses, or wheat, until the Spaniards arrived? They must first be crushed by force; conversion could come later.

But suppose a case when Indians yielded of their own accord, without a fight, and then became Christians of their own free will? Even then, argued Sepúlveda, since their inferiority was natural to them, they must never be allowed the same rights as Spaniards. So sinful were the Indians, indeed, that they could not even claim the right to defend themselves in a just war, any more, added Sepúlveda in illustration, than could the Jews, 'whose extermination God desired because of their crimes and idolatries'.

And if there happened to be some individual Spanish soldier whose conscience might trouble him? He too, declared Sepúlveda, had no right either to question the justice of his orders or to oppose any war to which his superiors might send him off to fight. Sepúlveda failed to sway the Council, but his friends in Mexico were so pleased with his effort that they sent him clothes and jewels worth two hundred silver pesos, 'to encourage him in the future'.

His arguments, with a word changed here and there, may still occasionally be overheard. The debate between Las Casas and Sepúlveda still goes on. For much of the twentieth century, it has lain at the heart of world politics, and led to world war.

The Emperor's fourteen advisers were expected to hand in written decisions, but their answers took an uncommonly long time in arriving – one cautious counsellor took seven years. The saintly but impractical Las Casas might be highly regarded at court, but he was an old man – and the Emperor, who admired him, was already talking of quitting the throne and retiring to a monastery.

In any event, the Council of Fourteen, men of sense and experience as they were, must have known they were being asked to decide the impossible. The heavy work in Spanish America had to be done – by the Indians, of course, and how else but under compulsion? Yet no one but a paid advocate could seriously claim that using Indians as forced labour was the best way of saving their souls. And no one who knew Spanish America could long pretend that forced labour – under some ingenious pretext or other – would ever become a thing of the past. All over the world for the next four centuries, men who called themselves Christian were torn this way and that, trying to find some sort of true answer to the questions once posed to the Emperor's Council of Fourteen.

In 1596, five Jesuit missionaries, one of them an Englishman called Tom Fields, had set to work in Paraguay, in South America, up the river Bermejo, in a difficult terrain amid the swamps and cane thickets of the Chaco. They made very little headway, because the nearest landowners, in what is now called Argentina, were on the look-out for Indians to work for them on the land. The missionaries found, to their disgust, that they were expected to wink at the recruitment, as forced labour, of the very Indians they had been sent to convert.

The Emperor Charles V's grandson, King Philip III, was by

this time King of Spain, and his confessor in Madrid was a
Jesuit, so what had been happening in Paraguay soon reached
the royal ears. Philip was a conscientious if not a very energetic
king. On 18 December 1605, Don Hernandarias de Saavedra,
the governor of Paraguay, was given a sharp reminder that 'even
if he could conquer the Indians on the Paraná by force of arms
he must not do so, but must gain them over solely by the sermons
and instructions of the religious'.

The principles laid down by Las Casas still had some effect
at court, and the Jesuits in Paraguay, thanks to their influence
over the king, were in consequence given an extraordinary
opportunity. Philip ordered that no converted Indian could be
made a serf. He must, instead, be exempted from taxation for
ten years. Two years later, the Jesuits were given royal letters-
patent for the conversion of all the Indians in Paraguay – a larger
territory than the present-day republic, overlapping into modern
Argentina and Brazil. And on 6 March 1609 came a royal decree
which, like so many others, might have been epoch-making
could it only have been given full effect. From now on, 'the
Indian should be as free as the Spaniard'.

But how, in the Spanish-American wilderness, might such
equality be made real?

The Indians with whom the Jesuits had to deal spoke Guaraní.
They were olive-coloured, thick-set, smooth-skinned and
communicated in a difficult language in which there were numbers only up to four. Guaraní often went naked, adorning
themselves by inserting an ornament in a slit in the upper lip.
They usually lived off corn and sweet potatoes, but sometimes killed and ate the prisoners they took in war.

The Jesuits made an effort to learn Guaraní, and once they had
won the Indians' confidence, they found them biddable and
quick to learn; even ready to forswear their cannibalism if beef
were provided instead. The Guaraní had already given up hunting
as their means of livelihood and taken to agriculture, so the
Jesuits found it not too difficult to bring them together into larger
villages, called reductions, since life in a community, as they saw
it, was the beginning of civilized behaviour. A Guaraní who
resented going to live in one of the Jesuit villages would have

two not very cheerful alternatives: unpaid labour, under the lash, on some plantation, or a free but grim existence as a hunter, in the impenetrable swamps of the Chaco. So most of them chose the reductions.

By 1609 the first Jesuit settlement, called Loreto, had come into being on the banks of the Paranapanema river. Five years later, 119 Jesuits were busily at work in the Paraguay mission, and by 1630 the Society had upwards of 40,000 Indians living in reductions along the banks of the great rivers Paraná and Paraguay and their tributaries.

São Paulo, in Portuguese-speaking Brazil, was the homeland of the *mamelucos* – desperadoes who lived by slave-raiding into the interior and selling their captives to the owners of sugar plantations. The Guaraní of Paraguay were a valuable part of the *mamelucos'* stock-in-trade, and they wanted no priests interfering.

Some of the reductions – Loreto and eleven others – were less than 300 miles from São Paulo. To the slave-raiders those mission villages were an ever-present temptation. The King of Spain's rule over Portuguese-speaking Brazil was weakening. The plantation-owners of São Paulo would offer high prices for hands to cut their sugar-cane. Thus, by defying the royal decrees which hitherto had given some protection to the Indians, the *mamelucos* could put a patriotic gloss on their dirty trade. Raids for slave labour on the Jesuit reductions would flout the King of Spain, help the sugar trade, and assert Brazilian authority on a part of the frontier where the Jesuits might be presented to the outside world as royalist interlopers.

In 1629, a large party of *mamelucos* from São Paulo moved upcountry along the banks of the Paranapanema. They carried muskets and lances, and were helped by Indian mercenaries armed with poison blow-pipes. After twenty years of living peaceably and prosperously in their villages, the Christian Indians were defenceless. By 1630, the *mamelucos* had accounted for over 30,000 of them, either killed or made slaves. In labour-hungry São Paulo it was a slave bonanza.

For the *mamelucos*, Sunday, when all the Indians of a village had come in to church, was a favourite time to attack. As a clever trick, they would sometimes dress up as Jesuits, so that the

Guaraní began confusing those who taught and helped them with those who killed and enslaved. The word spread among them that the Jesuits, too, were in the plot.

But most of these doubts vanished from the minds of the Guaraní after 1630, when the *mamelucos* herded 15,000 Indians back in chains to São Paulo. Instead of saving their own skins, as they might well have done, Fathers Maceta and Mansilla followed closely the procession of captives, down to São Paulo. Pistols were fired over their heads, to scare them, they were jabbed at with lances, yet they hung on obstinately, carrying the chains of the weakest Guaraní, confessing those near death. At other times the wild men from São Paulo had shown no compunction about killing a priest or two, but these sublimely persistent missionaries somehow kept them in awe.

When Maceta and Mansilla reached São Paulo, and sharply reminded the authorities there of the privileges in respect of the Guaraní Indians granted to their order by the king, they got no satisfaction. Europe had a sweet tooth; its taste for that delicious novelty, cane sugar, was insatiable, and when it is ripe, the cane must be cut.

The two Jesuits went further up the coast, to the royal council-general in Rio, but by now Brazil was tugging away from Spanish overlordship, and the royal governor, Don Diego Luís Oliviera, had almost no control over his rowdy Portuguese plantation-owners. As for the church – so the reckless Brazilians told the King of Spain's captain-general in São Paulo – if it meant parting with their slaves, they would rather be de-baptized.

In 1631, only three reductions were still intact along the river Paranapanema. For the past four years, the Jesuits in Paraguay had been led by Antonio Ruiz de Montoya, who had served in the mission for thirty years. When word arrived that the *mamelucos* were again on the march, Montoya called a conference. The Jesuits decided to cut their losses, abandoning San Ignacio and Loreto, which were as yet untouched – churches and houses, fields, flocks and herds, the work of twenty-two years – and move their threatened people inland, to a safer home.

From the destroyed reductions about one in ten had survived. About 12,000 Indians were willing to move off, rather than face the *mamelucos* again. For the first leg of their dangerous journey downriver, Father Montoya embarked them on 700 boats and rafts. Hardly had they left when in marched the slavers – to make bonfires of the splendid churches, and turn the row of cells where the priests had lived into a brothel. Indian women falling into the *mamelucos'* hands were closely cross-questioned: they wanted word of some scandal which might discredit the Jesuits with the world outside, but they had no such luck.

Disguising himself as an Indian, Montoya went off ahead, to spy out the land, and found his escape route blocked. Downstream, at an impassable waterfall, his Spanish neighbours had built a fort, so that when Montoya's gimcrack flotilla arrived they could entrap all 12,000 refugee Indians and march them off to their own plantations in Argentina.

So Montoya disembarked his 12,000, and led them on an appalling detour overland. The long column may well be imagined, plodding on staunchly as Indians always do, men with machetes clearing a track, and all loaded down – even the smallest boys and girls among them, if able to walk, carrying packs in proportion to their size. They travelled onward in endless rain through a tangle of rocks and vegetation, often dropping in their tracks from hunger. In front marched the black-robed foreigners, wearing incongruous, close-fitting cassocks, with flapped hats looped up at the sides, carrying the altar plate and sacred images. Leading the procession, said an eyewitness account, was an image of Our Lady, in whom the Guaraní had enormous confidence.

At last, they reached Jesuit reductions along the Iguazú river, which were further inland and had not yet been raided. When they reached safety, over 1000 Indians, having made their great effort, lay down and died of exhaustion. For the survivors, the Jesuits bought 10,000 head of cattle, and gave them a fresh start as ranchers. Two new reductions were built, named San Ignacio and Loreto, after the settlements the raiders had wiped out, and for five years, until 1636, the Indians from Paranapanema lived there in quiet prosperity. Then came word that the *mamelucos* from São Paulo were planning yet another of their big slave raids, this time deep into the interior.

For the Jesuit mission in Paraguay, this new threat was the

decisive turning-point. The Jesuits concentrated the Guaraní from their more exposed reductions on a site which could be better defended, a long and narrow stretch of land with the Paraná river on one flank, and the Uruguay on the other. Then Antonio Ruiz de Montoya was sent off urgently to Madrid.

The Society of Jesus offered to accept responsibility for arming the Guaraní with firearms, in their own defence. Many Jesuits in those days were old soldiers and, though not allowed to bear arms themselves, they would not have forgotten their drill and tactics. But the favour for which the Jesuits were asking – arms for the Indians – contradicted every prudent maxim of imperialist policy. Arm those you have conquered? Create a state within a state? Put an armed force in the control of a cosmopolitan religious society, obedient only to the Pope?

The Jesuits had then great ascendancy over men's minds in Madrid, but they might have been asking too much, had not Brazil just followed Portugal in separating from Spain. Somebody had to hold that exposed and defenceless frontier; it had better be the Indians.

The Guaraní soon learned enough soldiering to defeat such bandits as the *mamelucos*. They were strongest in cavalry – a Guaraní horseman would mount by leaping straight into the saddle, using his lance as a vaulting pole. All of them carried bolas and lasso. The mounted bowmen had 150 iron-tipped arrows apiece, but some had guns – long-barrelled English muskets, contraband, but the best procurable. There were guns for some of the infantry; the rest were murderously adept with sling and stone.

The Jesuits led their men into action, unarmed, and once battle had been joined it was their practice to succour the wounded from both sides. The Jesuits always made a point of reminding the Guaraní that they were free men, protected from enslavement by royal decree, and living on their own land – so their fighting morale was high.

There were usually two Jesuit priests in each reduction – a few hundred were enough to run all Paraguay. The older man was the local representative of the civil power, and responsible to the Jesuit Superior for administration. The younger, called *el com-*

pañero, performed the office of a priest, and only after years in a cure of souls – with all the insight this gave him into human nature – and when he was a perfect master of Guaraní, did his chance arrive to deal responsibly with practical matters.

Though only a handful of Jesuits controlled a population of about 120,000 Guaraní, their supervision was intent. Indians might here and there be given some specific authority, but they were never trained in self-government. They were kept in tutelage, and could never manage big decisions without the help of their philosopher-kings. This, as the Jesuits' many enemies in the outer world came at last to see, was Paraguay's weak point. Pull out the framework, and the structure would collapse.

Poll-tax of a dollar a year was paid, in the name of each reduction Indian, to their patron, the King of Spain, and this steady revenue helped to keep Madrid content. Otherwise, in Paraguay, the Society of Jesus had a free hand, and thus was given a chance, rare in human history, of organizing a new society from scratch – of giving shape and proportion to its own utopia.

For creating an exemplary social system the Jesuits were well equipped. They had all been given a rigorous intellectual training, over many years, in philosophy and theology, but Jesuit policy was also to master the secular knowledge of their time. So it turned out that the Jesuits in Paraguay were not merely theologians, but astronomers, musicians, architects, artists and practical technicians.

Moreover, they all thought along similar lines, and shared a unanimous belief as to the nature of Christianity. Thus they could always justify what they were doing to their own satisfaction; they had no doubts and, so far as an outsider can judge, no rivalry among themselves.

Presumably the Jesuits had renounced private ambition when they joined their order, and none had families to enrich at the public expense. So in Paraguay they could be disinterested. They had land, people, weapons, organization, and, unlike the plantation-owners, they were not obliged to make a living by exploiting the labour of others. So that by what they made of their opportunity – the greatest, perhaps, ever coming the way of any missionaries, Roman Catholic or Protestant – the Jesuits in Paraguay may be fairly judged.

Some names in the record tell of Englishmen taking a hand in the work. *Tomás Bruno natural de Yorca* is clearly Tom Brown of York, and *Esmid* is the usual Spanish bosh-shot at Smith. But almost every civilized country sooner or later sent men to help the work onwards in Paraguay, and this turned out to be useful, because the Indians began making a clear distinction in their minds between their priests, who came from all Christendom, and the Spanish or Portuguese, who threatened them from across the border.

The Jesuit idea of the good society was unlikely to have warmed the heart of any individualist Englishman or American. In Paraguay, until the very end, the Guaraní were never involved in any open disagreement concerning public policy, and those who look upon such a clash of opinion as healthy might have found the society stifling. There was no private judgement in religion or in politics. The possibility of a free press was inconceivable. There was no private property to speak of, and certainly no free trade. No one in Paraguay ever had a chance to make his fortune, and life was planned with an almost exasperating benevolence, down to the last trivial detail. But so far as we can judge, the Guaraní were happy; they have had a much worse time since. 'Such innocence prevails among these people', reported Bishop Faxardo to King Philip V on 20 May 1720, after a visit of inspection, 'that I believe no mortal sin is ever committed there.'

A Guaraní reduction was laid out like any other Spanish-American town, in a grid-iron pattern. The streets were terrace houses, one-storey high, in stone or adobe, with continuous, overhanging eaves, wide enough to walk beneath in the rains dry-shod. The houses were painted red and yellow ochre. They led in straight lines to a central plaza, where a statue of Our Lady stood beside a public well. The most conspicuous building would be a magnificent baroque church, built in stone and occupying one whole side of the plaza. The cemetery, bright with orange trees and flowers, was on another.

Public buildings grouped around the plaza would include a dispensary, with nurses called *curuzaya*, because their sign of office was a staff with a cross on top. There would be a home for widows and cripples, a free lodging-house for travellers, and a school with a Guaraní master which taught reading and writing. Each reduction in Paraguay specialized in one particular industrial technique – a tile kiln, a stamping mill, a primitive blast-furnace. If noisy or smelly, these industries were always located out of town, where they would cause no nuisance.

Much of the land was rolling plain, good cattle country, with green trees fringing the wide rivers. All buildings and land, like the flocks and herds and workshop equipment, were common property. The Guaraní had used canoes before, but now they learned boat-building, and eventually were running a fleet of 2000 vessels on the river Paraná alone. Relays of fresh horses were kept ready in eighty post-houses, and mounted postboys went overland from one reduction to the next, averaging a hundred miles a day.

On four days of his six-day working week, an Indian cultivated his own small-holding, and bartered his surplus vegetables in the village for his other everyday needs. That left him two spare days, on which a man might go and cultivate the plot of some neighbour kept busy on public service elsewhere – for instance, as ferryman or soldier – or he might be given a job of work to do for the community. Most of the villagers, however, on the two days which were not their own, went out to work under Jesuit supervision on the great field called *Tupamba:* God's property.

They crowded out from the village in the early morning, marching behind a band, and pausing at each of the crossroad shrines to pray. 'God's property' grew their seedcorn, and the crops which fed the sick and needy, or were put into store to buy necessities for the village from outside. Women took their own part in this communal labour by coming to a hall in the plaza every day to spin thread. The children, too, spun for an hour or two every day, and so were bred up from the start in the idea of working, not for themselves, but for others. The Jesuits had thought of everything.

Because each reduction had its own special product, trade between one reduction and the next was usually by barter – cattle being exchanged for cotton, sugar for rice, wheat for pig-iron. All transactions were strictly accounted for and open to inspection; there was an annual audit. The Jesuit Superior kept about $100,000 cash in hand, to finance foreign trade and pay the royal tax, but within Paraguay, transactions for cash were kept to a minimum, as if money itself were not to be trusted – almost as if it were the symbol of a treacherous and even selfish freedom.

The Indians learned, by slow degrees, to enjoy regular work instead of avoiding it, and in course of time they became remarkable craftsmen. The masonry of their churches – though now in ruins across a country which is sometimes desolate – has been cut from the stone with an exuberant felicity. Other Indians were skilful as printers, calligraphers, painters, bell-founders. Each trade was organized in a guild, and the guilds made sure, in mediaeval fashion, that the training of each apprentice was thorough and complete. Paraguay even made its own gun-powder.

Cards, dice and hard drinking were not allowed, but dancing and horse-racing were encouraged. The Guaraní could now satisfy their taste for meat: in Yapeyu, for instance, with its 7000 inhabitants, the butchers slaughtered forty beef cattle a day, and the Feasts of the Church were real village feasts. There were tens of thousands of Guaraní, and they all dressed alike – loose breeches and shirt, two woollen ponchos. Even the priests wore homespun. But, in procession, the village dignitaries were given splendid clothes to wear, of brocade and velvet, in bright colours.

So prosperous was the community that among outsiders the rumour began to sprout that the Jesuits had a secret gold-mine. Starting with a blank stretch of territory in South America, how else did you prosper than by working dumb Indians to death – best of all in a gold-mine? These rumours were investigated in 1645 and again in 1657, but the official denials were never believed. The Marquess of Pombal, dictator of Portugal, modernizer, admirer of Voltaire, a man who looked upon the Society of Jesus as the enemy of everything he stood for, had no difficulty a century later in convincing all educated Europe about the secret Jesuit gold-mine, hidden away in Paraguay.

Paraguay did have one valuable export – the herb tea called maté, which the Jesuits persuaded the Indians to drink as a stimulant, instead of alcohol. They also provided the outside world with maté, as well as shipping 50,000 hides a year down-river to Buenos Aires, along with some horse-hair, honey and wax. The export trade was nicely gauged to yield enough money for the royal poll-tax, and to meet the bill for Paraguay's strictly-controlled imports from Europe: scissors, knives, mirrors, but also incense, musical instruments, and English flintlock muskets.

The Indians' own leaders – *caciques* – were given a certain scope, but always as subordinates. No *cacique* could punish an Indian without the consent of a Jesuit. King Philip V once had the idea of promoting five hundred of these *caciques* to the rank of Knights of Santiago, but the plan was dropped when he learned to his chagrin that 'the *caciques* attached no value to such a distinction'.

Everyone in a Jesuit reduction attended mass – announced on fiestas by firing rockets and beating drums, as well as by church bells. The royal banner of Spain was prominently flown. Though the worshippers crowding into church might wear homespun, the nave itself was hung with imported velvet and brocade, and the altar was ablaze with candles. The grandeur was not personal, but collective.

Mass was often orchestral – everywhere in Paraguay, baroque music resounded. Indians who showed musical talent were taken up and taught by the Flemish Jesuit, Juan Basco, at one time chapel-master to the Archduke Albert. We know of an original opera called *Santiago*, and perhaps there were others. Music of course was safe, because although exhilarating it does nothing very much to provoke dissent. On the contrary, it unites men, even against their wills, as any conscript knows who has ever marched behind a band.

A price had to be paid for this material serenity. In a physical sense, the Jesuit government was never severe. After 1767, when Jesuit Paraguay collapsed, a careful stocktaking was made. Only a dozen pairs of handcuffs were found for over 100,000 people,

B

scarcely an indication of police terror. But morally, Jesuit control was absolute.

Plantation slaves all over America often rebelled; reduction Indians, never. At the height of the Jesuit experiment in Paraguay, so far as an outsider can judge, there was no disagreement of any kind, political, intellectual or religious. There were almost no differences of opinion; there was hardly any vice; there was no dissent whatever. Fortified frontier posts kept the outside world at a safe distance. Like Egypt under the Pharaohs – another civilization where money was unknown – Paraguay was static.

Elementary education in Paraguay was a long way ahead of other Spanish colonies, and some Indians even learned Latin, though little encouragement was given them to learn Spanish – the language of the hostile world outside. Whatever his moral qualities, no Guaraní ever became a priest in the Society of Jesus, or so much as a lay brother. The Jesuits, to do them justice, may privately have thought this imprudent, but in obedience they were bound to submit to the Council of Mexico, which in 1555 had forbidden an Indian priesthood.

Their rule in everyday life was simple: *he who does not work, neither shall he eat*. The lazy or drunken or violent were obliged to fast until they promised to reform. Extreme offenders were whipped; there was no death penalty. The most dreaded punishment of all, very rarely applied, was to be driven out of Eden – sent across the border, to where the plantation-owners lay in wait. If Paraguay begins to sound more than ever like a first-rate boarding school, with its set of clerical housemasters, infuriatingly wise and calm, and *caciques* as prefects, and expulsion as the ultimate punishment, one must bear in mind that the Jesuits had also a great reputation as teachers.

The sexual problems which so often upset a boarding school were eluded, since all the girls in Paraguay were compelled to marry at the age of fifteen, and all the boys at seventeen. Mishaps could occur; bigamy was a not uncommon crime. But though family life was encouraged in every possible way, and though there was plenty of spare land in Paraguay, the population never multiplied at the rate one would expect. Like Indians all over America, the Guaraní had little resistance to European diseases.

In 1735, measles killed 18,773. Smallpox carried off another 30,000, two years later.

In times of crisis, the King of Spain was able to call upon his loyal Guaraní for a service even more convenient to him than his steady revenue from the poll-tax. On fifty occasions between 1637 and 1735, the Paraguayan militia were called out to fight in the royal cause, thereby doing service for their special privileges. In 1678 they took part in a campaign to stop their traditional enemies, the Portuguese, from occupying Colonia del Sacramento, a port they coveted on the river Plate. In 1681 they helped defend Buenos Aires against the French. Between 1721 and 1735, as the revolutionary idea of independence began to stir in Spanish America and the colonists made their first attempt to throw off the royal yoke, Guaraní from the Jesuit utopia were the King of Spain's reliable horsemen. Even when plantation Indians rose in rebellion, the Guaraní had no objection to driving them back to work.

A policeman's lot is not a happy one. The Jesuit reductions in Paraguay, with their bizarre mixture of a mediaeval yesterday and a collective tomorrow, were at last to find themselves without a friend in the world.

In 1742, Gomez de Andrade, Portugal's governor in Rio de Janeiro, had hinted to his superiors in Lisbon how a wedge might be driven between the Jesuits in Paraguay and the simple-minded good-hearted King of Spain who had always been their patron. Suppose the Portuguese offered the following bargain: to give, in exchange for Colonia del Sacramento, an equivalent tract of land on the left bank of the river Uruguay, now occupied by seven Jesuit reductions, though just inside the formerly ill-defined Brazilian border. King and Jesuits would then be certain to collide.

For Ignacio Visconti, General of the Society of Jesus, the decision was painful, but he had no choice. Even though it meant shifting 30,000 Guaraní to new homes, his missionaries in Paraguay must evacuate those seven reductions along the river Uruguay – land they had tilled for over a hundred years, land they believed to be their own.

Not surprisingly, the Guaraní dragged their feet about moving. In 1753, when they became overtly rebellious, the governors of La Plata and Montevideo marched in with a combined Spanish and Portuguese force, a little more promptly perhaps than was necessary, and managed to provoke the Guaraní to a pitched battle.

The rumour had already reached Europe that the Guaraní were electing their own king – sixty-year-old Nicolas Neerguiri, ex-mayor of La Concepción. The rebels could rely, by all accounts, on the backing of about half their people, and a few of the younger Jesuits showed sympathy. Accounts are contradictory but some of the dissident Jesuits may even have gone with them to the field of battle, though they played no leading role there, and perhaps were no longer wanted.

The Guaraní were commanded in the field by their 'king', Nicolas, and by José, middle-aged, tall, taciturn, with a scar across one cheek, the mayor of San Miguel. But a quiet life in a planned economy, diversified by a little easy police work across the frontier, proved to be not much of a school of generalship. In their encounter with regular troops on 24 February 1754, the two *caciques* handled their men badly. An unfamiliar weapon, field artillery, scared some of the Guaraní out of their wits. Their militia scattered, though after this unlucky start some of them did better for themselves as guerrillas.

About half the Guaraní went submissively enough to their new homes, on the right bank of the Uruguay. The governor of La Plata was recalled to Madrid; he had been too zealous. A few Guaraní diehards fled to the Chaco, the usual sanctuary for those who shrugged off Christianity, for the Chaco, say the Guaraní glumly, is wet enough to put out the fires of hell. But once the fighting was over – and it did not take long – 14,018 of them refused point blank to cross the river. They would rather stay put, under Spanish and not Jesuit rule, on land they had been given every reason to think was their own.

The exchange of Colonia del Sacramento for the seven reductions fell through – a bad bargain, anyway – but even so, rather than let the Jesuits come back, the Spanish government kept control of the left bank of the Uruguay, just in case the mythical gold-mine might be located there. The 14,018 Guaraní who stayed on were their hostages. Paraguay's time was running out. Outsiders hungry for labour and for land had one foot inside the door.

This brief insurrection in Paraguay gave Voltaire an excellent argument in his lifelong campaign against the Jesuits. So far as his private religious views were concerned, Voltaire was approximately a Unitarian. The Jesuits in Paris had educated him and first encouraged his talents as a controversialist and man of the theatre, yet he detested the Society of Jesus: what it stood for was an infamy, and for this passionate hatred he may have had personal reasons, at which we can only guess. But the strong economic motives which made his many readers approve heartily of Voltaire's anticlericalism are quite clear. At a time when land was by far the best investment for men with money, the Roman Catholic church not only held vast amounts of property in France and all over central and southern Europe, but never died or went bankrupt. Its possessions would therefore never be thrown on the market; to any rich investor, church land was inaccessible.

Voltaire had therefore excellent reasons, public as well as personal, for not caring what success his old schoolmasters might be making of their collectivist missionary experiment in far-off Paraguay. Both their property arrangements and their sexual prohibitions were repugnant to him. In his witty short novel, *Candide*, he gave his readers a recklessly-travestied description of what went on in Paraguay – 'the fathers own everything and the people nothing – a masterpiece of reason and justice'. So immense was Voltaire's reputation that his travesty was taken, in his own time, for a sober statement of fact.

Candide still remains the one account of the Jesuit utopia which an averagely well-read man is likely to have encountered. But though his description of the economic reality in Paraguay might be wilfully misleading, Voltaire was in a larger sense being true to himself. The idea of land which could never be bought and sold – property held in common – was as repulsive to Voltaire as to his readers. They were men for whom possessions, money and pleasure were the liberating principles. And the Jesuits then typified everything that stood in their way.

Inside the church, too, the Jesuits had made enemies. Their founder Ignatius Loyola, had twice been put in prison by the

Inquisition. Jesuits had turned a cold shoulder to inquisitors ever since, and this reticence now cost them dear. Some of their missionary compromises in China – rice and tea in communion, for example, instead of bread and wine – were too clever to be wise. In an enlightened eighteenth century they were the bogey-men, much as the Jews were to become during a darker decade of the twentieth.

To the open delight of the Brazilian sugar-plantation-owners, the Marquess of Pombal had expelled the Jesuits from Portugal as early as 1759. In France, Madame Pompadour, the King's mistress, had never forgiven them for refusing her absolution: in 1764 she managed to persuade her royal lover to expel the Jesuits from France. At last a newly-elected Pope, Clement XIV, was forced by irresistible diplomatic pressure to insist, 'Sometimes we must cut down a mast to save a ship.' By 1773 the Society of Jesus had been formally suppressed. The cleverest opponents in their day of modern nationalism and unrestricted free enterprise had been broken, though a remnant around which the Society could later be revived lingered on in, of all places, Russia.

Exactly in what way King Charles III of Spain, a fervent Catholic, was duped by his Voltairean minister, Count Aranda, into expelling the Jesuits from all his dominions is still not historically certain. The story which Voltaire had helped to set going, that the missionary priests as a body had fought against royal troops in Paraguay, no doubt played its significant part. 'For me I see nothing so exalted', Voltaire had written, 'as the way the fathers make war here on the King of Spain and the King of Portugal, and in Europe are those same Kings' confessors.' But thanks to some kind of persuasion or pressure, on 2 April 1767 a secret royal decree was signed, expelling the Society of Jesus from all Spanish possessions.

A new and capable governor, the Marqués Francisco de Bucarelli, arrived at Buenos Aires in June 1767, and a packet boat from Spain reached him soon after with his secret orders for Paraguay. He was to give the Jesuits no warning, but strike. Like everyone else at the time, Bucarelli took it for granted that since they controlled both a private army and a tract of land the size of France, the Jesuits would fight tooth and nail to keep Paraguay. They were not very numerous – only 300 in all his jurisdiction.

Then Bucarelli had a stroke of bad luck. In the River Plate arrived two king's ships which had left Spain a few days after all the Jesuits there had been arrested. One of these ships was wrecked in the bay, and when the crew were rescued and set ashore, the astonishing news that the Society of Jesus was outlawed went around Buenos Aires quickly from mouth to mouth. At 10 p.m. on 9 July, Bucarelli discovered that his official secret was out. He arrested five merchants who had already tried to send warning upcountry, and instantly decreed the death penalty for anyone else who got in touch with the Jesuits. By two in the morning, he was on the march. The Guaraní militia, if mobilized, would enormously outnumber him – he had only a few hundred troops – but he still hoped for the advantage of surprise.

He struck first at the Jesuit college upcountry, at Cordoba – their headquarters, where new arrivals from Europe were taught Guaraní. The college had always been spoken of as vastly wealthy, but to his chagrin Bucarelli found only $9000 there.

A surprise of another sort was awaiting him at the reductions. Whether or not a warning had reached the Jesuits that he was coming – and in all likelihood it had not – they made no effort whatever to oppose the royal decree, but accepted their fate like lambs.

Seventy-eight Jesuits were marched in their manacles down to Buenos Aires, to be shipped off to Europe. These prisoners were seen by Louis de Bougainville, the French explorer then anchored in the River Plate, on his voyage round the world. He was a sceptic, a Voltairean, but a scientist, and the contrast between what he now saw with his own eyes and the tales current in Europe encouraged him to look more closely at the facts, and do the missionaries better justice.

All over Paraguay, a frenzied hunt began for imaginary goldmines. The Spaniards in Buenos Aires had never been able to believe that the mysterious inland civilization, prospering up there in the country of the great rivers, could have almost no use for gold except as church decoration. But Paraguay thrived, as we have seen, not from gold-mines nor from plantation-labour, but because of the highly sophisticated forms of property relation invented by Jesuit missionaries (with hints from Plato and More) and cemented into place by religion. They had taken their chance to create a utopia; now it was gone.

Yet another strict enquiry was made into the Jesuits' sexual morals, though nothing spicy came to light. Those marched to the coast in chains had been allowed to carry away their personal property – and, judging by the inventory, this did not amount to much. The first on the list, Father Pedro Zabaleta, was written down the possessor of ten shirts, two pillow-cases, two pairs of sheets, three handkerchiefs, two pairs of shoes, and a pound and a half of snuff. Father Zabaleta was better off for shirts than many of his brethren, but the most unwordly among them had at least one spare shirt, and nearly every Jesuit on the list took with him into exile a private stock of snuff. They had at least that one small self-indulgence.

According to de Bougainville, the last advice repeated to the perplexed Indians by the Jesuits, as they were marched off, had been, 'Get ready, my children, to hear many lies.' The *caciques* from the reductions were brought down, eventually, to Buenos Aires and ranged in the plaza, in a half-circle, to hear Bucarelli. He spoke to them from a balcony, telling them (and, we may be sure, in all earnest) that they were being saved from slavery, and that their possessions would now be their private property. 'It was easy to distinguish in their faces', said de Bougainville, who was watching, 'more surprise than joy.' He went on to observe, 'They had the stupefied air of animals caught in a trap.'

Franciscans were sent in to take the Jesuits' place in looking after, presumably, the moral welfare of the Guaraní. But though Franciscan missions elsewhere in Latin America had often been humane and imaginative, the friars were not adept in the local language. After so many years of being clearly understood, the Indians resented being shouted at in Spanish. So they made trouble for their new supervisors.

And indeed, with the best will in the world, the Franciscans could no longer have kept Paraguay going as an economic entity. Bucarelli had seen to that. On 14 May 1768, with an escort of dragoons and grenadiers, he had left Buenos Aires to put Paraguay in order. The Guaraní there found his grenadiers' tall hats very funny. But they had been trained in obedience; they gave no trouble; and later, when the joke was over and they grasped what was happening, their protests had a tone of innocent amazement.

A few simple administrative changes by Bucarelli had knocked the Guaraní community to bits. '*It is not convenient to leave* [the Guaraní] *entire liberty*' meant that those who did not quickly scamper away to the swamps of the Chaco were very likely soon to find themselves working for a taskmaster. '*Commerce with the Spaniards will be free*' ended the rigid control of foreign trade, which, galling though it may have been to some of the merchants down on the coast, at least had kept Paraguay out of their debt.

This transformation of common possessions into private property was carried out under strict forms of law. We have the official figures, and they speak for themselves. In 1767, when Jesuit ascendancy in Paraguay came to an end, there were 113,716 Christian Indians in 57 reductions. Buildings, cultivated land and means of production were held in common, and so were flocks and herds: there were 719,761 cattle, 27,204 horses and 138,827 sheep.

Five years later, there were only 80,881 Indians.

By 1796, there were only 45,000 Indians, and so the decline went on.

Rarely, except after a swingeing defeat in war, has a society to every appearance so viable crumbled so fast. The Indians disappeared – under the lash, or from disease, or into the swamp, or dying, as such simple people do, merely from the shock of change. In the former Jesuit utopia there are now a few ruins, kept up as a tourist attraction, which once were baroque churches. Here and there an inquisitive eye may detect an occasional not-unfamiliar flower: European orchard trees, once cultivated hereabouts, but long since gone back to scrub.

2 Come Over and Help Us

'If there were not merchants, who go to seek for earthly treasures in the East and West Indies, who would transport thither the preachers, who take the heavenly treasure? The preachers take the Gospel, and the merchants take the preachers.' *Antonio Vieira, SJ (1608–97), in his History of the Future*

'The Hand of God was eminently seen in thinning the Indians to make room for the English, it pleased Almighty God to send unusual Sickness among them, as the Smallpox, to lessen their Numbers, so that the English, in Comparison to the Spaniard, have but little Indian blood to answer for.' *John Archdale, a Carolina Quaker, in 1707*

Las Casas died in 1566, at the great age of ninety-two. In the century that followed, down the long North American coast, beyond the grasp of Spanish imperial power, a sequence of little colonies, Dutch and Swedish, English and French, won a footing. The wars of religion had begun in Europe. Protestants were fighting hard to survive, and North America became their safe refuge.

Though Protestants in Europe might be outnumbered, in New England they had a preponderance. In New England there were ten times as many Protestants as there were Roman Catholics in French Canada. So, logically enough, the first Protestant mission to the American Indians began in Massachusetts, the largest and most serious-minded of the English settlements. The missionary technique they tried there took up more or less where Las Casas left off, baffled, in Venezuela.

English Puritans escaping to Massachusetts had from the start been well aware that in some as yet undefined way they were responsible for converting or at least giving help to the Indians whose land they were now entering upon by force of numbers. The Massachusetts charter laid down, as one of the colony's purposes, 'to win and invite the natives of that Country to the knowledge of the only true God and Saviour of mankind, and the Christian faith'. The official seal of Massachusetts showed 'a poor Indian, having a label going from his mouth with "Come over and help us" '. But, as one observer pointed out, the Indians 'must be civilised ere they could be Christianised'. How was it to be done, and by whom?

In the autumn of 1631, a young Englishman called John Eliot landed at Boston with a degree from Cambridge University in his pocket. He was twenty-seven, a farmer's son, and before coming to America he had worked as a schoolmaster. The year following, Hannah Mulford, the English girl to whom John Eliot was betrothed, crossed the Atlantic to join him. Soon after, he was given charge of a congregation at Roxbury, as their minister.

For a Puritan minister, Eliot sounds to have been a cheerful man – 'affable and facetious rather than morose' – though conscientious in his duty, and generous to the poor. He was fond of a glass of wine, but would not touch hard liquor. Yet Eliot had his crotchets. For example, he thought well of beards, but detested long hair, and a wig he could never abide. He could prove from Corinthians that ' 'Tis a sinful abomination for a man to wear hair long on his head, and no hair on his face'. Most pastors in Massachusetts drew their stipend from the taxes; John Eliot insisted on living upon the freewill offering of his flock. He lived so high in the clouds as not even to recognize his own cow when it stood outside the front door. In short, though by all accounts a good and sweet-natured man, John Eliot was a thoroughgoing English eccentric, doing what he thought right, however odd it might seem to others.

The brunt of John Eliot's everyday life was no doubt taken by heroic Hannah, who bore him six sons, all of whom, in their turn, became ministers. Eliot himself was far less interested in milking cows or making ends meet than in his own fascinating neighbours, the Mohicans.

To show affection for Indians, or even intelligent curiosity,

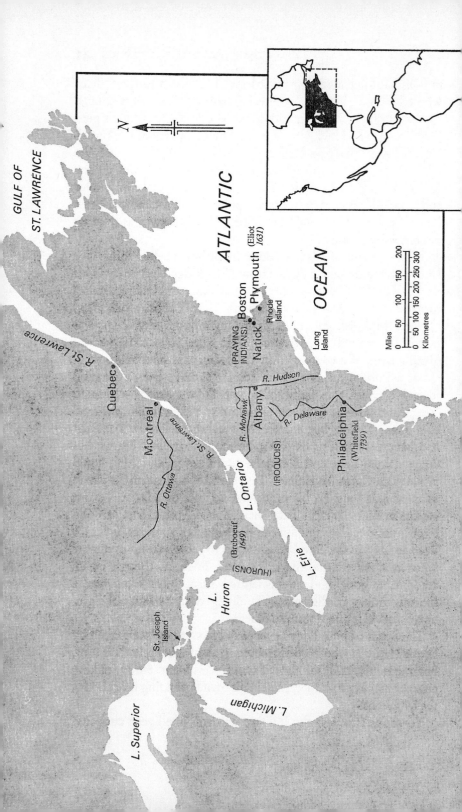

was uncommon in New England at that time. Cotton Mather, a scholarly and eventually famous younger neighbour of Eliot's, who was to write his life, never rose above the view of the Indians, then commonest in New England, that they were natural inferiors. Mather spoke sarcastically about how frightened the Indians had been at their first glimpse of a sailing ship – 'scared out of their wits to see the monster come sailing in and spitting fire with a mighty roar out of her floating side'. Another proof of Indian inferiority was their technical backwardness. They were 'abject creatures, never owners of so much as a knife till we came among them, their name for an Englishman was a Knifeman'. Even their strange, pagan piety was matter for Cotton Mather's scorn: 'They believe that every remarkable creature has a peculiar God within it or about it. They cannot conceive but that fire must be a kind of God.'

John Eliot saw the Mohicans through a different pair of eyes. He never for a moment shared his neighbours' contemptuous superiority. He loved the Mohicans, and knew for certain who they were: one of the lost tribes of Israel. Eliot ransacked the Old Testament for evidence and, of course, he soon found all he needed. Did not the Mohicans speak in parables, exactly like the Jews of old? Did they not anoint their heads, and give dowries, and mourn with a loud wailing? To Cotton Mather, however, much as to Sepúlveda before him, the Indians if they were indeed a lost tribe, which he doubted, were so sunk in sin as to be beyond all hope: 'The devil decoyed those miserable savages thither, in the hope that the Gospel of the Lord Jesus Christ would never come here to destroy or disturb his absolute empire over them.'

John Eliot began to study the language spoken by the Mohicans – a version of Algonquin, clotted with polysyllables, lacking the letter R, and disappointingly unlike the Hebrew he had learned at Cambridge. But he went on patiently reducing it to grammar and, by 1647, could speak Mohican well enough to preach his first sermon. He had attentive listeners.

His Indian neighbours were all the more willing to listen to new ideas because their own traditional life was breaking up fast. Since the strangers had landed from their ships and pushed inland, the old way of life was no longer self-sufficing.

New Englanders worked their own land, so they provided the Mohicans with that object-lesson in the virtues of hard work which Las Casas had hoped to demonstrate, more artificially, at Cumaná. Indians in Massachusetts, therefore, had less reason to fear slave-trader and plantation-owner than this new world of money-values which had overtaken them. A hunter who had bought a gun could excel a man who made his own bow and arrows – but afterwards, he must also go and buy more gun-powder. To acquire powder and guns and knives and iron pots and blankets the Indian was obliged to go off trapping for furs, which were bought or bartered in by the trader and shipped off to Europe. He thus became caught up in the mesh of world trade, with its perplexing cash-values and its wide-spreading ripples of price fluctuation. Trade brandy was poison to the Indian and here, as in Paraguay, quite ordinary ailments like influenza and measles were sudden death.

A surprising number of Mohicans took John Eliot's sermons to heart, and yielded up their old beliefs in favour of what he had to tell them, adopting instead the values of a culture to all appear-ances more powerful than their own. They were persuaded to settle and farm, and slowly they took up a way of life similar to Eliot's own, as a boy, on his God-fearing, hard-working father's farm in Hertfordshire. In belief, as in manner of life, they became in essentials no different from their English neighbours, thus disconcerting those who were secretly convinced that they must be natural inferiors.

By 1651, John Eliot had gathered his first Christian township together at Natick eighteen miles from Boston, the government granting the 'Praying Indians' a tract of four square miles to live on. By 1661 John Eliot had translated the New Testament for them, and two years later he finished the entire Bible – 'the whole translation written with one pen', as he whimsically boasted. The Indians made a great effort to give up polygamy, and were soon feeling quite as indignant as other Puritans in Massachusetts about fornication and drunkenness and Sabbath-breaking. There were similar missions on Nantucket and Martha's Vineyard, and four ministers became fluent in the Indian tongue; by 1674 their converts numbered 4000. John Eliot opened schools for the

Indians. They took to reading and writing with great keenness. Twenty-four were ordained as pastors and, according to Cotton Mather, two took degrees at Harvard. 'These praying Indians', he writes, 'quickly were for a more decent and English way of living.' The mission became celebrated on both sides of the Atlantic; where Las Casas could scarcely claim to have succeeded, John Eliot had triumphed.

The Praying Indians had, as it were, taken on a protective coloration to avoid extinction. They were never likely to give trouble; they were promising to be good. To a saintly dreamer like Eliot, the political aspect of what he had achieved may never have occurred, but Oliver Cromwell, a genius of power-politics who took a personal interest in Massachusetts, drew the obvious conclusion. If some Indians could be won over, why not all? If the Pope could swell his numbers by converting Indians, why not the Protestants? The English Parliament, dominated just then by extreme Puritans, needed no persuasion and, in July 1649, incorporated the Society for the Propagation of the Gospel in New England. By a church collection through England and Wales, £12,000 was collected – a fortune in those days. The estates of defeated cavaliers were going cheap; the money was invested in land, and rents from it financed missions to the Indians for many years to come.

Eliot's good intentions and the political hopes Cromwell had expressed were put to the test in 1675, in the first large Indian insurrection: King Philip's War.

King Philip – not of Spain, but the *sachem* or chief of the Wampanoags – had been given his ironical royal title because of the pre-eminent influence he had over those Indians, still resolutely pagan, who had begun to resent the thousands of Christian colonists disembarking from ships year after year, and pressing inland from the coast.

Philip looked down on the Praying Indians as renegades, but for several years he was conciliatory with the English, in 1671 even bidding his people give up their guns rather than offend the Puritans in nearby Plymouth. He would fight only when fighting could be avoided no longer.

'The sachems', as Mather recorded, 'did all they could that their subjects might not entertain the Gospel' – for, to them, the Praying Indians were traitors who had changed sides, and John Eliot 'in the wilderness, has been treated in a very threatening and barbarous manner'. One day King Philip met the minister a long way from home and, taking hold of a button of his coat, told him 'that he cared for his Gospel just as much as he cared for that Button'. 'I fear neither you nor all the sachems in the country,' had been Eliot's answer to threats. 'Touch me if you dare.'

The crisis arrived in 1674, when three Wampanoags killed a 'Praying Indian' called Sassamon, whom they believed with good reason to be a government informer. The three men were hanged, and the rebel Indians rose up, King Philip leading them into war with great courage and astuteness. He sought aid from England's rivals, trying to get help from the French and to buy arms from the Dutch on the Hudson river, as well as paying his court to the Mohawks, the nearest tribe of the warlike and formidable Iroquois Federation. The war was cruelly fought and, while it lasted, New Englanders lived in dread.

But too many of King Philip's own people had already rejected the way of life he was fighting to defend: very few Praying Indians went over to him. The Natick, Niantic and Mohican Indians offered themselves to the English as allies and, on 11 August 1676, an 'Indian traitor' led soldiers to Philip's hiding place, in a swamp at the foot of Mount Hope, in Rhode Island. For the next twenty-five years Philip's head could be seen in Plymouth, stuck up on a pole as a warning.

That no particular gratitude was felt towards the Praying Indians is not surprising. Massachusetts had suffered badly in the war. One man in every sixteen fit to bear arms was killed, and many civilians were massacred. Here were the Praying Indians, pretending to live like Englishmen, yet with the same faces as Philip's scalping warriors, a living reproach to men who had secretly prided themselves on their natural superiority, only to live for weeks in fear and trembling of men hitherto considered inferior. 'Some furious people', wrote Cotton Mather, 'clamoured for the extirpation of the Praying Indians as well as the Pagan Indians.' And, inevitably, they looked for a scapegoat. They 'vented a very wicked rage on our holy Eliot, because of his concernment for the Indians'. Had he not undertaken – at least by inference – to render all the Indians harmless?

Not everybody accepted killing off all the Indians as the ineluctable solution, but few wanted to help Eliot continue with his mission. The Praying Indians went on farming and praying and learning to read, but impetus was lost. Eliot towards the end of his life looked in a different direction.

Indians had never been of much use to the settlers in New England, as labourers. The saying went that when it came to hard work, one black was worth four Indians; and black slaves in considerable numbers were being shipped into North American colonies. As long ago as 1619 the first slave cargo had been sold to tobacco planters at Jamestown, Virginia, by the Dutch, and even in God-fearing Massachusetts, with its small farms and its cult of individual hard work, slaves were coming into use.

John Eliot had 'long lamented it with a bleeding and burning passion that the English used their Negroes but as horses'. When in his eighties – for Eliot, like Las Casas, made old bones – he managed to persuade some of the slave-owners living nearby to send him their blacks once a week, 'to enlighten them to the utmost of his power in the things of their everlasting peace'. His head might be in the clouds, but the old man could sense the American future.

John Eliot's translation of the Bible into Mohican is now a costly item for a collector of rare books. 'Prayer and pains, with the blessing of God, can accomplish anything,' he said in 1663, as he laid down the stump of his quill pen, after translating the last verse of the Old Testament. But no one reads the version of the Scriptures over which he took such pains; no pure-blooded Mohican survives; even forswearing drink and fornication could not save them. They were swept away, as Crèvecœur wrote a century later when most of them were gone, by 'particular fevers, to which they were strangers before, and sinking into a singular sort of indolence and sloth'.

The Mohawks, from whom King Philip sought help, were one of the five Iroquois nations – an Indian confederacy formed just before Europeans came to settle in North America. They lived south of Lake Ontario, in a strategic heartland between the Dutch in the Hudson Valley, the English in New England, and the French in Canada. The Iroquois were notorious for supple political ability, and for their ferocity. Over the years, they terrorized all their neighbours in turn.

The Mohawks bartered furs for firearms with the Dutch traders at Fort Orange – now Albany, on the Hudson river. Of the 800 Mohawk warriors, 300 carried arquebuses. In 1660, the league of the Iroquois could put 2000 warriors into the field – or more than the total of French settlers then living in Canada. At the height of their power, the Iroquois were raiding all the way from Hudson's Bay to Tennessee.

Emigration from France to Canada was under strict royal control; only Roman Catholics were allowed to go there, and all trade in Canada was monopolized by a royal chartered company. The church, too, interfered in trade, for example, forbidding for as long as it could the sale of brandy to the Indians.

From about 1630 onwards, the most prominent missionaries to the Indians in Canada were, once again, the Jesuits. As a rigorously educated élite under quasi-military discipline, they liked to speak of themselves as the soldiers of Christ the King – and, for them, Canada was to be a bloody battlefield.

The first Jesuits to arrive in Quebec started, as John Eliot had done, by grinding away at Indian languages. Their legs were sometimes pulled at first. When they needed to know some particular religious expression, the Indian instructing them would teach them an obscenity: this joke crops up all through missionary history. To learn how the Indians lived, some went out into the winter wilderness, sledging with Algonquin hunting parties. Others travelled long distances by birchbark canoe, and the instructions drawn up for them in Paris in 1637 are a measure of Jesuit thoroughness. 'Love the Indians', they were told, 'like brothers with whom you are to spend the rest of your life. Never make them wait for you in embarking. Take flint and steel to kindle their pipes, and light fire at night, for these little services will win their hearts. Fasten up the skirts of your cassock, so that you may not carry sand or water into the canoe. Do not ask too many questions. Take at once what they offer you, ceremony offends them.'

At long intervals, a great party of six or seven hundred Hurons would arrive at Quebec by canoe, and stay five days under the walls of the fort, to barter their furs and tobacco for edge-tools and iron pots. They came from near the great lake which now bears their name. The men went out hunting or fishing along the eastern shore; the women grew corn and beans, squash and tobacco.

The Hurons lived communally, amid thick woodsmoke, in bark huts which were sometimes over 200 feet long. They practised torture as a semi-religious rite – sharing out titbits of a prisoner's roasted heart among the small boys of the tribe, to help make the youngsters brave, and awarding the prisoner's head, boiled, to the chief to give him wisdom. There were certain diseases they thought they could cure by acts of mass fornication. But planting and trade were becoming an inducement to the Hurons to enter into a more civilized way of life. As warriors they were hardly as fierce as their enemies, the Iroquois.

Wandering Indians like the Algonquin, who lived altogether by the chase, were harder to come to terms with than a settled people who practised agriculture, so the Jesuits decided there would be more future in going to live and work in the villages of the Hurons. Among the first to make the journey to Lake Huron was Father Jean de Brébœuf, a powerfully built and tough-minded Norman nobleman. The journey was long – 900 miles – because of the detour made to avoid Iroquois raiding parties. De Brébœuf and his two companions carried loads at each of the thirty-five portages, and went all the way barefoot, rather than risk putting a shoe through the birchbark of a canoe.

Thus Jean de Brébœuf found himself at last in a stuffy bark hut on the shores of a great lake, a highly educated French gentleman, vowed to the service of God, aware that probably he had the rest of his life to spend amid these painted and tattooed men who wore the scalp lock, and stared at him from eyes always reddened with wood smoke. What notions of morality lay behind those blank, red-eyed, savage stares?

De Brébœuf soon found that everything a Huron saw or touched possessed a spirit, which might turn hostile. Therefore, to avoid mischance, all spirits must be propitiated. Any animal a Huron might kill for the pot had a spirit of its own, possibly an evil spirit. So did the net he flung into the lake, and so did the live fish struggling within it. Luckily, the smoke of tobacco had a particular spiritual value, and unfriendly spirits could be efficiently propitiated by throwing tobacco into the fire.

Oracles would come and speak to the Hurons as they slept. One particular tribal celebration was the Dream Feast – a sacred game of Guess-What's-In-My-Mind. On the morning of the Dream Feast, everyone tacitly agreed to pretend that, the night before, he had dreamed of something he very much needed. But nobody mentioned what it was. Dreamers ran from house to house, asking all the neighbours to guess.

You had to guess what your neighbour was pretending to have dreamed that he very much wanted. And if by chance you did happen to guess correctly, that signified good luck, because the guesser had miraculously penetrated right inside the dreamer's head. The last barrier between one person and another, the barrier of thought, had been broken.

Jesuit and Huron were not quite so different from one another as someone like de Brébœuf might at first have supposed. Each, according to his own lights, despised and each disciplined the body. Each had a mental preoccupation with pain; part of a Jesuit's training included a prolonged and intense brooding over Christ's passion. Both Jesuit and Huron were led, by their most private beliefs, to think a great deal about martyrdom – the Huron usually imagining himself as the torturer, the priest as the martyr.

Indian and priest alike were guided through life by visions. The Huron sensed that he lived in an implacably hostile natural world, where waking was confused with dream, and everything was possessed by spirits. For the Huron, the Christian way of looking at the world around him would mean submission, and it went against the grain of an Indian's upbringing to submit. The Jesuits therefore began by trying to impress the Hurons with their own all-round superiority. To set an individual example of goodness, and to preach the word, would hardly be enough.

The Jesuits' most dangerous rival was the tribal sorcerer, a cunning hunchback with a reputation for occult power. But luckily the Jesuits had brought with them several useful European gadgets, a clock, a magnifying-glass, a magnet, so they could easily score points against the sorcerer. The Hurons were greatly impressed. They thought the clock was alive, and wanted to know what it ate. 'All this,' the missionaries reported to Paris, 'serves to gain their affection, and make them more docile in respect to the admirable and incomprehensible mysteries of our Faith.'

As well as playing games with clocks and magnets, those Jesuits who in an earlier life had been soldiers advised the Hurons how best to fortify their villages against Iroquois raiding parties. They promised to bring in arquebusiers from Quebec, though it turned out that only a handful of men could be spared. The trouble was that in all French Canada there were not enough soldiers, or settlers either, to cope with the Iroquois.

The French Jesuits were soon sharing all the Hurons' hopes and fears, as well as eating their indigestible diet – usually a mush called sagamite, made of ground corn and smoked fish. Inevitably, they began to have similar unnerving dreams. Evil spirits arrived to torment the Jesuit fathers, in the guise of wolves or wildcats. The devil came in his favourite shape, as a desirable woman, but was vanquished, as usual, by the sign of the cross. Death made its appearance, as a skeleton. De Brébœuf, in one prophetic vision, saw a huge crucifix approach one night, from the direction of the Iroquois country, 'large enough to crucify us all'.

Then smallpox hit the tribe. The Jesuits nursed the sick, and promised them heaven as they lay dying. On earth, the Hurons had so often known hunger that they expressed a dread of starving up in heaven. The hunchback sorcerer, who had an inkling of what took place at mass, let it be known that in their chapel the Jesuits had a magical corpse ('the body and blood of our Lord') with which they were deliberately infecting the country-side; hence the smallpox.

When the chime of their clock came to be taken for a death-signal, the Jesuits prudently stopped the works. Since they themselves had no wish to be taken for sorcerers, they tried to counteract the tall stories their own conjuring tricks had put about, by fighting the epidemic. They fed the hungry, and nursed the sick, and made pets of the unruly children. By slow degrees, their tact, manly good nature and uncanny calmness reduced their opponents to dismay, and they were listened to. De Brébœuf himself made a great impression on the Hurons by accurately predicting a lunar eclipse, then, as the moon over their heads was gobbled up, warning them about hell-fire.

The Jesuits raised their own patch of wheat for sacramental wafers. They contrived wine for the chalice from wild grapes. By 1638, sixty converts were receiving communion in their little chapel. Among a people where trial marriage was the established rule, and divorce had always been easy, they did all they could to change those old customs and bring in Christian monogamy. The Hurons listened to these ideas but did not always get the point. Many thought baptism was a sort of vaccination – a safeguard against pestilence. Some chronic doubters were even worried about a shortage of tobacco in heaven.

No doubt some of the Hurons, like some of Eliot's Mohicans, turned to Christianity because it was all of a piece with iron pots and chiming clocks and obliterating eclipses; because it was the religion of these newcomers, who were so awe-inspiringly proficient. But many more must have had a great weight of nightmare fear lifted from their minds as the cult of propitiating evil spirits, and the practice of cannibalism, gave place gradually in their villages to everyday conduct influenced by a religion of brotherly love. Moral and technical superiority do not always go hand in hand: history has seen many technically expert barbarians. But to the Hurons, the moral superiority of the Jesuits may well have seemed authentic.

Yet in fact they were serving two masters, the King of Heaven and the King of France. As the royal government in Paris viewed the matter, by winning the hearts of the Hurons, the Jesuits were giving Catholic France a foothold on the midmost of the Great Lakes. They had a safe way forward, now, into the heart of America.

In their push down the St Lawrence river to Montreal, the French collided with the Iroquois. Lonely garrisons were threatened, stragglers were found scalped. In the spring of 1649, the end came for the Jesuit mission on the shores of Lake Huron. There were then eighteen black-robed fathers at work among a population of 20,000. The people had been gathered into fortified townships, but only eight French arquebusiers had arrived to defend them. Their Iroquois enemies by now had hundreds of guns; the Hurons would have to do their best with bow and arrow.

On 16 March 1649, an Iroquois war party appeared suddenly outside St Ignace, at a time when most of the men were away hunting. Only 400 women and old men were left to put up a fight. The little town was well protected, with a ravine on three sides, and a fifteen-foot stockade on the fourth. But there was hardly anyone to man the walls, so St Ignace fell quickly, and the Iroquois moved on to St Louis, three miles away.

Here, Jean de Brébœuf and another Jesuit were waiting for them, with a scratch force of eighty Huron warriors. They managed to kill thirty Iroquois, and to hold up their war party long enough for the women and children to flee to safety. As the Huron braves fought, the Jesuits encouraged the wounded, giving them baptism and absolution, and assuring them of heaven. But they were fighting against odds. The Iroquois overwhelmed the town, and carried off the two Jesuits as prisoners. In the next two weeks, fifteen Huron townships were captured or abandoned. Hurons who had escaped sought refuge on St Joseph's Island, about eight miles long and thickly forested, at the far end of the lake.

Some of the Jesuits managed to join them there, poling their possessions over to the island on a raft. Under their guidance, the Huron refugees, most of them Christian, began to build a stone fort with detached redoubts and stone walls twelve feet high. By the time winter came down, 6000 Hurons were crowded on St Joseph's Island. They were eating boiled and pounded acorns and all close to famine. On the shore opposite lurked the Iroquois, lying in wait to strike down anyone from the island who might cross over to fish or hunt. The Jesuits rationed out what food there was, using scraps of leather as ration cards, but as hunger got them in its grip, some of the Hurons defied the newfangled religious prohibition, and began to eat the bodies of the dead.

The priests managed at last to evade the Iroquois and lead the remnant of their people back to Quebec. They arrived there on 20 July 1650, and settled nearby, but dwindled away in numbers and vitality, year by year. There are still a few left.

John Eliot and the French Jesuits seem to have been engaged in much the same task, and to have encountered similar difficulties. But one was patronized by Oliver Cromwell, the other by Anne of Austria, Queen of France: the political rivalry between England and France kept them sundered. Just as only Roman Catholics were allowed in Canada, so the founders of New England described their settlements as 'a bulwark against the Kingdom of Antichrist, which the Jesuits labour to rear up in all places of the world'. The law was that any Jesuit entering Massachusetts should be hanged.

Jean de Brébœuf met the martyr's death of which his own dream of the giant crucifix had been a premonition. The account tells of his holding himself erect at the stake, conspicuously broad-shouldered, while the Iroquois went sedulously to work upon his trussed-up body. They had a cult not of loving-kindness but of physical pain. They put him to a series of tortures so devised as to be a diabolical commentary upon all de Brébœuf had done his best to preach.

They scorched him from head to foot in an imitation hell-fire of their own devising. To put a symbolic end to his exhortations, they cut away his lower lip, and thrust a red-hot ramrod down his throat. De Brébœuf is said to have stood all this without flinching. The Iroquois next hung around his neck a rosary of red-hot axe-heads. Before the French arrived in Canada there had been no iron to make red-hot, no rosary, and no imagery of hell, either. They baptized the Jesuit with boiling water. In a cannibal travesty of the eucharist, they cut bits of flesh from his body, and chewed them before his eyes.

They pushed forward a renegade Huron to taunt de Brébœuf.

'The more a man suffers on earth, the happier he is in heaven. We wish to make you happy. We torment you because we love you, and you ought to thank us for it.' They were evidently trying to get inside his mind, and break that, too.

They closed the windows of his intellect by putting red-hot coals into his eye sockets. Once the little gobbets of his living flesh had been chewed and swallowed, they cut open de Brébœuf's chest, to drink his blood. At last, the Iroquois chief tore out and ate the priest's still-beating heart. De Brébœuf was four hours under this torment, which he bore, they say, with such courage that 'his death was an astonishment to his murderers'.

3 An Asylum for the Oppressed

'What! Is it possible that any of my slaves could go to heaven, and I must see them there?' *A lady in South Carolina, 1711*

Solid joys and lasting treasure
None but Zion's children know.'
John Newton, 1779

Protestant missionary work in the early eighteenth century still meant trying to convert American Indians, in more or less conscious competition with Roman Catholic missions in Canada and Latin America; the rest of the known world was, as yet, hardly considered. George Berkeley, an Irish Protestant clergyman of great persuasiveness and sweetness of character, thought he knew how this could best be done.

His idea was to train the Indians themselves as missionaries – to build a college in some well-chosen place, a focus, and bring intelligent young Indians there from all over America. They could then be sent back home to preach the gospel. Berkeley even had a suitable place in mind. The archipelago of Bermuda, with its Shakespearian overtones, appealed to him as it had to Andrew Marvell in years not long gone by:

And in these rocks for us did frame
A temple, where to sound his name.
O let our voice his praise exalt,
Till it arrive at heaven's vault:
Which thence (perhaps) rebounding, may
Echo beyond the Mexique Bay.

In 1723, George Berkeley had a great stroke of luck. He was 38, and lecturing in Hebrew at Dublin, when at a dinner party he met a Miss Vanhomrigh – Jonathan Swift's Vanessa. So far as we know they never met each other again, yet so impressed was Miss Vanhomrigh on that one occasion by the young clergyman's wit and good morals that she left him half her fortune.

Berkeley was soon after appointed to the rich deanery of Derry – made for life. But the thought of the American heathen perishing for lack of the gospel gave him no rest. He blarneyed a sluggish Hanoverian Parliament into voting £20,000 for his scheme – though Robert Walpole, as the King's chief minister, had no serious intention of parting with the money. George Berkeley then gave up his own safe £1100 a year at Derry for a notional £100 in his own as yet imaginary college in Bermuda and in September 1728 set sail, 'in a hired ship of 250 tons', with his newly married wife and a few earnest friends.

The master of the ship was not up to his job, and 'could not find the island of Bermuda'. By steering northward, this shipload of idealists arrived, at last, on a coast which all on board expected to be inhabited by painted savages, but which turned out to be Rhode Island.

George Berkeley spent the next four years in Rhode Island, waiting with saintly patience for the £20,000 to arrive – it never did – and working away meanwhile at his *Alciphron, or the Minute Philosopher*, where, in a style of irresistible charm, he dismisses in turn all the varieties of freethinking current in his day, and advances instead his own view: that nature is the language of God.

Cynical old Walpole suggested to the Bishop of London that George Berkeley might as well be asked to come home, as he had found a better use at last for that £20,000. A soldier and member of Parliament called James Oglethorpe had put up to him an idea politically more advantageous than Berkeley's, yet philanthropical enough to satisfy those who wanted to redeem the Indians.

Wedged between the English settlement in Carolina and the nearest Spanish garrison, down in Florida, was a no-man's-land of swamp, cane-brake, sand-dune and pine wood where grew 'the famous Laurel tulip', or magnolia. Oglethorpe had already suggested a name for the place: Georgia. His idea was to found a military settlement in Georgia so as to defend Carolina against

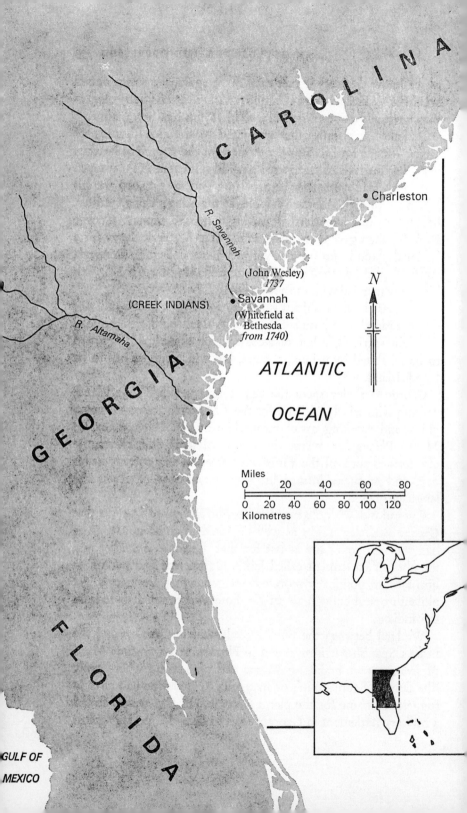

C A R O L I N A

• Charleston

R. Savannah

(John Wesley)
1737

(CREEK INDIANS)   • Savannah

R. Altamaha   (Whitefield at
                           Bethesda
                           from 1740)

ATLANTIC

OCEAN

N

G E O R G I A

Miles
0   20   40   60   80
0   20 40 60 80 100 120
Kilometres

F L O R I D A

GULF OF

MEXICO

Spanish attack from the south. But his new colony would be well thought out. Georgia was to become a kind of philanthropical, pragmatic Protestant utopia.

Oglethorpe was an Oxford man who had fought a campaign – under Prince Eugene, against the Turk – then gone home to enjoy an estate he had inherited in Surrey. He was thirty-three, a high churchman of Jacobite sympathies, and the pocket borough which went with his estate elected him to Parliament as a matter of course.

James Oglethorpe was the kind of English romantic – they occur in every generation – who hides his passionate idealism behind a stern mask of practical commonsense. In Parliament, though a Tory, he soon began making a nuisance of himself as the champion of the unfortunate. Whigs in eighteenth-century Britain were not distinguished by their social conscience; this was the time when, from Jonathan Swift to Samuel Johnson, the most forthright humanitarians were likely to be those who, in politics, had taken the Tory side.

In 1728, the year Berkeley set sail, Oglethorpe had been busy investigating debtors' prisons – the Fleet, the Marshalsea and the King's Bench. English law since the time of the Tudors had been harsh on poor debtors. When trade was slack, any poor tradesman lived in fear that some vindictive creditor might clap him in gaol: one Englishman in 500, on average, was in a debtors' prison, with little likelihood of getting out. 'What various misfortunes', wrote Oglethorpe, 'may reduce the rich and the industrious to the danger of a prison, to a moral certainty of starving? These are the people that may relieve themselves and strengthen Georgia.'

Oglethorpe had struck a nerve. Even members of Parliament – exempt though they were by privilege from imprisonment for debt – took up his plan to free the handiest of these poor debtors, train them in arms, and send them out with other Protestant unfortunates from all over Europe, so as to form in Georgia a colony which would serve as a buffer against the power of Roman Catholic Spain.

In 1732, George I granted the land between the Savannah and

Altamaha rivers by charter 'in trust for the poor.' Half Berkeley's money was paid over to the Georgia trustees, and every day hand-picked debtors were let out of gaol and drilled by sergeants of the Guards.

The Spaniards had a policy of enticing other people's slaves down to Florida, treating them well there, and enlisting them in black regiments. The next black insurrection in neighbouring Carolina – where slaves outnumbered free whites by six to one – was to occur in 1738, and chime in with a threat of war with Spain. Georgia was to be a military colony, so the trustees decided there had better be no fifth column: no Roman Catholics, and no black slaves either. Oglethorpe himself had at one time been a director of the Royal African Company, and he was careful to use arguments against allowing slaves into Georgia which sounded politically reasonable. This new colony, so he said, was intended 'as an asylum for the oppressed, and it is necessary not to permit slaves in such a country, for slaves starve the poor labourer'. But in private, James Oglethorpe had convinced himself that slavery was 'against the gospel as well as the fundamental law of England'; an uncommon view in those days. When the trustees also wanted to keep out Jews, he put his foot down.

Oglethorpe had also formed a good opinion of the Creek Indians, and held out high hopes of converting them. 'Nothing is wanting,' he explained, 'but one who understands their language well, to explain to them the *mysteries* of religion, for as to the *moral* part of Christianity they understand it and do assert it. They abhor adultery. Theft is a thing not known.' He began to look about him for the right clergyman to go out with him to Georgia, as a missionary chaplain.

Samuel Wesley was a high church parson in Lincolnshire, a better poet than some might think, and the father of nineteen children. He himself, when a young man, had contemplated going out as a missionary to Surinam. In the last days of his life, hearing of the Georgia project, Samuel Wesley wrote a letter to his old friend James Oglethorpe praising his intention to create 'a little world of your own in the midst of wild woods and uncultivated deserts, where men may live free and happy, if they are not hindered by their own stupidity and folly, in spite of the unkindness of their fellow mortals'. Samuel Wesley knew of old what it felt like to be in prison for debt.

Oglethorpe happened to meet Samuel Wesley's fifteenth child, John, on his way to court to present his dead father's master-work, *Dissertations on Job*, to the Queen (who, sitting amid her maids of honour, observed that the book was 'prettily bound' but failed to look inside). Oglethorpe at once bought seven copies at three guineas apiece – his old friend had left a widow – and made up his mind that this John Wesley, a Fellow of Lincoln College, Oxford, and a man of his own high church persuasion, was exactly the chaplain he needed in Georgia. He also took on good-natured, near-sighted Charles Wesley, John's younger brother and Samuel's eighteenth child, as his private secretary. John Wesley's stipend of £50 a year was paid by the Society for the Propagation of the Gospel, from the fund begun in Cromwell's time; it would also be his duty to carry the gospel to the Indians.

John and Charles Wesley were, at the time, the leading spirits among a group of serious young men, mostly clergymen, who amid a chorus of mockery from the rest of the university spent their time at Oxford in prayer and fasting, and in visiting sick prisoners. They had already earned themselves a sarcastic nickname: 'Methodists' (but then, 'Christian' was once a sarcastic nickname). 'They imagine they cannot be saved,' an onlooker bitingly remarked, 'if they do not spend every hour nay minute in the service of God – they almost starve themselves in order to be able to relieve the poor and buy books for their conversion.'

But in removing these two excellent young clergymen from the artificial atmosphere of Oxford, where a parson from a college had an invisible social ascendancy over any unlucky harlot or poor convict, Oglethorpe had blundered. Plunging them, unmarried, over-educated and inexperienced, amid the instinctive democracy of a frontier community hardly gave them a fair chance. Famous and effective though they were later to become, in Georgia the brothers Wesley, though always from the best of intentions, behaved like a couple of prigs. The fault was not all theirs. Like Oglethorpe and everyone else, they took it for granted that it would be possible to impose upon pioneer America the social relations which had in fact been left behind, in England, the moment the mainsail was hoisted.

Oglethorpe's first batch of debtors went across in *Anne* (200 tons). The men practised their weapon drill; the women knitted worsted stockings. *Anne*'s cargo included ten tuns of beer, and at Madeira they took in five more of wine. Oglethorpe planned to set up a brewery in Georgia, but to settlers and Indians alike rum would be banned. On Saturday, 19 June 1737, with John Wesley's approval, Oglethorpe introduced another new rule, to forbid fishing and fowling on the Sabbath. All the intentions for Georgia were rational and benevolent – as indeed had been the Jesuits', in Paraguay. But in individualistic North America, would this kind of well-meant paternalism ever work?

The first settlers were all Protestants down on their luck. But they had not much else in common, even language. Apart from the liberated English debtors there were some Moravians, who kept alive the teachings of the Czech, John Huss, and were pacifist. There were a couple of hundred Salzburgers – a handful saved and given a better chance out of the quarter of a million Protestants driven out of Salzburg at the point of the bayonet, not long since, by the Roman Catholic archbishop there. There were some Gaelic-speaking Highlanders: 'sober, industrious, friendly, hospitable people'. Drifters also began showing up in Georgia and breaking the rules, not least the rule against rum.

The leading men in Georgia most of all resented Oglethorpe's ban on slaves. Not only did this oblige them to do far too much hard work in this hot place themselves; they also knew they were losing a chance to make money hand over fist on plantations. Only the Salzburgers, the Moravians and the two Wesleys, so it would appear, were heart and soul with Oglethorpe. Tender-hearted Charles had but to see, once, in Carolina, 'a female slave whipped to the point of death by a dancing-master for over-filling a tea-cup', and his opposition to slavery was fixed for life.

Other arbitrary laws which in England could easily be enforced failed to be effective in Georgia. Dissenting sects who at home rejected the Church of England were nearly always the heirs of political extremists who, in the previous century, had fought on Cromwell's side against church and king. After royal government was restored in England, they had suffered penalties and were mistrusted. To John Wesley, with his high church principles, those who were not orthodox Anglicans could scarcely be considered Christians. But in America, the idea of mutual toleration among Protestants and even of equality between Protestant and Roman Catholic had taken root, at least in places like Rhode Island and Maryland.

Wesley refused communion to anyone – even to John Martin Boltzius, the saintly leader of the Salzburgers – who had 'not been episcopally baptized'. Even nominal Anglicans could not be sure of the sacrament unless they were men and women of conspicuously good life. Unless they were sick, he refused to baptize children otherwise than by total immersion. In Oxford – where dissenters were not then even allowed to take a degree – Wesley's behaviour might have been thought too meticulous, perhaps, yet justifiable. But in Georgia, the frustrated colonists exclaimed, 'We are Protestants, but, as for you, we cannot tell what religion you are of. We never heard of such a religion before.' In Savannah they told John Wesley frankly, 'There is neither a man nor a woman in the town who minds a word you say.'

Wesley was also disenchanted with the Creek Indians. He had spoken highly of them at first, as 'little children, humble, willing to learn and eager to do the will of God'. When they brought him symbolic gifts of honey and milk, asking him to teach them, he was touched. But the Creeks were less pure-minded than Oglethorpe had supposed. Wesley was soon denouncing them to the Trustees as 'gluttons, drunkards, thieves, dissemblers, liars, implacable, unmerciful, it being no uncommon thing for a woman either to procure an abortion or to throw her child into the next river, because she will go with her husband to the war. Whoredom they account no crime, and few instances appear of a young Indian woman's refusing anyone. Nor have they any fixed punishment for adultery.'

The Salzburgers, however, thought well of the Creeks. 'They love one another so that they venture their lives for one another.

C

When they promise a thing they keep their word. They account themselves gentlemen, and reckon working for hire to be slavery.' The Moravians built a school for them, and began a mission. The Moravians were the first to advance the obvious idea that mission work should never be an aspect of state policy, but an activity of the church and the church alone. But Moravians would not bear arms, even in defence of Georgia, and this was a military colony. So they were sent away, to find another home with the Quakers in Pennsylvania.

'Whatever increases the strength or authority of the body over the mind, that thing is sin to you' – so his mother, the formidable matriarch Susannah, had repeated over and again to John Wesley ever since he was little. Thus Wesley had been bred up to master the needs of his flesh, however inexorable, by an act of will. He was a grave, neat, small man, with dark curling hair, fine hands and polished manners – a man to catch a woman's eye, fascinating, a challenge. On the voyage out, while he tried to mortify the flesh by living only on rice and ship's biscuits, some of the matrons on board had tried, in vain, to entangle him.

The very rigour of his celibacy – and Charles's too – very soon led in Georgia to more scandal than if the brothers had been lax. Oglethorpe had more important things to bother with than screening his chaplain and his secretary from gossip; he advised them both to marry.

The chief magistrate at Savannah, Thomas Causton, was a man about to dip his hand, for at least the second time, into public funds – a rogue not yet exposed. Considering, perhaps how useful it soon might be to have a well-placed friend in the colony, Thomas Causton put his eighteen-year-old niece, Sophia, in John Wesley's way. Dressing Sophia 'all in white, and in the utmost simplicity, to please his taste', he dropped an unmistakable hint to the thirty-three-year-old clergyman: 'The girl will never be easy until she is married. I give her up to you. Do what you will with her.'

That, even for an unworldly parson, was a blatant trap. But Sophia was sweet and young, and John Wesley found himself liking her very much. Methodism had become a jocose byword at Oxford for 'endeavouring to reform notorious whores'. But this was a more innocent allurement – and one which nearly drove the good man out of his mind. Would the holiness towards which his mother, Susannah, had so continually directed him be lost from sight, in a cosy home-life with this delicious creature? Sophia offered him a cup of coffee. John accepted – how could he refuse? – and thereby broke his Friday fast. To ease his mind, he began translating some Moravian hymns, only to find that they, too, echoed his carnal preoccupation:

> My soul before Thee prostrate lies,
> To Thee, her source, my spirit flies,
> My wants I mourn, my chains I see;
> O let Thy presence set me free!

'I find, Miss Sophy,' he warned her, 'that I can't take fire into my bosom, and not be burnt.' After recourse to prayer on the 'complicated temptations of the married state', John Wesley, in the end, cast the girl off, telling her (and on St Valentine's Day, too) that he had made up his mind, 'if I marry at all, not to do it until I have been among the Indians'.

This was practically a jilt, and Sophia knew it. The Spaniards had begun to threaten the new colony. Oglethorpe was busily keeping the Creek chiefs happy with gifts of frogged laced coats and cocked hats, and had no intention of upsetting his delicately poised apple-cart by sending John Wesley on a fervent mission among them. Luckily for Sophia, another admirer, William Williamson, was standing in the wings. He proposed, she accepted, and Wesley, as the parson, was obliged to perform the ceremony.

A man more broke to the ways of the world might have managed to shrug it off, but John Wesley was wounded to the heart. His strictness had already made him enemies. When he hit on a form of words for excluding Sophia from holy communion, they pounced.

Wesley was indicted before a grand jury which included three Baptists, sixteen other dissenters, a reputed infidel, a Frenchman who could speak no English and a Roman Catholic who, strictly speaking, had no business being in Georgia at all. The principal charge was 'restricting the benefits of the Lord's Supper to a small number of persons, and refusing to it all others who will not conform to a grievous set of penances'. No civil court was competent in such a matter – an ecclesiastical court might have been – but the jury bought in a true bill. People in Georgia were not going to have a state religion imposed upon them. Wesley knew better than to stay and argue.

John Wesley broke bail and left Savannah, crossing the river 'as soon as evening prayers were over, about eight o'clock, the tide then serving'. He escaped through the woods to Charleston, Carolina, living on gingerbread, and there took passage in a ship called *Samuel* for England. His apprenticeship in Georgia had been brief, though sharp. Mission work was something other than he had supposed. His father, Samuel the poet, had also been mistaken in dreaming of Georgia as utopia. A handful there, like the Moravians, had followed Wesley's example, and tried to live by a strict religious rule. But most of the others, whatever they may have suffered in Europe for their principles, had gone to Georgia in the hope of accumulating property. They therefore carried with them the vices of acquisitive eighteenth-century Britain – greed, smugness, brutality, anxiety – as an invisible cargo.

John Wesley had developed the faculty of self-examination, and soon put his finger on the weakness of the missionary hopes which Oglethorpe's Georgia colony had at first awakened. 'I left my native country,' he wrote in January 1738, 'in order to teach the Georgian Indians the nature of Christianity. But what have I learned myself, in the meantime? Why, that I, who went to America to convert others, was never myself converted to God.' Europeans might go on seeking, sometimes from decent, sometimes from dubious motives, to sanctify the vast overseas market they had begun to exploit – to civilize and Christianize the new lands and people they were encountering. But what had been happening to their own faith, meanwhile.?

Though John Wesley's poet-father, Samuel, had been a high church parson, both his grandfathers had been nonconformist ministers, and both had suffered for their dissenting creed at the

Restoration. When, on his return from Georgia, Wesley began to brood in a different way upon his religious beliefs – he had been deeply impressed in Georgia, for example, by the Moravians – a half-forgotten, heroic nostalgia came crowding in upon him. This sentiment he shared, whether he knew it then or not, with many ordinary Englishmen of his time, including some who had emigrated as dissenters to America.

In Cromwell's time, the church to which a man gave his loyalty was likely to express where he stood politically. Thus, Baptists were more radical than Presbyterians; high church Anglicans were royalist. England after the Restoration was littered with sects, losing ground under persecution, which a generation before by preaching and pamphleteering had kept many respectable people, then doing well in the world, at a pitch of visionary exultation. Some of them – shopkeepers, craftsmen, farmers, merchants – had even dreamed of the reign of King Jesus as a practical possibility, here on earth.

But when John Wesley arrived back in England from Georgia the year was 1737. Cromwell had been dead for seventy-nine years, German George occupied the throne, and nobody – or almost nobody, except a handful of English or Scottish Jacobites, and a great many Irish Roman Catholics – dreamed of any radical social change. The secret of government had been found: to let sleeping dogs lie. Yet from the inconclusive and emotionally charged revolution of Cromwell's time, many ordinary, hard-working Englishmen, some of them now very prosperous, had inherited a sediment of democratic religious feelings and deferred hope, expressed in Biblical idiom. They did what everyone else did – earned their wages or tried to make their fortune – but meanwhile choked-off religious emotion and guilt mounted up in them, like water behind a dam. Money values, not spiritual values, now dominated, and the hypocrisy they imposed was an endless denial of the wild, millennial hopes of the civil war.

When John Wesley, on his way back from Georgia, began to ponder the significance of 'converted to God', the unresolved question was this: religious enthusiasm in the England of his day had recent associations with political and social upheaval. Was there a way in which religion might once again be made fervent and heart-rending – could, in fact, that buried revolutionary sentiment somehow be discharged – without disturbing the present advantageous set-up of civil society? Could the beneficiaries of a society in which a man now found fewer obstacles to making his fortune than ever before somehow keep the upper hand, by means of religion, over the disinherited, who shared in some degree or another his language and his principles, yet not his economic advantages? The Methodists in their Evangelical Revival gave a practical answer, and one which was to inform and colour almost all Protestant missionary work thereafter, as well as giving it great energy.

An evangelizing technique which had the effect of liberating those eighteenth-century men and women made unhappy by their own almost inexplicable sense of guilt was hit upon by a younger Oxford Methodist called George Whitefield, though it was soon after taken up and brilliantly employed by the brothers Wesley.

George Whitefield was unprepossessing – lank hair, small blue eyes, and in later life so obese that he had to go through a door sideways. But his voice was astonishing – varied, impassioned and extraordinarily distinct. Witnesses tell of sermons he preached in the open air which could be heard two miles away. He was a clergyman with all the talents of a great actor. As David Garrick once remarked, 'I would give a hundred guineas if I could only say *Oh!* like Mr Whitefield.'

Here is a snatch from one of his exhortations, taken almost at random from a shorthand version of a sermon. Declaimed with all the resources of Whitefield's voice, the emotional effect of such words as these on a huge, silent, guilt-ridden crowd may well be imagined.

I tell thee, O man; I tell thee, O woman, whatever thou art, thou art a dead man, thou art a dead woman, nay, a damned man, a damned woman, without a new heart.

After the dull and doctrinal sermons preached in the parish church, such rhetoric as Whitefield's was astonishing. Mediaeval friars had preached something like this, as had the more emotional

Puritan ministers of Commonwealth times. (Their printed sermons were easy to come by in the West Country when Whitefield was a boy, and in later life he was often tempted to identify himself with 'the good old Puritans'.) But in Methodist preaching there is something new, an aggressiveness. Whitefield's words knock at the heart like bullying hammer-blows. The men who make these assertions, these promises, are socially and economically in the ascendant: hot gospelling had begun.

George Whitefield had gone to the local grammar school in Gloucester – a place renowned in the civil war for standing a difficult siege in the Parliamentary cause. His widowed mother married again when George was nine, and he seems thereafter to have felt unloved. In school plays, cross-eyed though he was, he showed great talent in the girls' parts. At fifteen he left school, to fetch and carry for his mother as a pot-boy, at the Bell Inn.

Then someone explained to Whitefield how he could escape the drudgery of a pot-boy's life by working his way through Oxford, cleaning boots and waiting tables, in college, as a servitor; afterwards, he could take holy orders. So George Whitefield decided to alter his style. 'As once I affected to look more rakish, now I strove to look more grave than I really was.' And the piety he simulated soon became second nature.

The Methodists had by then been the joke of the university for the past three years. Whitefield went the whole hog, and soon after joining the Methodists was being threatened with expulsion by the Master of his college, for 'visiting the poor'. But combining the role of an exemplary Christian with fetching and carrying for his fellow students was galling for him. George felt solitary, out of sorts, loveless, as if an incubus weighed upon him. He fasted morbidly, prayed excessively, fell into neurotic fevers. He was well enough aware of his own latent theatrical talent, and this too became a source of guilt. 'Can I be a player,' he asked himself, 'yet go to sacrament, and be a Christian?'

The excessive intensity of the early Methodist way of life had driven more than one Oxford man over the edge, but a time came when, on George Whitefield, his ardours and austerities worked an instantaneous and as it were miraculous change. His neurotic tensions were one day all resolved, liquefied, turned to bliss, by what we may agree with the Methodists to term 'conversion'. Though a latecomer among them, Whitfield was the first of the Oxford Methodists, apparently, to experience personally this sudden clarification of the heart. The Wesleys themselves underwent a similar experience only after their lacerating apprenticeship in Georgia.

At the age of twenty-one, Whitefield went back home to Gloucester, no longer a pot-boy but a clergyman. So dizzily emotional was his first sermon – in St Mary de Crypt, the church where he had been baptized – that 'fifteen were driven mad'. The guilty depression which had weighed him down at Oxford was gone for good. The young actor-preacher, having plummeted to the depths of neurosis and emerged, soon found that he now had at the tip of his tongue a set of quivering cadences which would touch to the heart others in misery from sinful guilt or the dread of death. Like a great actor in a great role, he knew how to purge his listeners with pity and terror. Emotionally, he fed upon his own oratory, and from then until the end of his busy life, George Whitefield was never happier than when preaching at the top of his voice to several large audiences a day.

Once you were 'saved' – as Methodists employed the term – you were saved for life. Your sins were forgiven you; your faith had made you whole; guilt was a thing of the past. You could busy yourself about your worldly affairs with no bad conscience. Even the fixed social hierarchy was suddenly less oppressive, since you and your friends were saved, and your betters very likely damned.

Though John Wesley himself continued to live with apostolic simplicity, his lifetime coincided in Britain with eighty years of phenomenal prosperity: Bengal was conquered; factories and mines began to spew out wealth. Among the luckier of his followers, a feeling began to grow that doing well in the world was, in itself, a sufficient proof of goodness. In fact the organized sanctified anxiety of Methodism – its particular virtues of rigour, commercial honesty, the fruitful use of every moment, and a sense of trusteeship towards wealth – were also, of course, the very virtues likeliest to make a worldly success of a man in this newly industrialized Britain.

As time went by, a rift began to show between those Methodists who had risen in the world, and those who had not. Socially speaking, those who had done well were likeliest to be found in the evangelical wing of the Church of England. The least fortunate, many of them still working for wages and never likely to escape, went on worshipping in chapels even humbler than those of the most plebeian and democratic of the old dissenters. But all spoke much the same language, shared similar values, and would respond to the same appeal, were it pitched right.

When only twenty-three, George Whitefield turned his back upon the spectacular career opening up before him in England as a popular preacher, and took on the missionary job in Georgia which John Wesley himself had muffed.

This singular decision prompted the *Gentleman's Magazine* of November 1737 to break approvingly into verse:

> Go, loved of heathen! with each grace refined,
> Inform, enrapture each dark Indian's mind.

Unlike his strait-laced and exigent predecessor, Whitefield was admired in Georgia for his 'open easy deportment, without show of austerity or singularity of behaviour'. He had brought with him £1306 6s taken up in collections at his sermons 'for the poor in Georgia' before he left. His charity was timely; not all Oglethorpe's liberated debtors had turned out well as pioneers.

In Georgia, where John Wesley, the most distinguished figure among the Oxford Methodists, had failed so dismally, Whitefield triumphed. His dramatic way of preaching created a sensation. He enjoyed four months of gratifying success, and then several of 'the better sort of people', having summed him up, asked their young minister to go back to London and be their spokesman before the Georgia trustees. They wanted to sell rum, but they wanted, above all, to buy slaves. Their toast after every dinner in Georgia had been 'the one thing needful' – slavery.

William Williamson, Sophia's husband, had already worked out how to secure for himself the monopoly of the Georgia slave trade, once the trustees had lifted their ban. Wesley's old enemy, Thomas Causton, the embezzler, put his hand in his own pocket to pay Whitefield's passage from Savannah to Charleston, and thus speed his passage home. Nothing more, after those fulsome verses in the *Gentleman's Magazine*, was heard of a mission by George Whitefield to the Creek Indians. For the 'loved of heathen', fame did not lie that way. James Oglethorpe's comments on Whitefield's returning home to advocate slavery are not available, but then, a Christian abolitionist in 1737 was a rare bird, and Oglethorpe no doubt kept his own counsel.

Not having done what all expected of him, and gone off to convert the Indians, did not preoccupy Whitefield long. 'All wondered that I would go to Georgia', he declared afterwards. 'and some urged that if I had a mind to convert Indians, I might go among the Kingswood miners, and find Indians enough there.' This he did, once back in England.

In Bristol – then the second city of the kingdom – Kingswood was a byword for intimidation. The city had been refining West Indian sugar since 1654, using coal mined at Kingswood, on the city's outskirts. Men with black faces would surge towards the city, especially when bread was dear, to lead the mob and terrorize the rich. All over the country, other such masses of ill-fed, ill-clad, rejected and restless wage-earners were soon to germinate, as early industrial methods came into use. Here if Whitefield wanted them were pagan savages, and to spare.

Parsons of the established church, having found early Methodism heterodox, were beginning to withdraw their patronage. Early in 1739, George Whitefield was refused the pulpit in the great Bristol church of St Mary Redcliffe. So on 17 February 1739, he went outside the city, and preached in the open air to the Kingswood miners. Preaching out of doors to the unregenerate was a novelty almost unknown since the days of the mediaeval friars. John and Charles Wesley soon followed Whitefield's example: the emotional effect of their sermons upon the miners was astonishing.

The Kingswood miners had grown used to being treated like savages – like dangerous animals, prowling on the margin of society. Yet the vocabulary of the 'good old Puritans' must still have echoed somewhere in their minds, for in the civil war Bristol had been fought over, back and forth, and pitmen had then made notable soldiers. When they preached sin and redemption, the Methodists were using an idiom which echoed a heroic past, handed down in turn of phrase if not in actual reminiscence from father to son. These young parsons from Oxford were reawakening that dim verbal tradition which is all an illiterate man can know of his own history; they were arousing emotions which were the genuine substance of their minds. In familiar language they were offering the Kingswood miners a chance to resume their common humanity – to re-enter society. The Methodists' dramatic message of salvation – then a novelty – took the miners by storm. Everywhere in Kingswood, hymns were heard. A school was opened. Whitefield's miners like Eliot's Praying Indians were changed, no doubt for the better, but they were also tamed, and afterwards when the price of bread went up the merchants of Bristol could sleep more soundly in their beds.

Children, too, were treated by that rational secular century as little better than painted savages, until Rousseau began to advocate otherwise. Whitefield's next mission was to orphans in Georgia. The Methodist doctrine in those days was that first, as Susannah Wesley used to say of her own children, 'their wills must be broken.'

Some of James Oglethorpe's lame ducks, after reaching Georgia from prison or religious persecution, had failed and died there, leaving orphans. So Oglethorpe gladly gave Whitefield the 500 acres for which he asked, to support an orphanage called Bethesda. Whitefield had an eye for orphans who would make themselves useful. The colonists were soon appealing to Oglethorpe to stop the parson rounding up able-bodied orphans, busily at work for their near relations. Oglethorpe had to point out to Whitefield that he had been granted only 'helpless' orphans. The children he eventually gathered together, said Whitefield, were 'as ignorant of God and Christ as the Indians'.

The orphans camped on the site, without food or shelter, for Bethesda had had a setback when the Spaniards intercepted 'a schooner laden with 10,000 bricks', but happily, 'the Indians brought in plenty of deer.' The Creek Indians had by now seen enough of the colonists to become disillusioned with Christianity.

As their chief remarked, 'Christians get drunk! Christians beat men! Christians tell lies. Me no Christian!' The orphans, however, were too small to have an opinion in the matter.

Soon they were all hard at work, for Bethesda was to be self-supporting. From collections made on a nine-week preaching tour in Philadelphia, Whitefield brought back £500, together with four useful volunteers: a bricklayer, a tailor, and two maids. Staff at the orphanage were given only food and clothes; all necessities were bought from a common purse. But this rudimentary Christian communism for the very young – kept going, for the most part, by their own labour – depended on heightening the emotional atmosphere in which the unlucky orphans lived almost to the pitch of religious hysteria. Here is the day's time-table.

Orphans were out of bed at five o'clock in the morning, and down on their knees for fifteen minutes' private prayer. At 6 a.m. they met in chapel, for a psalm. At seven came morning hymn and public prayer, then breakfast, during which, at set intervals, the hungry youngsters were expected to lay down their spoons and stand up, to sing more hymns. During the forenoon they went to work picking cotton. Girls learned to knit and sew, and some of the bigger boys made clothes, or did carpentry.

At noon the orphans ate a meal, then came two hours of school, and two more hours picking cotton. Play was unprofitable – 'Satan's darling hours,' Whitefield declared, 'to tempt children to all manner of wickedness' – so any kind of play whatever was forbidden. After supper – interrupted, as breakfast had been, by hymns – came chapel services at seven, and catechism at eight, followed by another quarter of an hour's private prayer on weary little knees, and so to bed. Sunday, though a day of rest from field-work, was filled to the brim by four successive church services.

The terror, the hysteria, were near the surface. One day, according to a witness, the orphans were picking cotton 'when one of them exclaimed, "If we do not believe in the Lord Jesus Christ we shall all go to hell." At once the entire family [of orphans] fell upon their knees, and began to pray, "Lord Almighty, have compassion on us. Prick us to the heart. Pluck us as firebrands out of the burning." '

Benjamin Franklin had meanwhile become Whitefield's publisher. Though not greatly impressed by the gospel he preached, Franklin was shrewd enough to see that his writings would be a popular success. The great preacher was once so indiscreet as to say to Franklin, who made a note of it, 'The grand end of every Christian institution for forming tender minds should be to convince them of their natural depravity.' How indeed could conversion be assured if guilt were not first implanted?

After the colony had been yielded up by its trustees, in 1757, to the crown, slavery was at last allowed in Georgia. What was to have been utopia for the unfortunate became a place for dumping convicts. Whitefield's own attitude to slavery, too, had gone through more than one change since, as a young man, the settlers made him their advocate for 'the one thing needful'. In an early 'open letter' which Franklin published for him, Whitefield had dwelt on the dangerous side of slavery. 'Whether it be lawful for Christians to buy slaves,' he wrote, 'I shall not take it upon me to determine, but I am sure it is sinful, when bought, to treat them worse than brutes. I have wondered that they have not more frequently risen in arms against their owners.' But as soon as the work hitherto done by orphans on Bethesda could legally and more profitably be done by blacks, Whitefield showed an unctuous enthusiasm for the possibilities of the plantation system. 'Blessed be God,' he wrote, 'for the increase of the negroes! I entirely approve of reducing the number of orphans as low as possible; and I am determined to take in no more than the plantation will maintain, till I can buy more negroes.' In 1742 there had been forty-nine busy little orphans at Bethesda, but by 1769 there were only sixteen. The estate was then producing rice and indigo.

One black slave had been bought for Bethesda – at a cost of £30 – by the melancholy English minor poet, James Hervey, rector of Weston-Favell and author of *Meditations Among the Tombs*. George Whitefield as a sign of gratitude named the slave 'Weston', and promised the donor constantly to 'remind him by whose means he was brought under the everlasting gospel'.

The way he ran his orphanage – like a nightmare monastery

for the very young – shows up George Whitefield's less agreeable side, but he was not alone at the time in treating as sacrosanct all work which might be made to yield a profit. In Britain as in America, any available labour, white, black, female or infant was eagerly set to work, irrespective of its dehumanizing effect on the wage-earner, the orphan or the slave. Work of such a kind was regarded as good in itself – not only sanctioned and upheld by law, but even accepted without question by any wage-earners who happened to share their employers' religious views. The fatal twist given to St Benedict's simple little truth, *laborare est orare*, may be hard for us to contemplate, living as we do in an economy where work is becoming harder to find, as machines replace men. But the Protestant work ethic was, then, a code beyond all dispute.

The famous evangelist is more fairly judged by the oratory in which he was pre-eminent. His talent was for preaching to multitudes. More than any other minister at work in America before him, George Whitefield, by preaching to great crowds in the open air, articulated the Great Awakening: that singular renewal of Christian belief, which, during the 1740s, spread among American Protestants like wildfire.

Protestant refugees of every confession had taken ship to America, many for conscience's sake. The Great Awakening stirred them up and brought them together. They began to gloss over their doctrinal quarrels, and to seek a distinctively American cast of mind and tone of voice. Conversion became a common emotional experience, helping to form the new sense of nationhood: by 1748, the Great Awakening had increased church membership by 40,000 in New England alone.

While Whitefield was evangelizing in Philadelphia, in 1739, everyone in the city flocked to hear. On a good day – so Benjamin Franklin figured – the great preacher could make himself heard by an audience of 30,000. 'Many wept bitterly while I was praying,' Whitefield reported. 'Their hearts seemed loaded with a sense of sin.' 'It seemed as if all the world', Franklin himself remarked sardonically, 'were growing religious. One could not walk through Philadelphia in the evening without hearing psalms sung.'

Whitefield himself was better aware than most of the political and religious changes going on to form a new nation in America. In almost his last sermon, preached in 1770, six years before the outbreak of the American Revolution, he was to predict that America would become 'one of the most opulent and powerful empires in the world'.

His emotional outpouring in the Great Awakening was the last time Whitefield was to play a significant role. He drifted back to England, becoming chaplain to the widowed and pious Selina, Countess of Huntingdon – a lady who helped on the Methodist cause by building chapels in fashionable spas – Bath, Bristol, Tunbridge Wells. To raise money for a chapel in wicked Brighton, Lady Huntingdon sold her jewels. Evangelical religion was becoming the fashion.

George Whitefield, as its great exponent, was provided with a chapel of his own, in Tottenham Court Road, not far from London's theatres. He had already preached his sermons so often that they were dramatically perfect. As John Newton – a slave-trader turned evangelical parson – said: 'Many were the winter mornings in which I got up at four to attend his Tabernacle, and I have seen Moorfields as full of lanterns at these times as I suppose the Haymarket is full of flambeaux on an opera night. All our popular preachers are only his copies.'

In 1759, George Whitefield made the mistake of preaching a sermon against the playhouses. By now the theatrical profession thought of him less as a clergyman than as a competitor. Next year, Samuel Foote, the great comic actor, brought George Whitefield on stage at the Haymarket, foibles, obesity, gestures, stupendous voice and all.

Dr Squintum in *The Minor* was the great evangelist to the life. The play, Foote's performance apart, was a lewd farce. 'Dr Squintum washed me,' ejaculates the bawd in the play, 'with the soapsuds and scouring sand of the Tabernacle, and I became as clean and bright as a pewter platter.' But all Lady Huntingdon's influence with the Lord Chamberlain did not suffice to get it banned: even at Oxford, the mockery had been less cruel. In 1770, Whitefield died – he was only fifty-five, but his nerves had been shattered by emotional preaching. Two months after his death, Foote's parody was still playing to hilarious audiences, in Edinburgh, like a pantomime demon dancing on his grave.

When Whitefield died, John Newton, one of his more famous and interesting converts, had already been ordained for six years. He was curate of Olney, where the old slave-captain, with his hell-fire obsessions and his taste for writing hymns, was to drive his neighbour, the gentle and unfortunate poet Cowper, out of his mind.

> O, cleanse my leprous soul from guilt,
> My filthy heart renew

wrote the redeemed reprobate. In 1779 John Newton was presented – by Thornton, the banker – to St Mary Woolnoth, and thus became a prominent evangelical clergyman in the City.

His wealthy flock grumbled at his tedious sermons – Newton, though a formidable personality, had no talent for preaching. But now it mattered less, Methodism had arrived. The younger men no longer felt the same crying need to preach dramatically in the open air. Pulpits were theirs for the having – in London alone, the churches at the disposal of evangelical clergymen we reckoned to hold 30,000. The creeds of Wesley and Whitefield – they differed slightly, Whitefield making a sharper and more dreadful distinction between the saved and the damned – had successfully given a distinctive vocabulary and set of values to many of the new men growing rich as Britain industrialized.

Newton lived into the next century, and what he found hardest to reckon with was that the cause closest to his well-to-do parishioners' hearts should have become the abolition of the slave trade. John Newton had not seen the need hitherto to apologize for the ships he had commanded. After all, the ship-owner employing him, Joseph Manesty of Liverpool, had been a Methodist too.

'During the time I was engaged in the slave trade,' he wrote, 'I never had the least scruple as to its lawfulness. It is indeed accounted a genteel employment, and is usually very profitable. I considered myself a sort of gaoler or turnkey.'

> Strange and mysterious is my life,
> What opposites I feel within!
> A stable peace; a constant strife;
> The rule of grace, the power of sin.

His preoccupation on board, once he had seen the light, was the fight within himself against the ever-present carnal temptation of the manacled black girls, but by occupying his mind with Euclid and Holy Writ, and by constant prayer, he had manfully withstood.

In his old age, Newton began to edit his memories, almost managing to convince himself that, in his youth on the West African coast, he must have been, not a slave-dealer's runner, hunting up stock, but actually a slave himself. No one looks for truth on a tombstone, but John Newton's epitaph, composed by himself, is a sad prevarication.

JOHN NEWTON
CLERK

Once an Infidel and Libertine
A Servant of Slaves in Africa

4 Everything Belongs to Everyone

None of them know what it is to possess property in our sense of the word. If a native possess many articles of property he must distribute and cannot withhold; all his friends have a kind of positive claim, and to refuse to give would be shocking. Friendship is inviolate and is a kind of real relation in Tahiti. The friend was a partner in everything, the wife not excepted. It will be many years before they can advance much in civilization.' *Letter from Polynesia, 1824, by the veteran LMS missionary, William Crook*

'Rum, blankets, muskets, tobacco and diseases have been the great destroyers, but my belief is, the Almighty intended it so. Out of evil comes good.' *Edward Markham's journal, 1834*

'The white people will pray you all dead.' *Tonga chief, 1882*

On 19 June 1767, a British three-master, *Dolphin* (Captain Samuel Wallis), drew near to a South Sea island where no such monster as a full-rigged ship had been seen within the memory of man.

Around this island was the usual coral reef. Inland were volcanic mountains, 7300 feet high, visible sixty miles out at sea, and wrapped in cloud. The climate was benign – hot sun refreshed by sudden showers – and from the deck of *Dolphin*, as they approached, they could see a green and fertile coastal plain, where half-wild pigs and chickens picked up an easy living under the trees. There were groves of coconut palm, and another, less familiar tree, handsome, with shiny green leaves. Oval fruit the size of melons, hung down from its branches like Japanese lanterns. Breadfruit. The island was Tahiti.

Island women wearing robes of bark cloth had crowded to

the beach as the ship came near. Into their sleek hair they had stuck bright tropical flowers. Their buttocks, though not their faces, were elaborately tattooed.

Five hundred large war-canoes with threateningly high prows were beached along the shore. Four thousand men, armed with stone-age weapons, clambered into them and paddled valiantly towards *Dolphin*. From the deck of the ship came a puff of smoke, and a noise like the crack of a whip. One warrior was magically struck dead, and one was enough. The men in the canoes decided to be friends. They waved and shouted; they were as volatile as children.

As they crowded ashore, the men from *Dolphin* soon found that those women, waiting with flowers in their hair and their brown bodies lubricated with coconut oil, were only too eager to offer themselves. While the sailors took their womenfolk, the tattooed warriors stood by and watched and laughed and cheered them on.

People on Tahiti lived at ground level, without furniture, under a palm-leaf thatch to keep off the rain. Food was to be had for the bother of reaching out a hand. More than 40,000 people were then living on Tahiti – an island thirty-three miles long, and shaped like a disfigured dumb-bell. There were no snakes or fierce animals, but between the islanders from the big knob of the dumb-bell and those living in the smaller knob there was endless fighting.

These tribal wars gave the men on Tahiti an occupation; their life otherwise was almost entirely self-centred. As Captain Cook, the second British navigator to reach Tahiti, was later to observe with an almost envious regret, 'These people seem to enjoy liberty to its fullest extent, every man seems to be the sole judge of his actions and to know no punishment but death.'

The Tahitians most free with their favours were the youngest girls, from nine or ten years upwards. To the music of a wooden drum and a sharkskin nostril-flute they came merrily towards the seamen, performing the motions of 'a very indecent dance, singing the most indecent songs and using the most indecent actions, in the practice of which they are brought up from earliest childhood. In doing this they keep time to a great nicety.' Parents

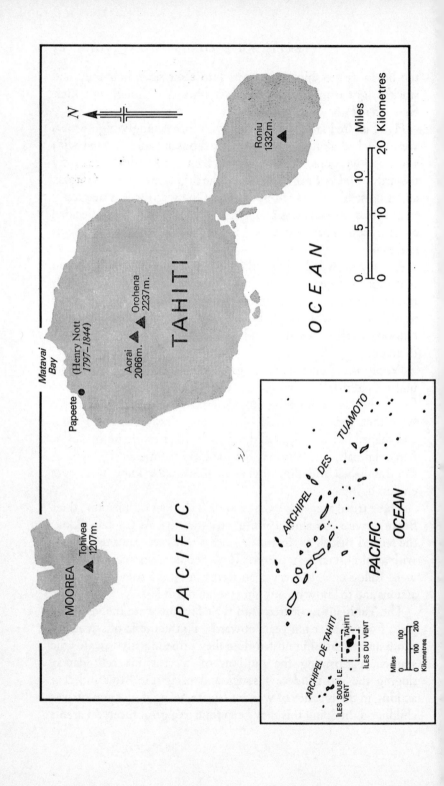

on Tahiti were of the opinion that an early deflowering made a daughter's menstruation easier. They would laugh tolerantly at the ingeniously complicated entanglements to which their small daughters introduced the sailors, remarking, 'Oh, let them alone. They are only children, and will grow faster for it.'

A girl who at last got pregnant would usually find a husband for herself, and leave the circle of dancers. Childbirth was easy on Tahiti, but infanticide was commonplace – this fact gave Thomas Malthus a simple and politically useful idea which has since gone round the world: that Tahiti thrived because its population never outgrew the food supply.

The Tahitians were great thieves, or, more exactly, they lacked any sense of property. Land on the island had never been bought or sold. As soon as a child was old enough to fetch down his own food by climbing a coconut tree, his parents lost control of him. Tahitians had magnificent teeth and splendid health, and spent much of their time surfing. When first their chiefs were offered alcohol, they turned up their noses at the beastly stuff.

The year after Wallis had rediscovered Tahiti, *La Boudeuse* brought Louis de Bougainville there, the good-natured French explorer who had observed the expulsion of the Jesuits from Paraguay, and the scientist who gave his name to bougainvillaea. This time *La Boudeuse* was met, not by war-canoes, but by twelve men coming off from the shore ceremonially with bunches of bananas: 'their olive branch'. On Tahiti, de Bougainville at once observed the men grew their nails long (as did French aristocrats) except for the middle finger of the right hand. Once sure he was a friend, the Tahitians approached *La Boudeuse* in such numbers that de Bougainville found it awkward to drop anchor.

He entertained them with flute, violin and bass viol, and by sending up rockets. They entertained him by letting their young girls make love to his sailors, to the sound of music. De Bougainville named the island *la Nouvelle Cythère*, after the place where Venus rose from the sea, and his account of thirteen days ashore there made Tahiti a part of Europe's romantic mythology.

In his *Supplément au Voyage de Bougainville*, Denis Diderot – encyclopaedist, courageous philosopher and occasional pornographer – took as his text the free sexual life on Tahiti, his real target being the taboos which the Roman Catholic church was so absurdly trying to impose on France: chastity, virginity, fidelity. Tahiti made good copy, but from what de Bougainville had reported, Denis Diderot perceived that Tahiti was in danger. What would European values and European products do to this paradise of the cult of pleasure?

'Here, everything belongs to everyone,' points out his fictional Tahitian, 'and you have preached us some such distinction, I know not what, between *mine* and *thine*.' With private property had come diseases, and with diseases, guilt. 'We take our daughters and our wives in common,' said Diderot's islander, but now the sailors, in their intercourse with the island's women, had 'lit in them a delirium never known. They have begun to hate themselves.'

Captain Cook's *Endeavour* dropped anchor inside Tahiti's reef the year after de Bougainville left. Cook stayed on the island three months, to establish the sun's distance from the earth by observing the transit of Venus. After three weeks ashore in Tahiti, twenty-four seamen and ten marines out of his crew of ninety had gone sick with venereal disease. Whether Wallis or de Bougainville had introduced these diseases to Tahiti became a matter of acrimonious patriotic dispute.

To the music of the nostril flute, the girls went on performing the same tantalizing gyrations, and the visiting Jack Tars returned the compliment by dancing the hornpipe. The little girls on Tahiti still gave themselves without any evident shame, but the price of an act of love was now an iron nail. The Tahitians were throwing away their stone-age tools. There was almost nothing they would not do for iron.

In 1773, the legend of a paradisal Tahiti was given a fillip by Sir John Hawkesworth's vividly romanticized account of Captain Cook's first voyage – an international best seller in its day. These were the halcyon years of enlightenment and rational pleasure before the thunderclap of the French Revolution, and Hawkesworth's account of Tahitian freedom was aphrodisiac:

> One page of Hawkesworth, in the cool retreat,
> Fires the bright maid with more than mortal heat:

She sinks at once into the lover's arms,
Nor deems it vice to prostitute her charms.

To radicals in France, Britain and the United States, the sexual eagerness and simple life of the Tahitians hinted at a daydream tomorrow. Could not everything everywhere always belong to everyone – somehow?

The first outsider known to have reached Tahiti was Pedro Fernandez Quiros, a Portuguese captain owing allegiance to the Spanish crown, who touched there in 1607. When, after 1767, British and French ships began making repeated landfalls at Tahiti, the nearest Spanish government, in Peru, took heed. The warship *Águila* was sent to take formal possession of Tahiti for Spain.

Two Franciscans from the college of Ocapa went with *Águila*. Though in their ten months on the island they made no converts, they were remembered and spoken of afterwards as singular men, who would have nothing to do with local women. *Águila* also brought to the Tahitians gastric influenza, another disease to which they could put up no resistance.

On his third Pacific voyage, Cook discovered that *Águila* had left behind a cross with the date 1774, claiming the island for Charles III of Spain. Underneath, Cook wrote his own inscription, with the prior date of 1767, claiming the island for Britain's King George III. Paradise was up for grabs.

The inn-keeper of the Castle and Falcon, Aldersgate Street, in the City of London, was a Mr Dupont, a godly man and for many years a fervent supporter of Whitefield's Tabernacle. Late in 1794 he acted as host, in the Castle and Falcon, to representatives of every shade of evangelical opinion, who had met there to found the London Missionary Society. Most of those who attended the meeting came either from industrialized cities or from the great ports. Their public appeal shows how well aware they all were of the powerful social impulse, generated by industry and commerce, which was urging them out to evangelize the world. 'Our merchants', they said, 'venture into burning and frozen regions, and trade with men of every colour and clime, for uncertain riches. Are there not yet among us numbers of ministers and pious youths who would gladly fly to the ends of the earth, bearing with them the glad tidings of salvation?'

From 1794 to 1817, their treasurer was Joseph Hardcastle, a prosperous city merchant and a keen abolitionist. After 1801, meetings of the Society were held in his counting-house at Old Swan Stairs, within sight of shipping on the Thames. Hardcastle's business premises got so lumbered up with curios sent back to him by grateful missionaries that, at last, the Society had to move elsewhere.

The reputation gained by John Eliot and the Jesuits died hard: almost the earliest proposal made in the society was to evangelize the American Indians. Mr George Burder was asked to investigate rumours that some North American Indians spoke Welsh. On 19 September 1796 he reported to the *Evangelical Review* that a Welsh prince had crossed to America in the eleventh century 'with a numerous train of followers'. Their Welsh-speaking descendants could still be found 'among the Choctaw Indians of the Mississippi and Missouri'. 'A host of zealous ministers of Christ in Wales', promised Mr Burder, 'would gladly undertake mission work among them.'

But Dr Thomas Haweis had read his Hawkesworth; his gaze was fixed on Tahiti, where, as he pointed out, 'savage nature still feeds on the flesh of its prisoners – appeases its gods with human sacrifices – whole societies of men and women live promiscuously, and murder every infant born among them.' Dr Haweis was accidentally running together in his mind Tahiti and New Zealand (where ten men from Cook's consort-vessel had been cooked and eaten by Maori in 1773). But the London Missionary Society agreed: the mission field should be the South Seas.

Captain Bligh offered to take a couple of missionaries out with him in *Bounty*. He was on his way to Tahiti, to collect seedlings of the breadfruit tree and deliver them to the West Indies, in the expectation that the tree which saved the Tahitians the trouble of working might in the West Indies provide cheap food for slaves. But the Bishop of London, who did not love the evangelicals, put obstacles in their way, so the Society bought its own ship, *Duff*.

Captain James Wilson offered to sail her to the South Seas without payment. Captain Wilson had fought at Bunker Hill, and afterwards been a prisoner of Hyder Ali's, in India. But having managed to make his pile by the age of twenty-five, he had come back, in 1783, to live a quiet life at Horndean, in Jane Austen's Hampshire. There he had undergone conversion. He sold his house and took command of *Duff*; possibly Hampshire was dull.

Of the thirty evangelical missionaries who embarked with James Wilson in *Duff*, only four were ordained. The rest of them were 'godly men who understood the mechanic arts'. Their task was not only to bring Tahitians over to the Gospel, but also to teach them the techniques of civilized living.

Six of the missionaries were married, and three of their children went along, too – a boy of twelve and two babes-in-arms. Even the crew of *Duff* had been hand-picked for their piety. On 9 August 1796 they all took communion together in Haberdashers' Hall Meeting House, then sailed away under the Missionary Society's flag, 'three doves argent on a purple field bearing olive branches in their bills', captain, missionaries and crew all joining in a hymn as they went down the Thames on the tide.

> Jesus, at Thy command
> We launch into the deep.

From Rio to Tahiti they sailed 13,820 miles in 97 days, without sight of land, and nerves became frayed. Most of *Duff*'s pious ship's company were Calvinist, believing with George Whitefield that salvation was for a predestined few, and that the rest of mankind was foredoomed to hell. After living cheek by jowl for five months they began to 'entertain a suspicion that Brothers Jefferson and Cock had Arminian tendencies' – followed, that is, the teaching of the brothers Wesley in placing no emphasis on predestination.

John Cock, when they pressed him hard, went so far as to say that, in his private opinion, 'Christ died for all men'. This would never do; in Romans VII St Paul clearly hints otherwise. 'The church of Christ aboard the *Duff*', as these believers termed themselves, decided to excommunicate Jefferson and Cock, but they let them back into the fold ten days later, when the culprits were ready to submit. The Society had evidently not sent easy-going, tolerant missionaries out to Tahiti, but men with a marked sense of their own superiority to the common run of sinners.

Out to *Duff* from the shore, on the day of their arrival in March, 1797, came seventy-four canoes. Half-naked, brown-skinned Tahitians began shouting 'Taio!' – 'Friend!' – as they clambered aboard. A hundred scarcely nubile little girls with flowers in their hair began dancing their way erotically along the deck. These young girls had been aboard warships and whalers before, but *Duff* was a ship of quite another kind. The dancers were chased over the side, and the deck cleared for divine worship. Thanks were given for safe arrival, the first hymn being 'O'er the gloomy hills of darkness'.

When the cooped-up missionaries went on shore to stretch their legs, yet more moral shocks lay in wait. Everywhere they saw the ugly symptoms of venereal disease. Since Captain Wallis's day, the population had been dropping away fast, going down in thirty years from about forty thousand to about sixteen thousand. Parents could no longer manage without foreign cloth and foreign iron; they still egged on their daughters to offer themselves, but now for payment. Worse still, the missionaries were horrified to discover that 'unnatural crimes which we dare not name are committed daily without the idea of shame or guilt. There are men who dress as women.'

Duff on her way back to London picked up a cargo of tea in Canton, and in this way made £4100 for the Society. Dr Haweis had already made a donation for the Tahitian mission of £500; they were almost breaking even. But Captain Wilson's commercial acumen misled the Society into believing from the start that their mission on Tahiti could and should be self-supporting financially, by working for God on some days and Mammon on the others. To their men on Tahiti they sent less help than was necessary, therefore the missionaries landing from *Duff* could never be single-minded in their religious vocation. One of them, for example, took his annual salary in calico, and though he made a good living out of bargaining it off, this was hardly what he had been sent out for.

After a little more than a year had gone by, of the thirty missionaries who came out in *Duff*, only seven were still busy on Tahiti. Some had gone on to other islands, several had lapsed from grace. In 1798, four of them were stripped and beaten; in 1799, three were killed in a small civil war. The island was beautiful but disheartening.

When the missionaries tried in their broken Tahitian to explain Christianity, they found that either the onlookers deliberately turned their backs, or 'complained of their diseases, saying that the English had brought them'. 'The children', ran a report to the Society of 3 April 1799, 'cannot bear to have their desires crossed, their actions prohibited and their wild ramblings controlled.' But the handful of English missionaries who stuck it out on the island, though never quite sure if they were being understood, had at least done their level best to denounce infanticide. They had set their faces solemnly against violence, and agreed never to take a hand in tribal wars. When *Nautilus*, an American sealer blown off course, arrived in Matavai Bay in March 1798, the missionaries did what they could to stop the Americans trafficking with the Tahitian chiefs in guns and ammunition. They protested against the immoral behaviour of seamen at liberty on shore. In a material sense they were rather badly off, but morally they had tried to do what they were sure must be their duty.

The bachelors among the missionaries were living in the midst of hair-raising sexual licence under a great personal strain. As early as 20 November 1797 the question had formally been raised, 'Was it improper for a missionary to marry a native woman?', and the answer had been forthright. 'To marry a heathen woman was directly contrary to the word of God.'

This was a setback for Francis Oakes and John Cock, who had found girls willing enough in all other respects, but not yet ready to embrace Christianity. On 1 August 1798 came the crisis, when Reverend Thomas Lewis defied the ban, and married a pagan Tahitian lass. The others excommunicated him, though he kept coming to services just the same, and even bringing his wife.

Mrs Lewis 'remained heathen, addicted to all the abominable practices of savage life'. As a companion, a Tahitian girl might well have many splendid qualities, but the Christian notion of fidelity would not be one of them. The amorous clergyman got embroiled with some of her relations, and was killed, probably murdered, on 1 November 1799.

Those evangelical missionaries on Tahiti in the early nineteenth century had set themselves a task which might on first consideration seem hopeless: to make people work hard for their living on the island of the breadfruit tree; to teach school when Tahitian children were spectacularly out of control; to impose sexual restraint upon girls taught lubricity by precept and example from the moment they were old enough to toddle. The missionaries intended to impose on the Tahitians the moral values which, in England, had made the factory system possible. One might also argue, therefore, that they represented progress. And certainly, all those intangible outside influences which had begun to break down the traditional way of life on Tahiti were working in the missionaries' favour.

When the Tahitians at last grasped what this salvation was that the English missionaries were so insistently offering, they had answered, simply and literally, 'We want no other salvation but to live in this world.' But their poignant response hid a groan of despair. Not only were imported ailments killing them off with hideous rapidity, but venereal diseases had begun to stain their sexual attitudes with the first hint of guilt. Now therapy for a sense of guilt and the dread of death were just what the evangelicals had to offer.

Economic change helped the missionaries, too. Into the mind of Pomare, the chief who ruled near the anchorage of Matavai Bay, the *Bounty* mutineers had put the notion that by using white marksmen armed with muskets he could probably make himself king of the whole island. Wars on Tahiti in days gone by had been like giant regattas – encounters between fleets of high-prowed war canoes. Now they were fought more destructively. Stone axes were becoming rare curiosities – and iron tools could be procured only from ships. Muskets won wars – but only these seagoing foreigners had gunpowder. The first trade coup in which the missionaries managed to involve the Tahitians occurred with the arrival from Botany Bay on 25 June 1801 of HMS *Porpoise*. The penal colony in New South Wales was running short of rations.

The missionaries gave the captain of *Porpoise* a helping hand to trade off knives, old iron nails, shirts and coloured bunting against 30,000 pounds of salt pork. Afterwards, pigs on Tahiti were wealth. Thus, however odd their clumsy sermons against promiscuous pleasure may at first have sounded, the missionaries had proved their worth as intermediaries with the now indispensable outside world. They had acquired prestige.

In his long campaign to become king of the island, tall, affable, pagan Pomare was running into trouble. Though secretly derisive of Christianity, and a little too fond of rum, Pomare was discerning enough to see that the missionaries could help him become the master of Tahiti. The missionaries for their part were ready to help Pomare, for how else could these wild islanders be made to listen but with the help of some established authority?

In January 1800, the brig *Eliza* arrived from New South Wales, bringing as passengers a missionary couple called Henry, and their young daughter Sarah. Out of *Eliza*, Pomare was given an eighteen-pounder carronade and two swivels, along with muskets and much powder and shot. A couple of the missionaries who happened, like the founder of their religion, to be carpenters rolled up their sleeves and made gun-carriages. Their pledge not to take part in native wars was shrugged off; the missionaries' candidate for king of Tahiti now had artillery.

The long-drawn-out civil war on Tahiti was not an easy time for the English missionaries. They used up all their soap, salt and sugar, and towards the end were going barefoot, having worn out their shoes. In 1805 they almost ran out of communion wine, and were glad to accept a couple of bottles of claret from the captain of a passing whaler. They went short of food, and had to scour the mountains for wild yams.

The moral strain, too, was severe; some lapsed. On 6 June 1800, Benjamin Broomhall, by trade a harness maker, announced that since he no longer believed in the immortality of the soul, he proposed no longer to submit to the restraints of the gospel.

Off he went to an inland valley, to live in bliss with a native girl. One of the newcomers, William Waters, after announcing his intention of teaching the islanders Hebrew, fell in love with Pomare's concubine, and at last went mad.

From 1800 to 1805, no letters reached Tahiti from home; the London Missionary Society had taken it a little too quickly for granted that by now their mission would be self-supporting. In 1803, when Pomare died, the missionaries transferred their allegiance to his son, who by custom adopted his dead father's name. By this time Henry Nott, formerly a bricklayer, and the toughest man among them, had learned enough Tahitian to preach an intelligible sermon, and a few converts were made.

Though they felt obliged to sponsor him as king, Pomare II was not quite the man they might have chosen. Herman Melville, author of *Moby Dick*, had seen Pomare II when ashore in Tahiti, and described him as a 'sad debauchee and a drunkard, and even charged with unnatural crimes'. The missionaries themselves reported home, more circumspectly, that he 'employs his time eating, drinking, and romping with his attendants'.

In 1808 a widespread rebellion against Pomare II's authority, pagan in its tone, drove him off Tahiti into exile on another island of the archipelago. The missionaries scattered to more distant islands, or else to New South Wales. Henry Nott was the only one among them to go into exile with Pomare II. Patiently Nott bided his time, diversifying his preaching with trading: in eight months of 1811–12, Nott and his partner made over £1000.

For three years the pagan rebels controlled Tahiti, and the reprehending voice of the missionary was no longer heard. The handful of native converts left behind on Tahiti had been captured or killed. Their corpses were wrapped in coconut leaves and taken to the *marae* – the place of rites – to be offered up sacrificially to the gods. The old gods ruled.

Meanwhile in his island exile, Pomare II was learning to read and write. Eventually he asked for baptism, explaining that he wanted to be 'happy after death, and saved on judgement day'. Nott temporized. Pomare certainly knew he would need to make full use of any moral influence the Christians might exercise on his behalf, if he were to recover his kingdom. He had his mission-

EVERYTHING BELONGS TO EVERYONE 95

ary, but he had his mercenaries as well – several dozen beach-combers, mostly English and some of them convicts escaped from Botany Bay.

They were armed with muskets, and were willing to take payment for their skilled marksmanship in girls and hogs. Pomare at last fought his way bloodily back to Tahiti with their help, Nott and other evangelical missionaries riding in on his coat tails. By the time the war had been fought to a finish – in 1815 – the island's population was down to 7000, or less than a fifth of those living there when Captain Wallis arrived in *Dolphin*.

Pomare II was in favour of schools, guns and trade; a moder-nizer. Pork meant wealth, and his method of collecting revenue was hard to evade: 'he has ordered every person to bring him a hog, or they are to be banished from the land, and go upon the reef'. The king's morals were deplorable, but not much could be done beyond insisting that, before baptism, he 'dismiss several of his great ugly male wives'. He was baptized at last, publicly, impressively, before 400 of his subjects.

Not only were the missionaries able from now on to manipu-late the king so as to enhance their own authority, but they were given a happy release at last from their own long and painful celibacy. In September 1810, Henry Bicknell and his wife came back to the island from Botany Bay, bringing with them 'four single young women, sent out by the Directors of the Missionary Society for the purpose of promoting the good of the mission'. As they waited for a passage in Australia, Reverend Samuel Marsden, chaplain at the penal settlement, had looked the pros-pective wives up and down, and reported to London, 'I very much approve of the females. They are modest, pious women.'

Modest and pious without a doubt, but what could have passed through the minds of these young women when first they met a corresponding number of lonely, bachelor missionaries on ribald Tahiti? Marital bargains were soon struck. Sarah Chrystie became Mrs Hayward, Ann Turner became Mrs Nott, Sophia Browning became Mrs Davies and Ann Spur became Mrs Scott. The Direc-tors in London had taken the opportunity, at the same time, to express their 'disappointment at the small degree of Improvement made among the natives in respect of Industry and Civilization'.

But the worst days were over; they would not have much longer to wait.

After his baptism, Pomare II's idols were despatched as trophies to Joseph Hardcastle's counting-house at Old Swan Stairs. In September 1814 there were ninety-two Christian worshippers on Tahiti; by December of the same year, 300. Church attendance went up and up; the tide had turned.

Some of the credit was due, though, to Pomare's warriors who would stand around on Sundays and drive slackers into church with thumps from their bamboo truncheons. A few pagans who rejected openly the offer of salvation were put to death. Not to be a Christian when King Pomare II himself had set the good example was seditious.

In 1817, a printing press arrived. The king, so the missionaries reported, had 'an extensive knowledge of the doctrines of the Gospel, but he is a slave to drinking'. The king himself tipsily printed off the first sheet of a New Testament in Tahitian, Henry Nott's handiwork, and the first copy of the finished book was presented to Pomare, 'half bound in red morocco'.

Ordinary Tahitians who wanted a Testament had, however, to buy one; the price was paid in hollow bamboos filled with coconut oil, because Tahiti's export trade in oil was now brisk. At least three thousand Tahitians, so the missionaries reported thankfully, had copies of religious books: the publishing business was thriving too.

Persuaded in 1818 that the day of 'Industry and Civilization', as he termed it, must at last have dawned, the director of the London Missionary Society sent out a Mr John Gyles to start a sugar factory. Mr Gyles had 'been in the West Indies, and witnessing the cheapness of labour by means of the negroes thought that the natives of these islands might be induced to labour in the same way'.

Some time earlier, a minor scandal had been caused by Henry Bicknell's deciding, though a missionary, to distil trade spirits on his own account 'from a native root called Ti'. This gave Pomare a hint. The rum he found so delectable was made from molasses: Mr Gyles's sugar factory might be no bad thing. His mind was influenced in a different direction, however, by some American sailors off a Nantucket whaler, who warned him that once sugar was grown in Tahiti the British might very easily come in and annex the place. And the missionaries themselves saw that, whatever their Society might have in mind, the time had come to take a firm stand: no distilling.

And no sugar boiling either, as it turned out, because the Tahitians were not yet broken on the idea of regular paid work. As Andrew Ure, the nineteenth-century eulogist of the factory system, had taken the trouble to point out, 'It is found almost impossible to convert persons much past the age of puberty into useful factory hands.' After a year of such disillusionment, Mr Gyles took ship with all his machinery for Australia.

By now the island's children, instead of climbing palm trees, were being herded to school, and there taught 'on the Lancastrian method' – the old-fashioned, sing-song method of class teaching, in which the monitors repeat in a chant what the master has just dictated, and the little groups of children around them parrot the lesson aloud, in chorus. The children on Tahiti, like the children in England, were learning the factory system in the classroom. A school report to London boasted that the little Tahitians could 'say the multiplication table offhand' as well as 'work out the most difficult long division sums without error'. Would the children show more willingness to work for wages than their parents?

In 1821, Thomas Bossom and Elijah Armitage arrived in *Tuscan*, a whaler, with machinery sent out by the London Missionary Society for spinning and weaving cotton. But even though the children of Tahiti had been so well drilled in school, thanks to the climate they could still live if they chose on fish and fruit, almost without effort. The missionaries' attempt to put their little fingers to work piecing cotton was another fiasco. Pomare himself was by this time owner of the brig *Queen Charlotte*, and by 1823 was trading in oil and other local products as far away as Port Jackson, New South Wales, as well as importing tea, sugar, flour and clothing, which he sold at a profit to his subjects.

In 1819, the missionaries had worked out new laws for Tahiti,

D

basing their legal code on the Old Testament prohibitions laid down by Moses. Missionary law was enforced by Pomare II all over the island, except at the anchorage of Papeete, nine miles from his capital at Matavai. Whalers would much rather call at Papeete than at missionary-dominated Matavai, and the anchorage was described by a contemporary as a 'vortex of iniquity, the Sodom of the Pacific'.

Thaddeus Bellingshausen, the Russian Antarctic explorer, dropped anchor at Tahiti in 1820. The place he describes bears little resemblance to the romantic island with which de Bougainville and Cook and all educated Europe had once been enraptured. The king, says Bellingshausen, is learning geometry. Sabbath observance is absolute. European clothes are worn, and the women no longer adorn their hair. In fact, many Tahitians, men and women alike, have taken to shaving their heads. There was less theft but more begging. The king himself tried to beg a bottle of rum from Bellingshausen, on the sly. Dancing, local music and the weaving of flower garlands were also banned, and tattooing severely reproved. Morality police went their rounds after dark, to snatch loving couples out of the bushes.

In 1823, another Antarctic explorer, Otto von Kotzebue, after calling in at Tahiti, declared that 'a religion like this, which forbids every innocent pleasure and cramps or annihilates every mental power, is a libel on the divine founder of Christianity'. The Tahitians were not only lacking in the urge to boil sugar or to spin cotton, they had lost all their everyday zest. Their splendid teeth were going rotten. They had even given up surfing.

Soon after Bellingshausen's visit, Pomare II became ill. The missionaries gathering around his bed 'gave him some medicine, and endeavoured to remind him of his sinful state' – the poor fellow had elephantiasis and dropsy – but they reported that 'he seemed to have no relish for religious conversation'. On 2 December 1824, Pomare II died. His heir was only a year old, so his sister became regent.

Henry Nott decided to 'crown' the baby, in due form, and to ask Britain's King George IV, in the infant's name, for the protection of the British flag. But a tangle of national rivalries was already complicating life in the Pacific. Were the British to reach out a hand and grab Tahiti, they would come directly into conflict with France and America. So George IV offered the infant monarch of Tahiti nothing more reassuring than his 'friendship'. In 1827, the child-king of Tahiti died, and the regent, a girl of seventeen 'given to youthful lapses of character', became queen.

In Papeete, childhood sexuality had become full-blown child prostitution. During the 1830s, about 150 whalers a year paid a call there. Seamen who signed on for the excessively long whaling voyages of those days were often hard cases, with a past to hide and a gift for raising hell. Matavai where the missionaries lived was unconscionably good; Papeete, nine miles away, was an inferno.

The missionaries on Tahiti had produced by this time enough growing children of their own to require a school. The headmaster of the South Sea Academy was John Orsmond, a man remarkable for having protested at the way the missionaries were supposed to live by trade. Orsmond set up his academy on a neighbouring island, where the whalers were unlikely to call, and with good reason. Missionary children of both sexes had the manichaean contrast between Papeete and Matavai always before their eyes. As Orsmond found, they were liable, very early in life, to react against evangelical severity, and decide to go to the devil. When this became notorious, the Society's directors, in 1829, made an order that no child was to stay on Tahiti longer than seven years in all, and no child over the dangerous age of fourteen was ever to remain there. With the best will in the world, the missionaries had helped into being a society not even fit for their own children.

After Pomare II died, some of the Tahitians began to defy the ban on tattooing. Their defiance was flagrant because a tattoo was indelible. An opposition had begun to stir.

By this time many Tahitians could read the New Testament well enough in their own tongue, and find out for themselves what divergences there might be between the reported words of Jesus and the deeds of the English missionaries. The Tahitians were not long in dreaming up a variant of Christianity more to their own liking. In 1827, people began talking about the sect of

Mamai, led by Teao and Hue, both church members, and both able to read and write. Their new religion administered the sacraments of baptism and communion, but also allowed erotic dancing – under the patronage of St Peter, St Paul and the Virgin Mary. Mamai tolerated drink and polygamy. Its policy was to drive the foreign missionaries off the island, and live their own kind of Tahitian Christianity, without interference.

When Mamai began slowly to attract followers, the English evangelicals were, to every appearance, on top in Tahiti and there to stay. They were ship-owners and traders, financially independent of their Society, and therefore not under very strict control. They determined modes of behaviour, they dictated laws. They had done their best to create, whole and entire, here in tropical Polynesia, that same cramped yet fervent society which they themselves had known, years before, in England, as God-fearing Methodist artisans. They had very nearly managed to transport the dark Satanic mills of cotton-spinning England to the palm groves of Tahiti. Considering how difficult life had been for them at the very beginning – hungry, lonely, in danger of their lives – the scope of their work had been astonishing. But for them, as for the Society of Jesus in Paraguay, three generations before, hidden difficulties were beginning to multiply. The Jesuits managed to keep their own artificial community going, year after year, by sealing off the frontiers. But what was to stop whalers calling at Tahiti?

In vain the evangelicals tried to legislate against the cargo of sin which every whaler brought ashore. By the late 1820s, there were laws against rape, sodomy, fornication, drunkenness, tattooing, dancing, singing and wife-beating. In 1834, when the royal family all signed the pledge against strong drink – though not with a very serious intention of keeping it – the missionaries passed one new law, forbidding the importation of spirits, and then another, making church attendance compulsory.

Yet the royal morality-police hardly dared venture into the grog-shops of Papeete, and all laws there were a dead letter. And well they might be, for the English missionaries were in fact legislating without possessing the sovereignty to which they boldly laid claim. They had tried to make London believe that the queen of Tahiti's word was law throughout the whole archipelago, but this was a pious fiction. Even on Tahiti itself, many of the inland chiefs were beginning to ignore the queen, and the missionaries' own influence over the skittish lady was spasmodic.

Nor, if the missionaries got into a mess, was the British government likely to step in and save them. In Australia and New Zealand, Britain already found herself over-extended. Tahiti in the Pacific power-game was only a dot in the ocean.

In 1836, a Columban lay brother called Murphy landed on a remote coast of Tahiti, giving himself out to be (as he very likely was) a carpenter. But Brother Murphy was also working in collusion with a French missionary society, and before coming ashore he had somehow learned enough of the local language to make himself clearly understood. He crossed the island to Papeete on foot, and there joined forces with two French Roman Catholic priests, Father François Caret and Father Louis Laval. A Roman Catholic mission had inconspicuously arrived.

Murphy's host on Tahiti was a sharp-witted Belgian Roman Catholic called Moerenhout, then acting as US consul. Moerenhout had come out to the island from Chile in 1828, as partner in a pearling syndicate. No doubt he was in on the plot from the start, for when the Americans summarily dismissed him, the French promptly appointed him as their own consul on Tahiti.

The powerful missionary effort which the Roman Catholic church was then commencing throughout the world was frequently timed to move in step with the patient efforts made by successive French governments to acquire more colonial possessions, in place of those they had lost with the defeat of Napoleon. To the more furiously atheistic aspects of the French Revolution there had been a reaction. Not all the French peasants who were Napoleon's best soldiers had been shaken out of their faith, so the Emperor brought back religious observance to placate them. Landowners had good reason for associating militant atheism with the guillotine. Intellectuals were finding nothing much to praise in the reckless destruction of religious art. In France, Roman Catholicism was, once again, an intellectual and social force.

The ban on the Jesuits was lifted, though they never regained their old supremacy, and several other energetic missionary orders were called into being.

Legally, the evangelical missionaries were on unsafe ground. De Bougainville, after all, had arrived on Tahiti a year before Cook. Those Franciscans from Ocapa were preaching there long before the London Missionary Society. The island had never been annexed, so that the French had as much right there as anyone else. While waiting in Valparaiso for a ship to Tahiti, the French priests had sent home to *Annales de la propagation de la foi* the following report, which hints clearly enough at the national conflict underlying the religious rivalry: 'The Biblical missionaries sent by the English societies appear to have undertaken, of late, to invade all the islands of the Pacific Ocean. The English government favours them for ends purely political; already they have printing presses, have started factories, and of course exercise great influence.'

The man called upon to cope with this French challenge on Tahiti was a former missionary called George Pritchard. He had come out in 1824 for the London Missionary Society, but was now acting there as if he were British consul, though his rank and status were not always quite in order. Never before on Tahiti had Pritchard seen such a direct blow struck at missionary authority. He was a narrow-minded man, and some of his reactions were hardly marked by common prudence.

Pritchard began by getting the queen of Tahiti to enforce against Murphy a law which gave her the right to stop any man coming ashore from a ship without her permission. But this law, as everyone knew, had been meant to discourage beach-combers, and Murphy was a missionary. Even so, the ship's captain who gave his passage was fined for landing him, and when Consul Moerenhout made it clear he would willingly pay the $30 fine, his offer was refused. On 14 December, Brother Murphy and the two French priests were dumped back unceremoniously aboard the ship on which they had come.

Six weeks later, on 27 January 1837, Father Caret was back again in an American vessel, *Colombo*, which called in at Tahiti on its way to Valparaiso. He tried to land from a ship's boat, and this time he and his companions were bullied back on board by a clumsy show of force. The ultimate folly was to come a year later, when the evangelical missionaries on Tahiti managed to set the entire civilized world against them. As if they were still living in the seventeenth century, they had all Roman Catholic teaching on Tahiti declared illegal.

Father Caret had appealed for help to the French government, as well as the Pope, and George Pritchard was foolishly providing him with a splendid case to argue. The British government in London tried to wash their hands of the matter. At the Foreign Office, Lord Palmerston described the expulsion of Father Caret as 'an uncalled-for act of violence' and condemned the Tahitian law against Roman Catholic teaching as 'an intolerable and indefensible edict'.

Moerenhout, now French consul, began making friends of the discontented chiefs inland. With the English missionaries publicly discredited, there was not much chance that the British government would intervene to save their necks, and the Tahitians were heartily sick of them. The French moved in, to fill the power vacuum. On 27 August 1838, a French frigate, *Vénus* (sixty-four guns, Captain Abel du Petit-Thouars) anchored off Papeete.

Captain du Petit-Thouars ran out his broadside, and made it known that within twenty-four hours he would bombard the little town, unless the French tricolor were saluted, and a compensation of $2000 paid to the maltreated French priests, together with an apology for the violence done them. What he asked was performed: who could argue with those guns?

In 1840, tough old Henry Nott went back to England, taking his completed Tahitian Bible translation with him to be printed. He presented a copy to Queen Victoria, argued the evangelical missionaries' case in London, and came back in triumph with a cargo of Bibles, but though he had managed to rouse a little national feeling against the French, it was all too late.

On 1 September 1842, du Petit-Thouars, by now an admiral, again dropped anchor off Tahiti, in *La Reine Blanche*, having just come from annexing the Marquesas Islands for France. The Admiral went on to annex Tahiti as well, and to impose religious toleration there at gunpoint, but he was going too fast for the political situation. A form of words was found which placated British public opinion while leaving the French in possession: Tahiti was to be, not a colony, but a protectorate. Not that the name made much difference. The French took over Tahiti formally as a colony in 1880, and have been there ever since.

The queen of Tahiti had been taken away from her island in HMS *Basilisk*, but after the political settlement she came back and was given a French pension of 25,000 francs a year, to keep her out of mischief. Old Henry Nott died in 1844, openly regretting the generous pagan society he had spent his lifetime trying to replace by a money-centred civilization. 'The great change manifested in the Tahitians', he was reported as saying on his deathbed, 'was a fruitful source of sorrow to him. Once, to speak was to secure a prompt and cheerful obedience, but now, nothing had charms but dollars.'

When, with the consent of the great powers, the French landed to 'protect' Tahiti, they did not have a walkover. A thousand Tahitians – an eighth of the population – went up with their guns to a fortified camp, high in the volcanic mountains. Towards the end, both the English missionaries' ban on Catholicism and their reliance on trade had been vigorously opposed by some of the younger and more liberal-minded men amongst them. Later, these younger missionaries took the credit for urging the Tahitians up into the mountains with their guns, though much of the inspiration also came from Christian rebels influenced by Mamai. Not that the Tahitians, armed with trade muskets, had much chance of defeating regular French troops, but they fought a good fight.

The French ringed the mountain refuge with forts, and for miles along the coast they cut down the breadfruit trees on which the rebels, and everyone else too on Tahiti, depended for their free food. French soldiers pushed their way over three successive stockades, losing seventy men. At last, in December 1846, for a bribe of $200, a traitor led the French by a back way into the rebel stronghold.

The last independent Tahitians surrendered on New Year's Day 1847, marching with their women and children to within a hundred yards of the French lines – effective musket range – and there kneeling in prayer before submitting. The French authorities were lenient with them. Political control on Tahiti was strict from then on, but there was little or no interference with moral conduct. Dancing revived, but the dances, said the old men, were never quite what they had been; the modes were sadder.

And the French put the local calendar right. Fifty years before, Captain James Wilson had been a day out in his reckoning so that, ever since landing from *Duff*, the evangelicals had obstinately persisted in going to church on Saturday.

The French authorities opened licensed brothels at Papeete. The prettiest of the Tahitian girls, who had been taught by English missionaries how to read and write and behave in a parlour, soon found a new vocation, as mistresses to newly arrived French officials. On the island, marriage as an institution practically ceased to exist. The population rose, but very slowly. After a century of French rule there were still only about half as many Tahitians as in the time of Captain Cook.

Most English missionaries left of their own accord. Those who tried to stay on were squeezed out by the French, who replaced them with French Protestants. There was one exception. John Orsmond, headmaster of the South Sea Academy, had been in the archipelago since 1817. He went over to the French side, heart and soul. The London Missionary Society expelled him, but he did not remain idle long. With amiable cynicism, the French made the veteran missionary their chief of native police.

5 Black Rebels

'The work performed by free men comes cheaper, in the end, than that performed by slaves.' *Adam Smith, The Wealth of Nations*

'Here's to the next insurrection of the negroes in the West Indies!' *Dr Samuel Johnson*

'The whites killed Christ! Let us slay all the whites!' *Slave warcry on Santo Domingo*

The first royal patent for the island of Barbados – the oldest English colony in the Caribbean – had spoken of 'the laudable and pious design' of 'propagating the Christian religion' there. In its early days, Barbados had been an island of small farms. There were 11,200 holdings in 1645, but only 5860 black slaves. On a small farm, tobacco could be grown. Sugar needed a plantation, and a big capital investment. To procure 100 hogsheads of sugar a year from 300 acres called for a capital of £14,000 – in those days, a fortune. And this capital would not fructify without labour.

Since a free labourer working in America for wages on a sugar plantation would soon find himself something better to do elsewhere, the men who cut the cane must be held in servitude: by 1667 on Barbados there were only 745 holdings, but 82,023 slaves. Many of those slaves were English, Scots and Irish.

From first to last there were 20,000 of them – cavaliers taken prisoner at the siege of Colchester, or trapped when proclaiming King Charles at Salisbury, Scots who had fought for their king at Preston or Worcester, and been auctioned off afterwards by the winners, not to mention unlucky youngsters kidnapped on some dark night in the back alleys of Bristol. Either as outright slaves, or as 'indentured labour', or virtual slaves, white men worked the plantations of Barbados until the civil war prisoners began to die out, towards the end of the century. They were replaced by imported black Africans. White men always had a better chance of running away than black, and since the child of a black slave was deemed to be his master's property, black slavery was a better long-term investment.

No doubt the earliest arrivals on Barbados had meant what they said about religion, yet by 1680, when sugar ruled, there were only five clergymen left. They reported gloomily that any attempt they made to instruct or console the plantation workers exposed them to 'the most barbarous usage'. Marriage and burial services were 'either totally omitted, or else performed by the overseers in a kind of prophane merriment'.

Christopher Codrington was born on his father's plantation on Barbados in 1668, in the palmy days of sugar. Before going to school in England, when he was twelve, one of his earliest memories would have been of seeing white men in servitude, cutting sugar cane, some of them unlucky old cavaliers. Codrington's father had amassed the biggest single fortune in the West Indies, and was made Captain-General of the Leeward Islands. In 1685, Christopher Codrington arrived at Christ Church, Oxford – a particularly exciting place, just then, for an intelligent young man.

Codrington's cheerful, sensual, sensitive face stares out at us from his portrait, under a full-bottomed wig. Rich and gifted, he soon became one of the 'Christ Church wits', moving in the same circles as Addison and Steele. Versification, yes, but Oxford in those days was also stirringly alive with high politics. The conflict in England between an authoritarian Roman Catholic king and an overwhelmingly Protestant and independent-minded people was at its height. The universities – which King James sought to control through his nominees, including a Catholic Dean of Christ Church – were then in the thick of it.

In 1688, James escaped abroad. Dutch William and his English wife, Mary, occupied the throne, and political power in England was to be shared thereafter, by and large, between the moneyed interest in the towns, and the Whig peers who dominated the countryside. For the individual seeking to make his fortune there would from now on be more freedom in England than almost anywhere in Europe. The principles of the Glorious Revolution

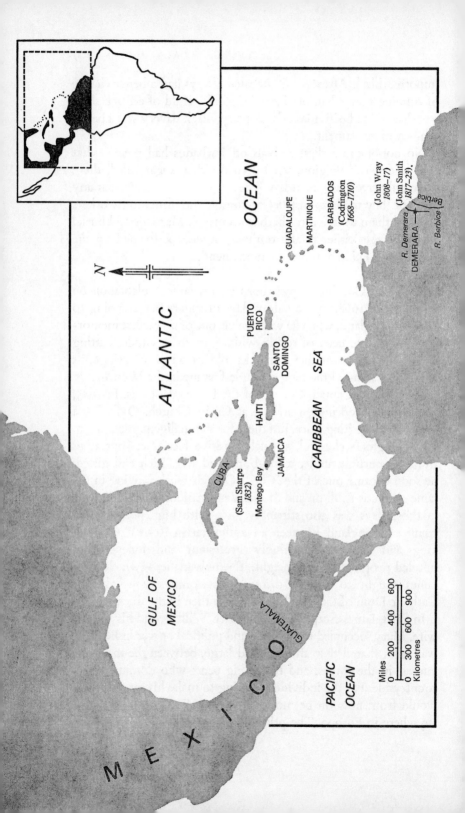

were later admired and taken to a logical conclusion by the Americans in 1776, and by the French in 1789.

In 1690, Codrington became a Fellow of All Souls. Three years later, he went out with Admiral Wheler's fleet to the Caribbean, and served under his father in the attack on the French island of Martinique – a failure. Next year he was off with King William, in Flanders, as a captain in the foot guards. He fought at Namur, and was promoted to command a battalion. In 1696, King William awarded him his father's old job as Captain-General of the Leeward Islands.

Codrington was scholar as well as adventurous soldier. In the intervals of fighting he had made friends with the poet Prior, and with Locke, the philosopher, accumulated a library of 12,000 volumes, and written satire. He went back to the West Indies, where he had inherited the family plantations, determined to stamp out the corruption, smuggling and oppression which had made English possessions in the Caribbean notorious. He was thirty.

Observing slavery on Barbados, not now as a small boy, but with the eye of a rich man who has lived through an upheaval when all the talk has been of freedom, Codrington knew better than to suppose it could be abolished overnight – but suppose it could be reformed and improved?

In 1699 he wrote to the Archbishop of Canterbury, asking for 'apostolical men, who are willing to take much pains for little reward'. Large estates worked by slaves made Barbados vulnerable to enemy attack: as well as more clergymen there, he wanted more small proprietors, as in the old days. 'I hope to provide for a great many five and ten acre men, the true strength of these colonies.' The sugar magnates were rich, he found, but not patriotic. When a neighbouring island was attacked by an enemy, they were seldom sorry: 'If a Sugar Island be lost, the price is raised.'

But slavery and sugar were generating prosperity on both sides of the Atlantic. The actual shipping across of black Africans might be in the hands of only a few dozen merchants in Liverpool, Bristol and London. But the guns and trade goods, beads and brass wire with which they were purchased on the West

African coast kept Manchester and Birmingham busy. A gun was the price of a slave, and soon Birmingham would be turning out 158,000 trade muskets a year.

Empty slave ships brought back cargoes of sugar to British refineries. Newfoundland prospered by shipping in salt cod to feed the slaves. New England sent barrel staves, and horses to turn the treadmills, and took back molasses to distil into rum, to sell to the Indians. The catchphrase went that ten blacks in the West Indies gave work to four men in Britain.

Slavery was at the heart of a huge and thriving vested interest, all through the eighteenth century. Therefore, in hoping to reform one of the sugar islands, merely by the light of reason and religion, Christopher Codrington, for all his wit, wealth and influence in London was bound to fail.

He was high-handed. He took a legal short cut in trying to clean up the island of Nevis, and the appeal against him was carried to the House of Commons. In 1703 he made a hash of his attack on the French island of Guadeloupe. He fell sick of a bloody flux, which he dosed rather too energetically with laudanum; he was past governing the Leeward Islands. Yet in his great house he lingered on, brooding over the possible reasons for his failure. Most of the planters were glad to get rid of Codrington as governor, though the man who took his place, Colonel Daniel Parke from Virginia, was so corrupt that in the end the colonists felt obliged to assassinate him.

Christopher Codrington spent his last few years ill, and dreaming of a return to England – 'If I live to see England, I will pass my life in my library and be buried in my garden.' He read hard, meanwhile, in metaphysics and church history. In 1710 he died, at the age of forty-two leaving his 12,000 books to All Souls. He put up £1250 for a monument to his own father, in Westminster Abbey, and £20 for his own gravestone. He provided his natural son with £40 a year, and £500 when he came of age – 'it's my Desire he should be Bred up in the Sea Service.' Then came the surprise.

Codrington willed his 'plantations continued intire, and 300 negroes at least always kept thereon, and a convenient number of Professors and Scholars maintained there, all of them to be under

vows of poverty, chastity and obedience, that they may endear
themselves to the people, and [do] good to men's souls while they
are taking care of their bodys.'

'The design of the bequest', as the local rector pointed out
to the Society for the Propagation of the Gospel, who were to
administer the property, thus becoming slave-owners against
their will, 'was the maintenance of monks and missionaries to be
employed in the conversion of negroes and Indians; which design
he took from the conversation of a learned Jesuit of St Christopher's, between whom and him there passed several letters upon
the antiquity, usefulness and excellence of a monastic life.'

Monasticism in its day, as Codrington knew, had redeemed
much of Europe – and England, in particular – from pagan
barbarism. But when the early Benedictine monks brought
literature, music, architecture and religion to the Anglo-Saxons,
their work had not been financed by the forced labour of kidnapped black Africans. The first missionary monks did their
own hard work. Codrington's heir, not surprisingly, claimed that
such a popish bequest was not legal. The lawsuit was the first of
many delays.

Queen Anne, however, a churchwoman heart and soul, was
enchanted with Codrington's scheme, and the Admiralty gave
orders to ship in timber for it from other islands. The Society
itself sent '160,000 well-burnt bricks, and two tons of iron bars,
assorted'. Provision was made for the spiritual needs of the 300
slaves on the estate. They had a chaplain, and a catechist who was
also a surgeon. By the standards of the time they were exceedingly
well treated. They were given Saturday off, to dig their gardens,
and all day Sunday for religion.

But Codrington's hard-headed neighbours had no intention of
letting the parsons spoil the slaves. In the corrupt tropics, with
pickings to be made, all went slowly. The heir's lawsuit dragged
on; Queen Anne was dead, and England's new king, George of
Hanover, spoke only German. The iron bars rusted and the royal
timber rotted. The mere preliminary of putting up buildings for
Codrington's college took over thirty years, from 1713 to 1745.

The college opened its doors at last, not as a monastic establishment, where 'apostolical men' might possibly learn to emulate

the notorious Jesuits of Paraguay, but as a free grammar school for twenty lucky little white boys. The trustees announced one other minor change. 'Celibacy', in the palpitating tropics, 'had been found to be impractical.'

A fleet and an army sent out by Cromwell in 1655 had taken Jamaica. The purpose of this expedition, as John Milton had declared on Oliver Cromwell's behalf, was 'promoting the glory of God and enlarging the bounds of Christ's Kingdom'. The Spanish settlers in Jamaica – thin on the ground – were chased out with not much difficulty. But when they fled to Cuba, they left behind them five hundred of their black slaves, who took to the mountains, and under their leader, Juan de Bolas, with the help of the feverish climate, fought the English to a standstill.

In the long-drawn-out campaign, even the army's chaplains died wholesale of fever, and the general had to write home for some more, 'forasmuch as we conceive the propagation of the Gospel to be the thing principally aimed at and intended in this expedition'. On 14 August 1659, 1701 Bibles were given out to the troops, to keep up their morale. The next docket on file in the archive is 'to pay unto John Hoy the summe of twenty pounds sterling – for fifteen Dogges brought by him for the hunting of the Negroes'. Yet Bibles and bloodhounds alone did not suffice. In 1663, the English were obliged to put an end to the war by offering the fifty surviving Maroons thirty acres apiece and their freedom, if only they would lay down their arms.

The island had been forcibly populated by Cromwell with English unemployed, Scottish convicts and two thousand kidnapped young Irish. By 1670, there were 57 sugar works on Jamaica, producing 1,710,000 tuns a year. By 1673, the number of slaves had increased from 1400 to 9504. In 1684, when black slaves were predominant, a big slave insurrection broke out on Jamaica – the first of many.

There was money in sugar – and on Jamaica, as on Barbados, some well-intentioned men tried to do good with their fortunes. Between 1667 and 1732, 218 endowments were made on Jamaica for schools and churches – but the income from them almost all went into the pockets of embezzlers. From one education trust alone, Alderman William Beckford, radical, friend of John Wilkes and perhaps the wealthiest commoner in Europe, was found to have pocketed £50,000.

In 1735, the Maroons' independent status was confirmed by treaty. They were content to be employed thereafter, like the Guaraní in Paraguay, as policemen, being paid 'mile money' by the government for hunting runaway plantation-slaves out of the mountains. In the bloody slave-uprising of 1766, the Maroons' boast had been that they brought in every rebel, dead or alive, within a month. But as the Maroons gradually found sweethearts and wives among the plantation slaves, they became less stony-hearted, and therefore less reliable.

In 1795, at the height of the Jacobin scare in the Caribbean, the Maroons, though numbering only a couple of thousand, were provoked by what most people at the time judged to be administrative idiocy into taking up arms on their own behalf. Word flew about Jamaica that they were being egged on by French agents. The rumour was false, but when in their first armed clash the Maroons killed thirty-four British with no loss to themselves, there was panic.

There were 30,000 free white men on Jamaica, and a quarter of a million black slaves. Old resentments against the planters' police were being forgotten. A hundred slaves had already escaped into the mountains to join the insurgent Maroons, and the fear was that thousands more might follow. No time for half-measures.

A price of $300 was put on every Maroon's head, and $150 on the head of any slave who joined the rebellion. Thirty-six hounds specially trained for hunting down black runaways were shipped over by schooner from Nicaragua. But in fact the Maroons were not the intrepid revolutionaries of the planters' worst nightmares. They had a horror of bloodhounds, and once they had been blockaded by the bounty-hunters in a waterless tract of mountain, thirst and dogs broke their will to fight.

The survivors were shipped off in three transports, *Dover*, *Mary* and *Ann*, convoyed by HMS *Africa*. They were kept aboard in such strict confinement that seventeen died. Once in Halifax, Nova Scotia, the Maroons were paid wages for working on the fortifications, but after their life in the tropics, they found the weather appalling. A chaplain was appointed to oversee their welfare, and the seven worst months were spent in school, but during that winter potatoes and flour ran out. So they all downed tools, and demanded to be sent to a warmer climate. Since keeping the Maroons under constraint had been costing the British government £10,000 a year, they were shipped off to Sierra Leone in West Africa – which not long after was to become a most remarkable social laboratory, a place where by and large the missionary experiment had a singular success.

Until the 1780s, critics of slavery in Britain had been a handful of conscience-stricken Christians, like Charles Wesley or General Oglethorpe, or monomaniac reformers, like Granville Sharp, or warm-hearted literary men, like Johnson and Defoe. But disgust at slavery was spreading out from individuals to sects – by 1774, any member of the Society of Friends keeping up a connection with the slave trade was expelled. Yet in June 1783, when the Quakers handed the Prime Minister, Lord North, a petition against the slave trade, he warned them in all earnestness that 'abolition would be found impossible' since the trade in slaves 'had in some measure become necessary to almost every nation in Europe'. Conscience might have pricked, but most commonsense Englishmen at the time, and for that matter most Americans, would have found themselves obliged to agree with Lord North.

The decisive turnabout came with the independence of the United States. The 600,000 slaves then at work in Carolina, Georgia, Virginia and the rest of the thirteen states were deducted from the total number living under the British flag. Thus the only remaining great vested interest in Britain still committed heart and soul to the slave trade was sugar. In 1783, sugar was still of paramount importance. Business worth £4,250,000 a year was being done in 1783 with the West Indies – or twice the value of the trade then transacted with all British India. But a decisive change was coming. India was soon to become a great new textile market, Britain's export of cotton goods there and elsewhere rising enormously, from about £1,000,000 in 1785 to over £30,000,000 in 1830. Britain's pattern of trade, contingent for the past hundred years on slave voyages, was radically changing.

As sugar lost its pride of place in the British economy, those enlightened individuals who had always been critical of the slave trade found that their ideas were now acceptable to a large and powerful group of the new rich, whose ideas were tinctured by evangelicalism, and who looked upon the well-entrenched and over-represented men of the sugar trade as their rivals, both in business and politics. This was the great turn-around in evangelical opinion which had baffled John Newton, and caused him to prevaricate on his tombstone.

Thus by the end of the eighteenth century, during the political campaigns in Britain against the slave trade and for an enlarged parliamentary representation, the most energetic men of the respectable, God-fearing, acquisitive middle class once again found it possible to identify their own political aspirations, as in the time of Cromwell, with the will of God. And once again, as in Cromwell's time, they carried with them in the cause many poorer men. The horrors of the factory system were still no more than rumours; the wealth it generated was an astonishing fact. The men who controlled the evangelical missionary societies were always eminently respectable, but a great deal of money to finance their work came henceforth from the pockets of the decent poor, and the men they sent abroad as missionaries were quite likely to be plebeian, eccentric, and sometimes even radical. Over the abolitionist movement has always hung – as Cobbett and Hazlitt pointed out – a whiff of hypocrisy.

Yet political and economic motives were tangled, even contradictory. This may perhaps signify that for ending the trade in slaves, the moral motive, particularly in Britain was, finally decisive. Whatever the Whitefields of this world may choose to preach, Christian believers are certain, sooner or later, to find themselves wholly at odds with any economic or political order which buys and sells, or even hires, people on such terms that their lives are no longer their own. The doctrines taught by Christ have to be deformed out of all recognition to condone the treating of people as things, and the historical reason for this Christian intransigence is self-evident.

Chattel slavery – universal in antiquity – flouts those simple restraints which alone keep the monogamous family in being – and, for better or worse, such a family has thus far been the living cell of our society, the final source of its moral values. A family, by contrast with the competitive and perhaps hostile world outside, needs for its survival a certain measure of unselfish cooperation. Unless carefully limited by law, slavery makes almost impossible this simple human need to establish a small alternative society, based not on power and greed but love. In 1783, any slave marriage in a British colony was precarious, because the partners in it could at any moment be sold and separated, though on a similar plantation in a colony under the Spanish crown an owner's freedom was more circumscribed. A slave in a Spanish colony had by law to be prepared for baptism and sent to mass, could never be separated from his wife and must be given a chance to buy his freedom; but this in plantation society was exceptional. Elsewhere, the children of a slave marriage were doomed to be commercial objects, with a price on their heads, from the day they were born. They could be orphaned by the scratch of a pen.

Primitive Christianity had taken form in direct opposition to this moral offence, hence the sexual directives always deeply embedded in its teaching. When a slave-owner – in a Roman villa as on an American plantation – had the whim to gratify his love of pleasure, a slave's body was always there, to be raped or degraded. But though violated during life, a Christian slave knew that his invulnerable soul would escape damnation after death. He could survive his martyrdom, thus becoming halfway human again, even in servitude. Christian belief enabled many slaves to hold up their heads and urge on their own freedom.

The abolitionist movement had setbacks in France and America and succeeded sooner in Britain not simply because the economic situation was, on balance, politically more favourable to Manchester than to Jamaica, though this of course gave the movement impetus. A systematic attempt to abolish the slave trade by popular demand would stand a chance of success only in a country where ideas might circulate unhindered, and where men were free, by and large, to associate politically. France under Napoleon was not such a country, nor – for a short time –

was England under Pitt. There were few such countries then; there are not many more now.

In Britain, then, there was an influential group in the middle class with strong economic and political motives, who were using public opposition to the slave trade to advance their other ambitions too. They were free to associate, and to campaign. But the emotion, the energy, which brought other men in behind them was derived, in Britain, from Christian belief. The campaign therefore escaped from the hands of those who had at first assumed control, and has had repercussions which still continue.

A blind economic process – such as the industrial revolution – generates questions, yet cannot of its own accord provide answers. Practical men who in their everyday lives attack and solve practical problems always do so, whether they admit it or not, in the light of abstract ideas, which emerged, perhaps many years before, from the heads of thinking men: there could have been no steam-engine without Euclid. That is to say, answers often exist long before the practical questions to which they will correspond are posed. Essential ideas are sometimes preserved for long ages in the cultural continuum of our society, before the time arrives when they may at last be given effect.

Now religion is an old and particularly tenacious element in our inherited culture, colouring the thoughts and words even of downright non-believers. If the official who considers it his duty to send a dissenter to a gulag advocates when he does so a 'merciless struggle' – the phrase is current – against the ideological enemies of the regime, he thereby pays unconscious tribute to the notion of mercy. The liberating ideas which Christianity has obstinately preserved have not always, as the missionary record shows, been put to good use. Yet they were always there, accessible, seeds beneath the snow.

William Wilberforce was the son of a wealthy merchant in the Baltic trade at Hull – a port outside the ambit of the slave traffic. Hull had a tradition of sending radical MPs to Parliament – from Andrew Marvell, the poet, to David Hartley, the inventor and friend of Benjamin Franklin, who stood up and moved a quixotic anti-slave-trade resolution in the House as early as 1776.

Wilberforce himself was very small – his nickname was 'the Shrimp'. He was helplessly short-sighted, and effeminate in demeanour, but with a talent as a mimic, and a singularly beautiful voice. When, at the age of twenty-one, he took Hartley's old seat in the House of Commons, he soon earned another nickname: 'the Nightingale'.

Wilberforce had been intimate when at Cambridge with young William Pitt, who was to rise very fast in politics, becoming Chancellor of the Exchequer when only twenty-three. The two sprigs of MPs shared a house for a while at Wimbledon, where they revelled in duck and asparagus, turtle and venison, not to mention the healthy country air, but their nights were busy, too. 'No pious parents ever laboured more to impress a beloved child with sentiments of religion,' Wilberforce admitted later of his life as a young man on the town, 'than my friends did to give me a taste for the world and its diversions.' Night after night he gambled in St James's, at Brooks's and Boodles'. But while other young bucks were plunging for thousands, Wilberforce prudently limited his losses to £100 a night. He was evidently not beyond redemption.

Serious conversation with his old schoolmaster, Isaac Milner, later to become Dean of Carlisle, brought raffish young William Wilberforce to a dead stop. 'What madness is all this,' he wrote, 'to continue easy in a state in which a sudden call out of the world would consign me to everlasting misery: and that when eternal happiness is within my grasp.' Milner headed Wilberforce towards Reverend John Newton, the retired slave-trader, now rector of St Mary Woolnoth, and a clever man at dealing with a sensitive youngster, unnerved by dread of death and the fear of hell. Wilberforce resigned his clubs, made heavy contributions to charity, and announced his conversion.

'God almighty has set before me', said the young Member of Parliament, perhaps a little grandiloquently, 'two great objects, the suppression of the Slave Trade and the reformation of manners.' He therefore became active in the Society for the Suppression of Vice (which at one time wanted to stamp out Sunday newspapers). But in taking up abolition, Wilberforce had discovered his true political role.

Pitt was Prime Minister. And here was his close friend, Wilber-force, now a saint, to serve as a useful link between all those wealthy and powerful if sometimes wrongheaded evangelicals outside Parliament, and the cool Whig politicians of the day, Grenville, Whitbread, Fox, Burke, Pitt himself, who often might be glad of their political support.

In 1787 the Abolition Committee was formed – Quakers were the mainstay. Brilliantly led by Thomas Clarkson, the abolition-ists were making a vast impact upon opinion. Clarkson, though a clergyman, had all the skills of a great investigative journalist. He found out and published the small, grim facts about the slaving ships which operated from British ports. He made a nerve-racking collection of iron manacles, thumbscrews and mouth-openers, the slaver's tools of trade. He knew to a nicety, and could illustrate with hideous diagrams, just how many Africans could be crammed into a ship's hold. To those who used the last-ditch argument that the slave trade was, at the very least, a 'nursery of seamen', he pointed out that the shanty meant what it said:

Beware and take care of the Bight of Benin,
There's one comes out for forty go in.

Of 3170 seamen on the muster-rolls of the 88 slavers which left Liverpool in 1787, Clarkson discovered that only 1428 had returned; 642 were dead, or lost at sea. As soon as they got to the West Indies, most of the rest deserted.

Cowper and Coleridge wrote poems for the movement, Wedgwood made and sold a propaganda cameo. The question of ending the trade in slaves was put in Parliament, in the halcyon days of Enlightenment, two months before the taking of the Bastille, when every man of goodwill in Europe was an abolition-ist. Necker, the French king's chief minister, had already proposed ending the slave trade by agreement among the European powers. During the debate, Wilberforce collapsed from sheer nervousness, and the strong dose of opium prescribed for him by his eminent medical practitioner, Dr Pitcairne, made an addict of him for the rest of his life: a predisposition to vice is never wholly overcome.

There were others at the time, besides philanthropists in Europe and propertied men in the West Indies, who held views on slavery. The seven hundred thousand slaves, for instance, had a strong opinion of their own. Abolitionist propaganda liked to portray the black slaves as helpless and even childlike victims. But plantation slaves repeatedly formed their own clandestine organizations, and though their attempts at insurrection were usually beaten down with great brutality, yet the fear of slave revolt accelerated political change. In British colonies, the rebel slaves' idiom was usually taken from the Bible; elsewhere, they used the libertarian phraseology of the French Revolution. But the slaves helped to break their own chains: between 1678 and 1832, there were twenty-seven serious slave rebellions on Jamaica alone.

At one time, because of this haunting fear of black uprising, the Jamaica planters themselves toyed with the thought of abolishing the slave trade. In 1774 they decided not to import any more slaves, but to breed them, since too many recent arrivals had been Ashanti warriors, hard to handle. But the moneyed men in Britain who did well by financing the shipment of slaves managed to overrule them.

Slaves were still arriving from Africa by the boatload, yet sugar was in decline. In the last seven years of the trade, 63,045 blacks were landed, yet from 1799 to 1807, 65 Jamaican plantations were abandoned, 32 sold for debt, and nineteen-twentieths of the cultivatable land on the island was owned by absentees. Sugar – which, as Adam Smith asserted, had once been the most profitable crop in the world – was being grown on Jamaica's exhausted soil both in excess of demand and at a loss. To make matters worse, Napoleon's clever chemists had found out how to make sugar from beet.

In 1789 the population on the great sugar island was 291,400, yet hardly five hundred of them were church-goers. Since religion, in Jacobinical times, might serve as a useful restraint, an Act was passed in 1797 requiring Anglican rectors on Jamaica to instruct the plantation slaves on Sundays. Hitherto, this had been forbidden – the average run of clergy on Jamaica were once described as 'much better qualified to be boatswains to privateers than ministers of the Gospel'.

The Anglican church on Jamaica, torpid for over a century, was so closely identified with authority that it never had a chance with the blacks. Among free people of colour – most of them living in the ports, though not until 1828 allowed to own property – Methodism had by now taken hold. But out on the plantations, black Baptists had reached Jamaica from the United States after Britain's defeat there. The plantation slaves, when not indulging in the cult of *obeah*, were worshipping, sometimes secretly, at their own Baptist meetings. There had been black Baptists on Jamaica for forty years before the first white Baptist missionaries arrived.

Obeah was syncretic – knocked together out of scraps of traditional West African belief, which was all the baggage the slaves had been allowed to bring over with them. The world of spirits could be controlled – said the *obeah*-man – by little fetishes of bone or rag, called duppies. Enemies might be despatched by a deadly poison, held under the finger-nail, chickens were used in a blood sacrifice, there was much ritual drumming and dancing. As time went on, some of the minor aspects of *obeah* began to colour the behaviour of the Baptists too: there was great emphasis on the Spirit. A neophyte would spent the hours before his baptism in the woods, fasting, and waiting for the Spirit to descend upon him, and inform him in a dream.

The sacrament of baptism was highly regarded by black Christians, for it freed a slave from the power of the *obeah*-man who, as often as not, was the driver, or plantation foreman – a man who carried a short-handled cart whip with a ten-foot lash always slung around his neck, a whip capable of drawing blood, his sign of authority. The Baptist class ticket became the 'passport to heaven', a more powerful fetish than any duppy, an antidote to morbid fear.

The French announced, in a brief moment of revolutionary euphoria, that the Declaration of the Rights of Man applied to all human beings in French colonies without distinction of colour. Jacobin principles went round the Caribbean like wildfire, and though the French authorities soon after changed their minds, the ideas they had by then let loose could not so easily be whistled

back into the box. On the prosperous French sugar island of
Santo Domingo, the ideas of liberty, equality and brotherhood
were at once taken to heart by the slaves, as an expression of their
natural right.

Santo Domingo was then Britain's fiercest competitor in the
sugar trade, and black men there outnumbered white by sixteen
to one. The slaves rose up, British troops invaded, and for the
next six years the island was fought over, back and forth, by the
redcoats, until a thousand plantations had been destroyed, and
the prosperous rival sugar economy was wrecked.

Pitt was in two minds. If Santo Domingo, with its cheap
sugar, could eventually be captured by British troops, then a
new lease of life for the sugar trade might possibly be justified.
Those devastated plantations would need to be restocked. On
the other hand, said Pitt, abolition might turn out to be the best
available means for discouraging 'negro Jacobinism'. In fact, from
the ruins of France's sugar colony emerged Haiti, the modern
world's first independent black republic. Thereafter, all slaves on
other Caribbean islands were well aware that on Haiti, for better
or worse, black men shipped across as slaves were now governing
themselves.

With opponents of slavery being damned by the sugar magnates
as Jacobins, the tide of enthusiasm receded so fast that from 1797
to 1804 the Abolition Committee never met. Wilberforce
meanwhile was associating himself rather ostentatiously with any
repressive action the anti-Jacobin British government might
choose to take. 'God defend us from such poison!' he exclaimed
after reading Tom Paine's *Age of Reason*. He supported the
Combination Acts – which outlawed trade unions – and the
suspension of Habeas Corpus. He let the slave question go, and
busied himself instead with the British and Foreign Bible Society,
which met in that counting-house in Old Swan Stairs to which
the missionaries on Tahiti were to send as trophies the wooden
idols of Pomare II.

The panic died down at last. About 1804 the movement revived.
At its heart, as an organizing centre, was a clique of rich and strict
evangelicals, neighbours, and many of them connected by marri-

age, which became ironically known as the Clapham Sect.
Henry Thornton, the banker, Charles Grant, of the East India
Company, John Venn, rector of Clapham, whose son, Henry,
became the most intelligent missionary administrator of the
century, Zachary Macaulay, father of the historian, were some of
them; they launched foreign missions, too. The founding of the
Church Missionary Society was first discussed in Wilberforce's
rooms in 1799; Thornton became treasurer and John Venn the
first chairman. As these shrewd men of conspicuously upright
life saw the future of Britain, commerce, Christianity and
colonization were to go hand in hand.

The anti-slave-trade campaign organized after 1804 by the
Clapham Sect swept all before it. The bill to abolish the slave
trade was passed in 1807, by Charles James Fox, in his short-lived
Ministry of All the Talents. Twenty-three days before the British
bill was given royal assent, Thomas Jefferson approved a Bill
of Congress which prohibited the import into the United States
of slaves from abroad, though allowing an interstate coastal slave
trade – a useful loophole. A ban on the slave trade became general
throughout the civilized world. The French nursed rueful hopes
of continuing the traffic, at least for long enough to restock their
sugar colonies, but at Waterloo they were the losers, so they too
gave way.

By 1815, only Portugal and Spain were shipping out slaves
from West Africa. A British squadron cruised up and down the
coast there, to put down smuggling. At first, the smugglers were
French, though American smugglers soon joined them. In 1811,
the slave trade had been declared a felony, punishable by trans-
portation. From 1822 onwards, the Abolition Committee turned
its attention to putting an end in the British Empire to slavery
as such.

Even among the West Indian planters there were of course a
few evangelical devotees who took a line of their own. One
such was Mr H. H. Post, of Le Resouvenir, a plantation eight
miles outside Georgetown in the new colony of Demerara in
Guiana. Demerara had changed hands six times since 1781. The
French and Dutch had ruled there, but the colony was now British

and the soil there could still produce sugar at a competitive price. Mr Post sent to the London Missionary Society for a minister, and on 1 February 1808 John Wray arrived. He was then twenty-seven and landed in Demerara as the last ship to import slaves legally sailed out.

Critical though his neighbours were of this risky experiment, Post spent £1000 on a manse and chapel which held 600. Wray reported cheerfully, as his mission continued, that there was less 'dancing, drumming, intoxication'. *Obeah* – the cult of fear – was in retreat.

By this time, Wilberforce, Macaulay and Stephen had shrewdly got themselves appointed to the Commissioners for Managing the Crown Property in South America. Le Resouvenir changed hands. Sunday once more became a day of work, and women were whipped in the fields, so Wray was sent off to make himself useful at Berbice, along the Guiana coast, where 1143 slaves had in 1811 become Crown Property. At Berbice, the death penalty was inflicted for practising *obeah*. Those who sang 'certain songs' in the hearing of slaves from other plantations risked a hundred lashes, and a white who allowed his slaves to sing was fined. Already the planters in Demerara were developing a dread of insurrection.

When the governor stopped the slaves at Berbice being taught to read and write, Wray, with Wilberforce and the others in the background, felt confident in setting him at defiance. Planters nearby soon tried the other tack: 'If you will give up all that non-sense, we will soon put you in the way of making your fortune.' But they mistook their man.

John Wray had a broad, good-natured, hook-nosed face, and a straight, countrified gaze – hardly the man to take a bribe. John Smith, the missionary who came out in 1817 to replace him, was gimlet-eyed, sharp-featured and consumptive: his portrait has a look about it of the predestined martyr. He was told by the governor, on arrival, 'If ever you teach a negro to read, and I hear of it, I will banish you from the colony immediately.'

By 1823, John Smith was preaching to an average congregation of 800. In the same year, as a step towards full emancipation, the House of Commons ordered that the field labour of slaves be limited to nine hours a day. They also prohibited the flogging of women, which hitherto had been prevalent and commonplace. Of 68,921 floggings, usually of twenty-five lashes, recorded as having been given in Jamaica during one year, 25,094 were inflicted on females. Wood-engravings of half-naked black women being flogged in the fields had helped make the planters odious in Britain with both the prurient and the prudish. Flogging women was indefensible, but cutting down the working day was quite another matter. Hitherto, a day of fourteen hours had been worked in sugar plantations, rising to nineteen hours after Christmas, at the height of the cane-cutting. A nine-hour day, now the legal maximum, was a shorter day by far than wage-earners in Britain then worked in mill or mine. It would mean putting up the price of sugar; for the planters, it might mean bankruptcy.

Then why should the slaves ever get to hear of this new law? The governor decided for the time being to keep secret the news of the shorter working day; all time gained was to the good. His decision was a piece of folly, for of course the secret could never be kept. White men confided in their black mistresses, or were overheard by their house slaves when in their cups, and the news soon leaked out to the plantation hands.

On Sunday, 17 August 1823, representative leaders of the slaves called a clandestine meeting, and decided by going on strike to force Governor Murray's hand, and oblige him to announce the shorter working day. Their leaders must have been well respected, for despite the great risk 13,000 men came out at their call. They had trusted John Smith with their secret, and so elevated was he by their confidence that he blazoned his sympathy with them abroad· by preaching on the text, 'If thou hadst known, even thou, at least this day, the things which belong to thy peace! But now they are hid from thy eyes.'

Smith also took it upon himself to warn the slaves' leader, Quamina, not to shed blood, and he went so far as to hint to a nearby estate manager that he had better look out for trouble. Like many of the other well-intentioned and radically minded missionaries then in the West Indies, Smith was in a painfully ambiguous position. What exactly was he, here in Demerara – the mouthpiece of his patrons in Britain? Of a respectable middle-class movement there with both religious and political objectives? Or was he heart and soul with his flock, and willing therefore to run their risks and share their fate? This time he had gone too far to draw back.

The governor, riding at the head of a cavalry detachment, clashed with blacks armed with a few flintlocks and their cane-knives – usually described in reports afterwards as 'cutlasses'. Shots were fired, martial law was proclaimed and, since the local Presbyterian minister happened to be a downright supporter of slavery, his church was turned into a barracks. Some of the slaves had tied their cane-knives to poles, in a desperate hope of using them as pikes against the cavalry. But in a running fight with a well-armed militia commanded by the planters themselves, the result was never in doubt. In the desultory fighting, 200 blacks were killed and many taken prisoner, but not a single militia-man lost his life.

Several hundred prisoners were at once killed in cold blood. Colonel Leahy, who despatched twenty-three with his own hand, was voted 200 guineas by the approving planters to buy himself a dress sword. Forty-seven ringleaders were hanged, the severed heads of some being stuck up along the roads as a warning. Seventeen others were given prodigious floggings – five of them receiving a thousand strokes. Those tough enough to outlive such punishment were afterwards sent out to work in the fields, loaded with chains.

Once word of this policy of terror reached London, where the abolitionists were becoming a power in the land, there was of course an uproar. Stringent orders were at once sent out by fast sailing-packet – they arrived in Demerara in time to save the lives of the last fifty prisoners waiting in gaol under sentence of death.

The planters had been out from the start to get John Smith. He was gaoled two days after martial law had been declared – though a minister of religion – for 'refusing to take up arms'. On 13 October 1823 he was brought for trial by a court-martial, and five weeks later found guilty of inciting the slaves to rebel by preaching, and of not informing the authorities that an insurrection was intended. No detail usual in trials of this type was lacking. Black prisoners were offered a chance to go free, if only they would give suborned evidence against John Smith. Outgoing letters with news of the trial were held up. The Anglican chaplain in the garrison, Rev. W. S. Austin, was convinced of John Smith's innocence and said so – he was forced to leave Demerara. John Smith was sentenced to death by hanging – with an ironic recommendation to mercy. All knew there was no need to risk putting a noose around the pastor's neck. Lock a consumptive man in a stagnant cellar in a tropical climate, and his days are numbered.

Smith died as they expected, on 6 February 1824 – three days before an order arrived from the Colonial Secretary, peremptorily releasing him from the death chamber and calling him back to Britain. Mrs Smith had until now voluntarily shared her husband's imprisonment, but she was not allowed to follow the coffin. Governor Murray ordered his body to be buried by night, in secrecy. The mortal remains of John Smith were tumbled into an unmarked grave, for fear the slaves might regard him as their martyr.

The strike in Demerara in 1823 was put down no more ferociously than other slave insurrections in the British West Indies years before. But in a political climate where every action discreditable to the sugar magnates and their minions would be seized upon, perhaps exaggerated, and thereafter used against them relentlessly in London, such repressiveness was folly. Under the barrage of clever publicity from their political opponents, the planters began to lose heart. They still had their own militia, they controlled their courts of law, but they had lost confidence in any future.

So they made gestures of defiance. On Jamaica there was already loud talk of seceding from the Union Jack, and going over to the Stars and Stripes. In 1829, the Jamaican House of Assembly voted by a large majority to retain the right to flog women in public, and at the same time decided to punish 'by whipping or imprisonment with hard labour' any blacks 'teaching or preaching as Anabaptists or otherwise' – brave words, though the planters and their attorneys in the House of Assembly were well aware that what they pronounced would at once be vetoed in London. Their behaviour was deliberately, flagrantly provocative – and in the last days of 1831, just before emancipation, their provocation had its effect: the Jamaican slaves rose in revolt. Fifty thousand took part, and the violent strike – it never had time to become an effective armed uprising – was afterwards called by the blacks themselves the Baptist War. The House of Assembly too decided afterwards to put the blame for the outburst on 'the preaching of the religious sects . . . but more particularly the sect called Baptists, which had the effect of producing in the minds of the slaves a belief that they could not serve both a spiritual and a temporal master'.

The focus of the rising was Montego Bay, where a Baptist missionary called Thomas Burchell – lately gone home to England on a visit – ministered to a large and well-organized church numbering 1600 members, with separate classes on most of the nearby plantations. Sugar was by now in decline. The planters' grip over their slaves had slackened – as early as 1827, the number of runaways living in shacks on abandoned plantations, or else hiding in the mountains, had been estimated at twenty thousand. From information – sometimes optimistically exaggerated – which reached them through the missionaries, the black slaves still at work in the fields had a broad idea of the political changes in Britain which were bringing about emancipation. Near Montego Bay, everyone was eager to believe the story now being put around that Thomas Burchell himself had sailed away to England to make sure of their freedom: all slaves to become free men, so the good word went, at Christmas.

That summer, a loose-knit clandestine organization had been formed among church members by Sam Sharpe, an intelligent and literate slave in Burchell's congregation, a man always highly regarded and well-treated by his master. Under cover of a prayer meeting, local Baptist class leaders had come together, and pledged themselves with an oath that, after Christmas, when the cane would be ripe for cutting, they would lead their people out on strike unless the planters at last paid them wages.

Just before Christmas, a brutal incident sent passions rising high. A black woman was seen carrying home a piece of sugar-cane from the field. If she had indeed broken it off and kept it for herself, the offence was trivial. But Colonel Grignon, a militia officer and attorney for a property near Montego Bay, ordered her to be flogged.

The head driver was told to carry out the sentence on her with his ten-foot cart-whip – but the woman happened to be his wife. When he refused, the second driver was called upon to carry out Grignon's sentence – but the woman was his sister. So Grignon sent for the police. The slaves, this time provoked too far, came out against them with cane-knives, threatening to throw them all in the boiling sugar-vat. Man, wife and brother-in-law then ran for their lives.

The strike was to begin after Christmas but, with tempers rising high, so did the arson. There was almost no bloodshed, but on one sugar estate after another fires broke out, until the torch had been put to buildings on 160 estates. In an armed clash with the slaves at the head of his militia, Colonel Grignon disgraced himself. He beat a retreat to Montego Bay, and there excused himself by spreading a tall story, readily believed, that he had been 'attacked by 10,000 men, who came down upon him in four columns'. On Christmas Eve, two regiments in the Westmorland Militia, with freed men of colour in their ranks, were disarmed, for fear that they had come under Sam Sharpe's influence and might join the rebels.

Martial law was declared. The Navy shipped two regiments of regulars to Montego Bay, and stood offshore. At first the blacks thought those warships had been sent by the King to break their chains, for they had been told that King George, like William Wilberforce, was their friend. They were soon undeceived.

For a long month, the planters took their revenge, until at Montego Bay a woman doing her shopping would not bother to turn her head at the sight of yet another black man being hanged. Hardly a dozen whites lost their lives in the vast uprising. Upwards of four hundred black rebels were killed out of hand, a hundred prisoners were shot or hanged after drum-head court martial. Some were shot by planters after being pardoned by the governor as demonstrably innocent.

Slaves who ran for the mountains were tracked down by bloodhounds shipped over from Cuba, a bounty being paid on

E

each pair of human ears brought in. Possession of a Baptist class ticket was purged by five hundred lashes in public – fifty lashes being given at each of ten successive street corners in Montego Bay. Seventeen Baptist or Methodist chapels on Jamaica were wrecked. The last rebel to suffer death, on 23 May 1832, was Sam Sharpe – at a solemn execution intended as a public example. From the scaffold, Sam Sharpe 'in a new suit of white clothes' made use of the chance they had given him. Solemnly he denied that the missionaries had organized the uprising. With the noose around his neck, his last words were, 'I depend upon the Redeemer who shed his blood on Calvary for sinners.'

The persuasive arguments of those economists, from Adam Smith to Ricardo, who were advocates of the wages system, were soon to be contradicted on Jamaica. Abolitionists had always said confidently that with money as their incentive, liberated slaves would go to work in the cane-fields more readily than when under duress. But those good men in Clapham could not have tried cutting cane. Sugar-cane is like giant nightmare grass, and the leaf edges, face-high or underfoot, are sharp enough to cut the unwary in the flesh. The stem has to be severed twice – each time with a shearing blow forceful enough to cut off a man's hand. Cutting sugar-cane is somewhere in between hard work and stiff punishment – no one would do it who could find something better.

English Baptists bought land on Jamaica, and by 1838 had planted 3000 of their followers in free villages, as smallholders. The Methodists too joined in, though less enthusiastically, and until the 1840s the English missionaries on Jamaica were usually listened to with respect. In 1831, there were 10,000 Baptists, in 1845 34,000. But here, no less than on Tahiti, they wore out their welcome.

The missionaries condemned drumming, dancing, traditional Christmas festivities, and concubinage. Even the blowing of conch shells was made illegal. They failed most conspicuously to impose their own strict sexual mores upon a population hitherto held down but now won free, where young women considered marriage a form of slavery, and seven out of ten children were born out of wedlock. Slowly the Baptists from England lost ground among the 'noble free peasantry' they boasted of having helped bring into being.

By 1865 there were 50,000 small properties on Jamaica and, in the wake of a great religious revival in 1860 (when '20,000 souls were saved'), many distinctively African elements entered the Baptist cult there: trances, dreams, prophesying and public confession, wild dancing and flagellation, even ritual sex orgies. Jamaican behaviour drifted even further from the punctual frugality characteristic in Britain of chapel-folk, and appropriate to a society based on factory production. But modes of behaviour based on forgiveness and lovingkindness persisted on Jamaica, and a cheerful travesty of Christian dogma and liturgy could still be overheard in the corrugated-iron chapels there, even though the puritanism of the foreign missionaries was by and large forgotten.

6   The World Upside Down

'The faithful missionary is liable to be involved in many questions of a social and political kind, and he cannot always escape the reproach cast upon his Divine Master of being the enemy of Caesar, and of turning the world upside down.' Henry Venn, Secretary of the Church Missionary Society

Before abolition came suddenly into vogue, in the 1780s, the most persistent individual philanthropist to befriend the slaves had been a scholarly eccentric called Granville Sharp. All through the first three-quarters of the eighteenth century, rich West Indians visiting London had been in the habit of bringing their black domestics with them – and the sight of these unlucky slaves breathing English air wounded Granville Sharp to the core. He had no great personal resources – the grandson of an Archbishop of York, he had a clerkship in the Ordnance Office. Yet by intelligent and high-principled obstinacy, Sharp had at last extracted, in 1772, a favourable judgement from the Lord Chief Justice. 'As soon as any slave sets his foot on English ground,' announced Lord Mansfield, 'he becomes free.'

There were fourteen thousand of them, suddenly made free. Considered merely as property, they had been worth £700,000. What was to be done with them now? The question did not arise. The judgement had made free men of them. A free man looks out for himself, to sink or swim.

The wages system was new to them, and a good many freed slaves failed to find a niche in it. The rookery of St Giles became their refuge, a stone's throw from Whitefield's Tabernacle, and nicknamed the Holy Land. This vast warren of tumbledown houses on the fringes of fashionable London hid the West End's criminal population, in a rotting slum so full of traps and boltholes that until the 1840s, when New Oxford Street was driven through the middle of it, police and magistrates hardly dared show their faces there. The freed slaves, begging on the streets, soon became known as St Giles's Blackbirds, and the scandal grew when they were joined by black ex-soldiers – men, formerly slaves who, having served on the British side against their old masters in the American War of Independence, had by chance been demobilized in London.

Inshore of the Banana Islands – where John Newton, in his unregenerate young days, had been a slave-trader's runner – the view from a ship's deck, after passing the monotonous Sahara coast to the north and reaching the no-less-interminable African coastal swamp thereafter, is broken abruptly by a mountainous headland, twenty-five miles long. The Portuguese in their day of imperial splendour had seen a resemblance between the promontory and a lion's head, and called it Sierra Leone. Pitt agreed with Granville Sharp that the St Giles's Blackbirds might as well be sent to Sierra Leone. He offered them free transport, and six months' maintenance thereafter. So, in the spring of 1787, under the auspices of the Committee Relieving the Black Poor, four hundred blacks from London accompanied by sixty whites were shipped out – most of the whites were whores.

A hundred and forty of these uprooted unfortunates died on the voyage – a mortality higher than that aboard most slavers. Twenty square miles of St George's Bay were sold and formally ceded to the British crown by the local chieftain, King Naimbanna. A noble fellow called Patrick Fraser, recently ordained by the Bishop of Ely, had volunteered to shepherd the Blackbirds and their ladies. They reached their new home, so he reported glumly to London in July 1787, 'at the beginning of the rainy season' – and the rainfall in Sierra Leone averages upwards of 150 inches a year. Patrick Fraser soon got homesick; the task he had accepted was impossible.

There were, for one thing, other black men already living on that fever-ridden coast, and they resented being pushed out. The locals knew how to build a hut and plant a crop. The black men from London had no such useful skills: some had been soldiers;

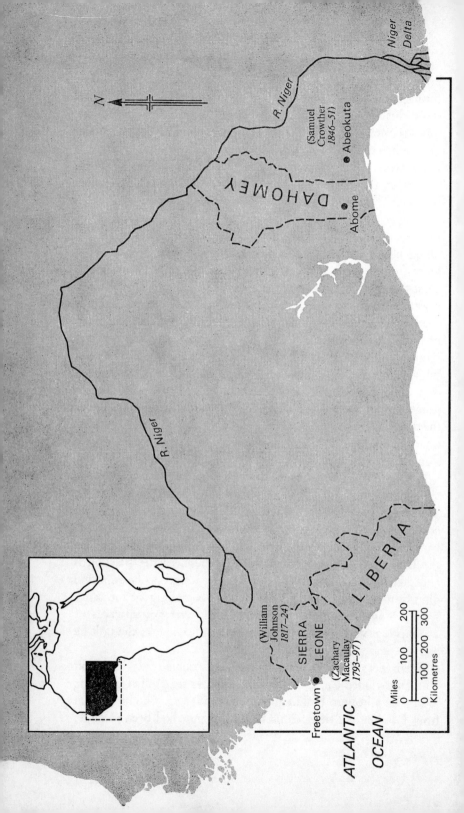

N

Niger Delta

R. Niger

(Samuel
Crowther
1846–51)
● Abeokuta

DAHOMEY

● Abome

R. Niger

LIBERIA

(William
Johnson
1817–24)

SIERRA
LEONE

(Zachary
Macaulay
1793–97)

Freetown ●

Miles
0   100   200

0   100   200   300
Kilometres

ATLANTIC

OCEAN

many had, fifteen years before, been little blackamoor slaves in ostrich-feather hats, meant to look decorative as they held up lady's train. When the salt horse and hard tack landed from the ship ran out, they went hungry. Within the first year, half of those who had survived the voyage out were dead, most often of fever. And there were other dangers: north and south were the barracoons of slave traders, both French and British, to whom a black man was a valuable animal. Freedom was bitter – some openly declared they would rather go back to slavery in the West Indies.

In 1789 some English Jack Tars, hardly expecting to find English-speaking harlots on their run ashore, went off afterwards in their hilarity and smashed up a nearby native village. Hoping to finish off all these intruders the chief retaliated by wiping out the settlement on St George's Bay. But the government in London was by this time taking it for granted that the right place to send unwanted black men was Sierra Leone; moreover, the Admiralty had its eye on what is now Freetown harbour – by far the best along the West African coast.

In 1791, Wilberforce and his friends made it easier for the government to secure this port without political opposition by launching the Sierra Leone Company, under a royal charter, and with funds of £240,000, much of the money raised by subscription among wealthy evangelicals. The Company's aims were 'the civilization of Africa and the abolition of the Slave Trade'. The device of a chartered company – which could occupy a prospective colony without compromising the government – was later found useful for taking the Union Jack into Rhodesia, Kenya, Uganda and Nigeria. Missionaries might go first, and even alone – but they could expect a chartered company at their heels soon after.

Sixty St Giles's Blackbirds had survived. They were rounded up, and the settlement got ready to await the arrival of 1100 blacks from America, who on 28 March 1792 were landed by Lieutenant John Clarkson, RN, from a convoy of fifteen vessels. These were yet more of the black men who had fought on the British side against their former American masters – men who, after defeat, had moved north to Nova Scotia with the United Empire Loyalists. Some of them, while in America, had been reached by the aftermath of Whitefield's teaching in the Great Awakening, and were practising Methodists. Of these converts, a hundred were still busily alive in 1811, when Reverend George Warren arrived as a Methodist missionary (he himself was dead within a year). Evangelical Christianity reached West Africa unaided, and of its own accord.

The black Americans had not only their own religion, but many had their own opinions, too. In the years of fighting after 1776 they had heard much talk of liberty, and were, therefore, not easy men to handle. They refused to dig and hoe at the company's mere bidding, and demanded democratic rights – though to the wealthy philanthropists running Sierra Leone at the time, the very word *democracy* was anathema.

In 1793, Wilberforce and his fellow directors sent out to Sierra Leone a twenty-five-year-old Scot called Zachary Macaulay – a son of the manse, and one of twelve children. Macaulay when he was sixteen had gone out to a sugar plantation on Jamaica as what was then euphemistically called a 'book-keeper' – the lowest and least-considered of plantation employees, the man who was sent to work out there, under the vertical sun, and drive the slaves hard.

The young Scot was gawky, deadly serious, with a totally impassive face, and was later described as having no sense whatever of the ridiculous; he was all will-power and high principle. In Jamaica, Zachary Macaulay, with his father's homilies echoing in his ears, did his best to 'alleviate the hardships of a considerable number of my fellow creatures, and to render the bitter cup of servitude as palatable as possible'. By twenty-four his fortune was assured – he had risen to manage the plantation. But the job disgusted him. To his father's alarm, he threw it up and came back to London, where Wilberforce recognized at once that an experienced and humane slave-driver who was also deeply pious might be just right for Sierra Leone. And so it proved.

Zachary Macaulay plunged into the chaos waiting for him there, and worked a miracle. He was obliged to turn his hand to everything – he was judge and clerk and diplomat, he preached the

Sunday sermon and in the absence of a chaplain even performed marriages. Unless a crop were sown they would starve, so he got them out into the field with hoes, apportioning the easiest tasks to blacks who could read and write, and thereby giving a fillip to education. He started a library of improving books, he set going a printing press. Then, in September 1794 – Year II of the new French Republic – disaster struck.

Eight French sail under Commodore Allemand, in *Experiment*, out of Brest, were led into the anchorage at Sierra Leone by an American slaver captain called Newell, who was very familiar with the coast, and wanted to get back some of his own runaway slaves who had found sanctuary with Zachary Macaulay. The squadron moored close inshore, and for two hours poured musket-shot and grape into the defenceless settlement, then sent an armed landing-party ashore.

The French seamen were undisciplined and in rags. While Newell led a gang of them in search of Macaulay and his own runaway property, the other sailors exchanged their rags for women's finery, and began plundering at leisure. They burst open every drawer and cupboard, and wrecked the printing press in search of money. Discovering that the day they landed happened to be Sunday, the revolutionary sailors assured Macaulay that 'the National Convention has decreed that there is no Sunday, and that the Bible is all a lie'. Commodore Allemand himself, Macaulay later discovered, sat down to dinner in his cabin aboard *Experiment* to a chorus of fresh-faced ships' boys, singing 'La Marseillaise' in lieu of grace.

'The view of the town library', Macaulay wrote in his report, with a certain primness, 'filled me with lively concern. The volumes were tossed about and defaced with the utmost wantonness; and if they happened to bear any resemblance to Bibles, they were torn in pieces and trampled on.' Nor had science fared better at their hands. 'The collection of natural curiosities next caught my eye,' Macaulay wrote. 'Plants, seeds, dried birds, insects and drawings were scattered about in great confusion.' By the time the French had left, in mid-October, they had burned the buildings at Sierra Leone to the ground, shot twelve hundred hogs, mainly in sport, and left the unlucky blacks there with nothing but 'a little flour, a little brandy', and the clothes they stood up in.

Help came from London, and Macaulay spent a year getting the place on its feet again. In 1795 he went home, and came back the year following to cope with a black insurrection, bringing with him a cargo of evangelical missionaries. Even though from now on there would be no need for him to preach sermons and bless brides, Macaulay did not think much of them. 'The Baptists under David George,' he reported, 'are decent and orderly' – though he went on to charge them with 'neglect of family worship, and sometimes unfairness in their dealings'. Lady Huntingdon's Methodists were a particular affliction to Macaulay, because 'the lives of many are very disorderly, and a rank antinomianism prevails among them' – that is to say, knowing themselves safe through grace they were prone to indulge in sin. The thorn in his side was, however, Moses Wilkinson, a Wesleyan Methodist who launched such an enthusiastic revival among those black infantrymen who had been touched by the Great Awakening that their fervour led to scandal.

A missionary's career in Sierra Leone was usually brief, though Zachary Macaulay, well-seasoned in Jamaica, argued to the end of his days that everyone else was mistaken, and the climate in Sierra Leone was really excellent. Of the six missionaries, all under forty, who on 12 October 1797 set sail for Sierra Leone in the Company's ship, *Calypso*, three were dead of fever within six months, and a fourth was sent back as undesirable. With the colony once more on its feet, Macaulay had in that same year gone home, taking with him twenty-nine hopeful boys and five clever girls, for a school he planned to set going in Clapham. He began a partnership, not long after, as a West African merchant, and the firm was soon worth £100,000. Freetown, with its 300 newly built houses and 1200 inhabitants, was prospering too. In 1798, the British Treasury, well aware that the Admiralty had its eye on Freetown harbour, relieved the Clapham philanthropists of the financial burdens of administration and defence. In 1800, the rebel Maroons, discontented with their life in freezing Nova Scotia, arrived to add to the problems of everyday life in fever-ridden Sierra Leone.

On 1 January 1808, after the trade in slaves had been abolished by law, Sierra Leone was made a British Crown colony. By then there were 1871 inhabitants. The place was so notorious for sickness and riot that in the twenty-two years to 1814 there were seventeen changes of governor. As Sydney Smith wryly observed, Sierra Leone had always two governors, one just arrived in the colony, and one just arrived in England. The missionaries managed, after 1804, to cling on and dig in, but sixteen of the twenty-six men and women missionaries reaching Sierra Leone before 1817 died there. The place earned the nickname of the White Man's Grave.

From 1808 onwards, a British naval squadron was on duty, blockading the West African coast against slavers. And where were the Royal Navy to dump what they called their 'recaptives' – the slaves they had rescued? Where else but at Sierra Leone – and thus the problem of governing the place grew worse. Those rescued Africans might have been kidnapped by slave dealers anywhere along the coast from Senegal to Angola. They arrived speaking such a variety of native tongues that they could hardly communicate with each other, much less with their rescuers. New arrivals, often living skeletons, were crowded promiscuously into huts. In their hopeless rage they sold what clothing had been given them, refused point blank to work, and shut their ears against the exhortations of any white man who might know a little of their language. They were numb with despair.

The bodily suffering of any man or woman sold into slavery might be real enough, but almost always the moral shock – the sense of loss – was worse. A third of the slaves surviving the sea-passage and actually reaching America were likely to die of a broken heart within three months of landing – the dealers called the process 'seasoning'. To be 'shipmates' – to have crossed the Atlantic in the same slave-ship – was often a stronger bond for the survivors than the older tribal loyalties which had been broken off short.

But to be kidnapped into one ship, 'rescued' by another, then landed on a wet and feverish peninsula among Africans all jabbering different tongues, must have deepened their bewilderment to a stupor. Yet out of this confused misery the evangelical missionaries managed to set going a viable new society, educated, civilized and lasting until now.

No less than their contemporaries who went out to Tahiti, they were overweeningly confident that they knew best – that what they preached was the final truth. Their evangelicalism was vigorously driven onward, so to speak, by the steam engine: God's will, as they interpreted it, and the energetic historical process finding expression on the West African coast in victorious naval cruisers, prosperous traders and bewildered recaptives, were all one.

Missionaries who volunteered to work in the White Man's Grave, in the days before modern tropical medicine, took their lives in their hands, and by this time in Sierra Leone they all knew it. The loss of life was hair-raising. Of seven Anglican schoolmasters and five wives who landed in 1823, six died the same year, and all but two within eighteen months. The Methodists in fifty years' service to West Africa lost sixty-three missionaries and wives by fever and shipwreck. Between 1804 and 1824, of seventy-nine men and women sent to Sierra Leone by the Church Missionary Society, fifty-three died. Officials fared no better; between 1821 and 1825, four governors died.

Yet the human situation the evangelical missionaries had to confront in what span of life might be granted them coincided marvellously well with their own passionate and simplified theology. The black men dumped back by the navy in their midst had all been given their own foretaste of hell. They must now either give up all hope – lie down and die in their crowded, starving, fever-ridden huts – or else decide to renew their lives; be born again. An idiom of survival and renewal was already on the tongues of the black Methodist veterans who had fought in America. From shock, the ex-slaves were psychologically ready to shed the traditional languages and customs they had left behind them. Nova Scotians, Jamaicans, Blackbirds, missionaries were communicating already in a picturesque kind of simple English, and this was another unifying factor. There was a basis for a new start.

The conspicuous missionary hero in Sierra Leone was William Johnson. He had been born in Hanover – then united to the

British crown – and after the Napoleonic wars came to London, a poor man, to take a job in a sugar-refinery. There, as a wage-earner, he experienced conversion. In 1817 he sailed with his wife and others for Sierra Leone. Johnson was then twenty-seven, and could sympathize from personal experience with the recaptives: he too had been a poor man trying to keep his head above water in a country where everyone spoke a strange language. Johnson lasted seven years in the White Man's Grave, and in that time he made his mark.

Recaptives were pouring in: from 1808 to 1858 the Royal Navy landed between 60,000 and 70,000. In the settlement called Regent, which Johnson was given to oversee, lived 1400 of them. Within two years, the hopelessness and chaos which Johnson met on arrival had been overcome. Land around was under cultivation; there were nineteen paved streets, decent houses, a school, a hospital. There were 258 communicants and a very much larger number of worshippers – since only those willing to give up the polygamy traditional in Africa were admitted to the altar. They went on Sunday to a stone church built with their own hands. Johnson must have been a phenomenal all-rounder, for he found time to train masons, carpenters, blacksmiths and even tailors.

A measure of the change wrought by incessant missionary activity in the everyday life of Sierra Leone is given by the criminal statistics. In 1812, from a population of four thousand, forty criminal cases were brought before the judge. A decade later, in 1822, only six cases were brought before the Chief Justice, the Hon. E. Fitzgerald, from a population of six thousand – the crime rate having fallen in ten years from one in a hundred to one in a thousand – and there were no criminal cases whatever from villages where missionaries lived.

Here as on Tahiti, the Roman Catholics eventually made their appearance, not from France this time but from the United States, which was busy establishing its own colony of freed slaves in Liberia. On 29 November 1843, Monsignor Barron from Philadelphia, Vicar Apostolic, landed at Freetown with seven priests and three lay brothers. Within a few weeks, eight of the ten were dead.

The missionaries in Sierra Leone usually pushed to the back of their minds those tenets of Christian teaching which obliged them to treat the black man as a perfect equal. For this there is perhaps some excuse: abolitionist publicity always pictured the black slave as a suffering child – a kind of simpleton – and the missionaries for their own part were uncritically confident of everything their own particular England stood for, from Sabbath observance to dark satanic mills. So in Sierra Leone they preserved their own status: in the first forty years, only three black clergymen were ordained.

Henry Venn, administering the Church Missionary Society in London, was among the first to see that this would never do, and his view prevailed. By 1860, English missionaries had begun to withdraw from Sierra Leone and hand the church there over to black clergy, of whom by 1882 there were twenty-three. The colony's population was then 60,000. The Church of England had made 14,000 converts, and another 20,000 had become Methodists, Baptists, Presbyterians and Roman Catholics.

This was the high point so far of professed Christianity in Sierra Leone. There has since been, proportionately, a long, slow decline, and the reason is clear. Black Christians are men of some education, living near the coast, descended from strangers who arrived abruptly from without, and the clients, at least in other men's eyes, of the colonizing power. Once the heroic early days had faded from memory, the church under its native clergy marked time. Many Africans in the hinterland were Muslim – even by the 1860s, Muslims in Freetown had come to outnumber Christians. Islam was not a cat's-paw of colonial Britain: moreover, Islam allowed polygamy. Conversion to Islam depended not upon a profound inner transformation of psyche and ethos, but was brought about simply, by the repetition of a verbal formula – *la illāha ill'Allah Muhammed rasul Allah!* – a ritual ablution and the saying of set prayers. The conversion of black Christians by black Muslims began then, and still goes on.

In 1822, Lieutenant Leeke, RN, of the blockade cruiser *Myrmidon* landed a cargo of recaptives at Freetown. Among them was a small boy about eleven called Adjai, intelligent, a Yoruba from what is now called Nigeria. A missionary called J. W. Weeks taught him carpentry, and when he was baptized, on 11 December 1825, Adjai took the name of Samuel Crowther. He had been a model pupil, and was sent in 1825 to Islington, where for a few months he taught in a parochial school, arriving back at Sierra Leone at the age of nineteen, a dandy in a blue suit, white stockings and beaver hat. His new style of life was too much for the missionaries. They took Samuel Crowther's mattress away from him, as an unnecessary luxury, and soon had him walking barefoot again: there was to be no aping of the white man. But Samuel Crowther was too secure in his belief to be daunted by a snub. Had he not, when rescued by the Royal Navy, been in an almost literal sense redeemed from hell? He married happily, and spent the next few years as an exemplary teacher.

In 1842, John Venn's son, Henry, became Secretary of the Church Missionary Society (just as James Stephen's son, who was Venn's brother-in-law, became Permanent Secretary at the Colonial Office, and Grant's son, Lord Glenelg, Colonial Secretary – the second generation of the Clapham Sect were clever at establishing themselves in the centre of power. Their remoter descendants took a literary turn: E. M. Forster was a Thornton, Virginia Woolf, a Stephen. There was also a link between missions and nonsense. Edward Lear's brother Charles was a West African missionary, and surprised nineteenth-century Leatherhead when he came back to die, bringing home with him a black wife called Adjouah; Lewis Carroll's brother was for many years a cheerfully eccentric chaplain on Tristan da Cunha.) Henry Venn's enlightened policy, for the next thirty years, was to respect native customs – though strictly drawing the line at polygamy – and, by encouraging a native pastorate, to make the church African.

Samuel Crowther's journal came into Venn's hands, and he was so impressed that, in 1842, he had the young teacher brought back to Islington College. In 1843 the Bishop of London ordained Samuel Crowther priest, and on 4 August 1846 he was sent as missionary to Abeokuta, in present-day Nigeria – inland from Lagos, and then a notorious slaving centre.

Near Abeokuta, Crowther came across an illiterate old Yoruba woman called Afala, who had been bought out of slavery by her daughters. She proved to be his own mother. Crowther baptized her, and after three years in Abeokuta had formed a church there, in the midst of the contraband slave traffic, with eighty Yoruba communicants and five hundred worshippers.

Such was the demand at the time from sugar planters in Cuba and Brazil for contraband West African slaves, that any black who could be landed there was worth five times his purchase price and cost of transport. Even if two out of three ships were intercepted by the blockade, the slaver was still in business. Henry Venn's view was that only a prosperous legitimate trade would cut the ground from under the slavers' feet. 'You must show the native chiefs', Venn explained, 'that it is more profitable to use their men for cultivating the ground than to sell them as slaves. When once the chiefs have learned that lawful commerce pays better than the slave trade, the work of the squadron will soon be at an end.' Venn got missionaries to send him samples of such local produce as cotton, ginger, palm-oil and ebony. Without telling the Church Missionary Society, of which he was a paid official, he bought four hundred pounds of arrowroot, as an experiment – and launched the West African arrowroot trade. By 1859 Venn was able to report exuberantly, 'There are now 200–300 gins at work in Abeokuta . . . cotton is flowing into England in a stream.'

On Monday, 3 March 1851, the obscenely cruel king of Dahomey had attacked Abeokuta with 150,000 warriors. Reverend Samuel Crowther, who knew better than anyone how slavery was ruining everyday life in the hinterland, went back to London to confer with Lord Palmerston, who already had his eye on Lagos as the port commanding all the water-borne commerce coming down the Niger.

Dr Scholefield, Regius Professor of Divinity at Cambridge, had once taken some of Samuel Crowther's answers to questions set on Paley's *Evidences* with him to Trinity, 'to show some of our Trinity Fellows, who maintain that the African mind is incapable of apprehending an argument'. This readiness to use the intellectual powers of black men, like Venn's eagerness to make them entrepreneurs, was second nature to evangelicals of the Reform

Act generation, whose ideas had been formed when Britain was the undisputed workshop of the world. But the slow loss of Britain's manufacturing monopoly coincided with a growing esteem for Darwin's *Origin of Species*, and a sceptical reaction set in. The coming men were beginning to think that the best way to make sure of a market might be to seize it by force, and keep competitors out by tariff. This led them to consider the black man, logically enough, not so much as a customer or a trading-partner or indeed as a fellow-Christian – for 'loss of faith' was the keynote of the times – but as a natural inferior, who would hew wood and draw water for them, in colonies as yet to be marked out on the map.

A sanction for such a belief could not very easily be found in the gospels – as Sepúlveda had discovered, three centuries before – so recourse was had to the newer authority of science. The catch phrase, 'survival of the fittest', might crudely oversimplify Darwin's hypothesis of natural selection, but it soon became the conventional wisdom of advanced men with faith in the future of the British Empire. And the young discipline of anthropology was soon ready with arguments to justify treating black men as natural inferiors – arguments still being used, here and there, to beat Christians and other egalitarian optimists over the head.

In 1866, in the *Popular Magazine of Anthropology*, J. C. Nott, MD, described as 'the greatest living anthropologist in America', announced that 'the brain of the negro is nine cubic inches less than the brain of the white man, and the large-headed races have always ruled the earth and been the only repositories of true civilization'. The papers read before the Anthropological Society of London take up a similar refrain. In his presidential address to the Society's third meeting, Dr James Hunt declared, 'Statesmen have yet to be taught the practical value of race distinction and the absolute impossibility of applying the civilization and laws of one race to another race of men essentially distinct.'

'The negro brain', claimed yet another anthropologist, 'bears a great resemblance to a European female or child's brain, and thus approaches the ape far more than the European, while the negress approaches the ape still further.' There was, therefore, excellent scientific justification for white men to keep women, children and niggers under their thumbs. The sentimental and interfering missionaries were of course in their way. One anthropologist in 1865 even cast a lingering and regretful glance back to the good old days in Britain when slavery was legal. 'Our mistaken legislature has done the Negro race much injury', he announced, 'by their absurd and unwarrantable attempts to prevent Africa exporting her worthless or surplus population.'

In 1864, Samuel Crowther, a living denial of all these recent scientific theories, was made Doctor of Divinity at Oxford, and consecrated bishop. The beams which held up the roof of his own alma mater, Fourah Bay College – founded by the Church Missionary Society in 1827 – were the masts of captured slavers. Crowther was a prudent bishop, restraining Venn's impatience, and in the next seven years ordained no more than eight Africans. Polygamy was the great stumbling block. For Roman Catholic priests vowed to celibacy, this sexual difficulty was even thornier: until 1896, there was no non-European Roman Catholic bishop anywhere.

The 'export of surplus population' century after century had grotesquely deformed West African society. Dahomey, which attacked the city of Abeokuta when Samuel Crowther had a mission there, had evolved a method of terrorizing its opponents and future victims by a cult of skulls. The intelligence service of the Royal Navy's blockade estimated that Gezo, King of Dahomey, made £60,000 a year from his part in the slave trade. In his capital, Abomey, skulls were heaped up by thousands. They were stuck over doorways, and in rows along the palace ramparts. The skulls of his enemies formed the floor of the royal bedroom. Skulls made tops for royal walking-sticks.

The King of Dahomey's most cruel and effective soldiers were women – many of them prisoners, frightened out of their minds and then retrained as warriors, for in Dahomey the object of war was not to kill but to take prisoners. After a war the King sold his men captives off as slaves, but many of the women and children he absorbed into his own nightmare society. A little world had been created in Dahomey wholly denying mother-love and family affection, and based absolutely on fear. The King's Amazons – there were four thousand of them – went into action carrying polished human skulls as drinking cups. When by happy chance he got his hands on a Christian prisoner, King Gezo's son, Gléglé, would crucify him.

In the mind of the gentle and sagacious Bishop Crowther, the contrast between what the influence of the slave trade over many years had made of Dahomey, and what Christian teaching had helped the slave-trader's victims in Sierra Leone to achieve, was indelible. Not unexpectedly, he associated the Christianity in which he had been bred with free trade and the wages system, and therefore was not keen to be pushed too fast in any new direction.

Just as the audacious racialist ideas tossed into the air by anthropologists in the 1860s had become club commonplaces by the 1880s, so at the same time, among the blacks, the obvious slogan of 'Africa for the Africans' came to the fore. But, protested Samuel Crowther, with Dahomey in mind, ' "Africa for the Africans alone" is to claim for her the right to continued ignorance, to practise cruelty and acts of barbarity as her perpetual inheritance.'

A traitor to his people? In a twentieth-century context, that is perhaps what he sounds. But if in the western world there are any restraints on cruelty, other than those we inherit, sometimes indirectly and unawares, from Christianity and the family-based virtues it has set itself to nurture, they were not much in evidence on the West African coast in Crowther's lifetime.

7 Among the Heathen as an Equal

'It is much to be lamented that the Gospel with all its attendant blessings cannot be introduced into any heathen nation without the introduction of the crimes and diseases which obtain in civil society.' *Samuel Marsden on New Zealand, 1820*

'I was prepared to go even to Sierra Leone, to cancel, as far as my efforts might, one item of the debt of sin and woe which England's commercial prosperity has entailed upon the sons of Africa.' *George Augustus Selwyn, 1841*

Georgia in its latter days was no longer used as a refuge for liberated debtors, but as a dumping ground for Britain's criminals. Therefore, once the United States had won their independence, some new convict settlement elsewhere had to be found. While the government made up its mind, the unlucky convicts were kept for years aboard hulks – old, dismasted wooden warships, at anchor in estuaries. West Africa was suggested, but sending convicts to the White Man's Grave would be a sentence of death.

Sir Joseph Banks, a man of science who had gone on Captain Cook's first voyage, suggested that Botany Bay, near present-day Sydney, on the east coast of Australia, might do very well for convicts, and this was agreed. The first fleet set off for Botany Bay in 1787 – nine transport-ships escorted by two men-of-war. Some of the 565 male convicts had been transferred straight from the hulks. They had lived in chains aboard wooden ships for years. The 192 women convicts were kept elsewhere in the fleet, separate from them. There were also forty free women – most of them the wives of the couple of hundred marines sent in the fleet to overawe the convicts. Though all the condemned men and women were kept under hatches – as on slave-ships – once at sea their manacles were knocked off.

The convicts gave little trouble, and thanks to conspicuously good management, only twenty-three died – the death rate in the second fleet out was to be ten times higher. Some no doubt were monsters of criminality, but the law in those days was harsh on the poor. Many were being transported for offences we should now find trivial.

With the help of Captain Cook's old pen-and-ink chart, Captain Arthur Phillip, RN, sailed his convoy on 18 January 1788 into Botany Bay. The women convicts were put ashore first, then the male convicts and their guard of marines. The voyage out had lasted eight months, and some of the unluckier convicts had neither seen a woman's skirt nor set foot on dry land for years. Males and females, whether convicts or guards, all fell gladly upon one another. Australia – so the legend goes – began with a dionysiac orgy.

Marines and criminals very soon resumed their proper stations in life, and next Sunday there was a church parade. The convicts, male and female wearing their blue-and-yellow jackets, stood inside a hollow square of scarlet-clad marines, to hear Captain Phillip, RN, read prayers and go on to recommend heartily those who felt uneasy at any part they may have taken in the debauch to put matters right by an offer of marriage. Some took him at his word.

The first convicts to arrive had by and large been picked out for their usefulness as farmers or craftsmen. But they were in a new antipodean climate, with unfamiliar seasons. Crops failed, food ran short, and the pilfering of such rations as remained was soon a menace to the very existence of the colony. Captain Phillip seriously wondered whether to maroon the most notorious of his pilferers among the cannibals who lived on New Zealand. But being cooked and eaten was too extreme a disciplinary sanction, so the least tractable of the convicts were transported, instead, to the Pacific, to the loneliness of Norfolk Island. By 1791, when the third fleet of ten ships had set on shore its cargo of 1865 convicts (of whom 144 were prostitutes), the first British settlement in Australia numbered 4000 souls.

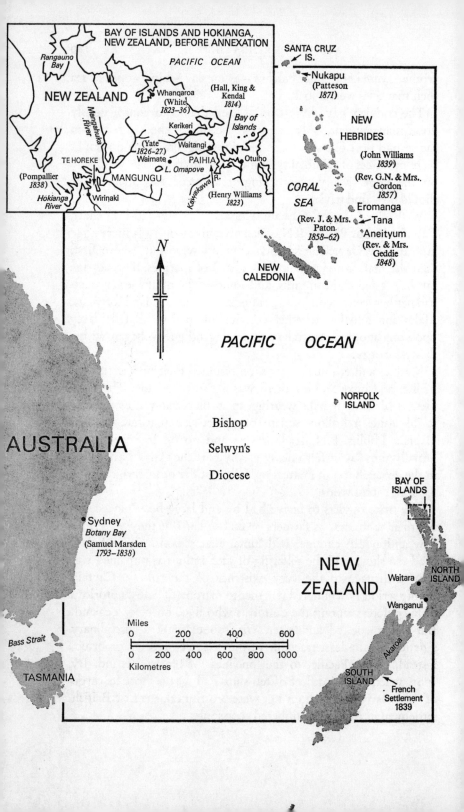

BAY OF ISLANDS AND HOKIANGA,
NEW ZEALAND, BEFORE ANNEXATION

Rangauno Bay

PACIFIC OCEAN

NEW ZEALAND

Whanqaroa (White *1823–36*)

(Hall, King & Kendal *1814*)

Mangahuka River

Kerikeri

Bay of Islands

(Yate *1826–27*) Waitangi

Waimate

TE HOREKE

PAIHIA

Otuiho

L. Omapove

MANGUNGU

Kawakawa R.

(Pompallier *1838*)

Hokianga River

Wirinaki

(Henry Williams *1823*)

SANTA CRUZ IS.

Nukapu (Patteson *1871*)

NEW HEBRIDES

(John Williams *1839*)

(Rev. G.N. & Mrs. Gordon *1857*)

CORAL SEA

Eromanga

Tana

(Rev. J. & Mrs. Paton *1858–62*)

Aneityum

(Rev. & Mrs. Geddie *1848*)

NEW CALEDONIA

N

PACIFIC OCEAN

NORFOLK ISLAND

Bishop

Selwyn's

Diocese

AUSTRALIA

BAY OF ISLANDS

Sydney
Botany Bay
(Samuel Marsden *1793–1838*)

NEW ZEALAND

Waitara

NORTH ISLAND

Wanganui

Bass Strait

Miles

0   200   400   600

0   200   400   600   800   1000

Kilometres

TASMANIA

Akaroa

SOUTH ISLAND

French Settlement 1839

Between 1788 and 1834, a hundred thousand convicts were sent out. They had all been sinners, but so are most of us; some were Irish rebels. Their sentence was servitude – they were used as forced labour, and most of Las Casas' old arguments in favour of the American Indians applied to them, too. Their spiritual welfare was not entirely neglected. Reverend James Dixon, a Roman Catholic priest who had fallen foul of the law, was set free in 1803 so as to 'exercise his clerical functions'. Even out on godforsaken Norfolk Island there was a compulsory church parade. 'Once a week we are drawn up on the square,' reports an eyewitness, 'opposite the Military Barracks, and the soldiers are drawn up in front of us with loaded muskets and fixed bayonets; and a young officer then comes to the fence, and reads part of the service.'

Convict labour in such masses made this new land flourish. Sydney by 1836 was a city of thirty thousand people, with land there fetching £12 an acre. Convicts still outnumbered free men, and their presence engendered dread: hangings during 1833–4 averaged more than four a week. But a proof that convict labour was the secret of Australian prosperity is given by the petition from West Australia, where workpeople were harder to come by. As late as 1850 they wanted a penal colony set up in their midst, too.

'There's no God in Van Diemen's Land, nor ever shall be,' was what the men transported there said about Tasmania, which lingered on as a penal colony until 1853. For its five thousand original inhabitants, Tasmania was not a comfortable place, either. In 1830, a long line of beaters, most of them convicts, were sent out to move systematically across the great, wet island, driving the Tasmans before them, so that they could all be shot down like two-legged vermin. Only a couple of hundred escaped with their lives; they were shipped off to small islands in Bass Strait. By 1847 half Tasmania's 60,000 population, too, was convict. The last Tasman died in 1876.

Samuel Marsden was born in 1765, the son of a Yorkshire blacksmith of strong evangelical principles. After a few years in the village school, Marsden started work at the forge; William

Wilberforce at the time was a Yorkshire MP. Noticing that young Samuel Marsden was a man of brains and force of character some rich evangelicals encouraged him to study for the ministry, so at twenty off he went, a grown man among schoolboys, to learn his Latin on the benches of Hull Grammar School. His wealthy patrons sent him up to Cambridge, but after a couple of years, they began to wonder if Samuel Marsden might be too rough and ready for an English parsonage.

The convicts in Australia needed a chaplain, so Wilberforce arranged the appointment, and on 26 May 1793 Marsden was ordained priest, 'for the service of the Church in the settlement of Botany Bay'. He arrived there after the usual long voyage to find the colony in extreme disorder and almost starving. Major Francis Grose of the New South Wales Corps was now in charge, and drunkenness, gambling and sexual licence were the rule. The Corps had a monopoly of the sale of spirits. The officers bartered drink for the corn crop, then sold the corn back to the government at a profit of five thousand per cent.

Grose had abolished the convict's compulsory attendance at church. He made his newly arrived chaplain a magistrate, and gave him a hundred-acre land grant, along with five convicts to work the place. Marsden, when any other such chance came his way, never hesitated to acquire more land and the convict labour necessary to make it bear fruit. By 1802 the Reverend Samuel Marsden, JP, had 650 acres worked by ten convicts. By 1804 he owned 1720 acres and ran 1200 sheep. But he was also conscientious in enforcing law and order. In the spring of 1800, the Irish prisoners were said to have planned a rising: he condemned Patrick Galvin to 300 lashes for refusing to betray them by revealing where the pikes might be hid. In 1809 Marsden shipped out five Merinos, and at the same time he introduced Australian wool to Yorkshire's woollen men, in Leeds. But this heavy-handed, enormously self-confident and instinctively acquisitive Yorkshireman was also hot against sin. Along with his belief in hell-fire went a single-minded fervour for missionary work.

In 1808, Samuel Marsden applied to the Church Missionary Society for men to go to the cannibal Maori in New Zealand.

Runaway convicts had already settled there, along the shore of
the Bay of Islands, a harbour eleven miles across, at the tip of
North Island. Whalers called in there to replenish their supplies,
and the convicts were managing to survive because they were
useful as middlemen in the trafficking between ships and the
Maori tribes on shore.

The year following, Marsden's plans for a New Zealand
mission had a setback when seventy passengers and crew aboard
a British ship *Boyd* (600 tons) were killed out of hand by Maori.
Boyd's captain had made enemies of them by flogging one of
their chiefs – personages considered sacred. Of *Boyd*'s four
survivors, two were children who happened in the midst of the
massacre accidentally to have touched a chief: his sacred touch
made them inviolate, so their lives were spared when all the rest
were killed and eaten.

By 1810, not only was Marsden officially forbidden to launch
his New Zealand mission, but the New South Wales government
had begun to discuss sending over an armed force to exterminate
the Maori. Three English missionaries arrived, and eventually
they were shipped across – William Hall, a joiner, John King,
a shoemaker, and Thomas Kendall, a man of some education
and property, who in England had run a school. To keep in
touch with the missions he was supervising in Tahiti and hoped
to launch in New Zealand, Samuel Marsden bought a small
hermaphrodite brig, *Active* (110 tons) – his plan was at the same
time to make £1000 a year out of her in trade.

On 15 December 1814, Marsden landed Hall, King and Kendall at the Bay of Islands. Their instructions were 'to introduce
among the Natives the knowledge of Christ, and in order to do
this, the Arts of Civilized Life.' Their first step was to buy a
farm for twelve axe-heads – the chief's signature on the deed
being a copy of the tattooed volutes on his face, a pattern of
whirls which was his sign manual. The Maori had never seen an
animal larger than a pig – Captain Cook had landed pigs – and
they were fascinated by the horse, the bull and the cows which
Active put ashore. Next year a miscellaneous cargo was landed
which had been chosen to impress them: bar iron, tools and nails,
knives, and forks, twelve gross of Jew's harps and a box of pea-

cock's feathers. The Maori had been making hard work of tilling the soil and building canoes with their stone-age tools. They showed great eagerness to lay their hands on metal hoes and axes. for forty-eight axe-heads they sold their missionaries 13,000 acres.

And here they were – three God-fearing, hard-working, well-intentioned Englishmen, with their wives and children, on the edge of a hilly, evergreen, forested country, where ferns grew nine feet high and the kauri pines were as high as a church steeple. Volcanic springs spouted coloured mud, there were swamps thick with bulrushes. The climate was no worse than in the south of England, but what of the cannibals? The missionaries may have felt about them as did the Romans of St Jerome's day, when discussing the dreaded savages up there beyond Hadrian's wall. 'When I was a boy in Gaul,' writes the saint, 'I beheld the Scots, a people living in Britain, eating human flesh; and although there was plenty of cattle and sheep at their disposal, yet they would prefer a ham of a herdsman or a slice of a female breast.' Then the Scots; now the Maori.

With his Tahitian experience in mind, Samuel Marsden was liberal with good advice. The missionaries in New Zealand were to keep the Sabbath, and have a public service. Hard work would keep them out of mischief, for 'if you indulge in idleness you will be ruined'. While cultivating their land, they were to seize every chance of talking with the Maori, conversing about sin and salvation, for example, 'when employed in planting pota- toes and sowing corn'. Marsden ordered his men above all to keep out of tribal wars: 'Tell them you are forbidden by the chiefs who have sent you out.' Kendall, the only one who became fluent in Maori, was soon teaching their children and healing the sick, as well as lending a hand on the farm.

By 1819, the three missionaries had ploughed wheat-fields, planted fruit trees, begun a boarding school for Maori children – and Kendall had started work on a Maori grammar. Though in the past year or so over a hundred Maori had been killed in clashes with traders and escaped convicts, there had been no retaliation on the mission. To all appearances they were success- fully achieving, here in New Zealand, that 'Christianization by patient, peaceful means alone' which Las Casas had advocated but failed to achieve himself at Cumaná.

In 1815, Samuel Marsden took three Maori chiefs over to Sydney, to impress them with civilization. They were shown smiths hammering iron and carpenters sawing wood. They saw a ship launched. On Sunday the Maori chiefs saw the convicts muster in their particoloured jackets, under armed guard, to hear a hellfire sermon. They may even have met, after dark – for it would not have been easy to avoid them – women from the overcrowded Female Factory at Parramatta, which took its nickname of Mrs Gordon's Fashionable School for Young Ladies from the sergeant's wife in charge.

Under the care of Mrs Gordon and her two dashing daughters were 481 female convicts who had behaved badly or tried to run away. At night they were turned out into the street, to earn their bread by prostitution. The Reverend Samuel Marsden had in 1801 described the Parramatta Female Orphanage to Wilberforce as 'the foundation of religion and morality in this Colony'. But he refused to baptize any of the 112 babies who in due course were born to Mrs Gordon's Fashionable Young Ladies, in case at the christening ceremony one of them might blurt out the name of some respectable citizen as the father.

Vice prevailed at the Bay of Islands, too, though the vice of hypocrisy had not yet taken root there. Traders were beginning to call in for flax and timber, convicts were by now keeping grogshops and distilling gin. For the gift of a blanket, any Maori chief living nearby would happily prostitute one of his female slaves, or even offer a night with one of his own less highly regarded concubines. For a musket, you could have his daughter. By 1830 – claimed the *Sydney Herald* – the chiefs around the Bay were making £11,000 a year from theft and prostitution. Into New Zealand's stone-age society, money and its uninhibited code of conduct had arrived.

Dollars – American or Mexican – were current in the Bay of Islands, and there was at one time a shabby trade in gilded farthings, but barter still went on briskly. As well as pimping their own womenfolk, the chiefs were also learning how to make a legitimate business profit from the whalers. Tribal wars could now be turned to great advantage, since any prisoners taken in them could be set to work in the field, growing potatoes. The chiefs would exchange their potatoes and pork aboard the whalers for gunpowder, with which they would fight more tribal wars, and capture more slaves, and thus grow more potatoes.

Venereal disease soon became as rampant in New Zealand as on Tahiti, but the imported ailment which most harrowed the Maori was tuberculosis. Infanticide became so common that the missionaries often saw newborn babies thrown to dogs or pigs.

The Maori as a people were intelligent and generous. Dreams powerfully affected their conduct. Dreams reported by the old women were carefully discussed on the morning after, in case they might yield some insight useful to the community. Maori who could afford concubines might take them, but adultery was frowned upon, and though individual ownership of land was not yet the custom, the boundaries of tribal properties were clearly recognized.

Since the missionaries were obliged to keep on good terms with the chiefs, for them to condemn prostitution outright might have been imprudent, but they would now and then try to save an unborn baby's life by offering the pregnant girl a garment in exchange. The girls around the Bay of Islands would answer that they could get more in one night from a whaler than a missionary was likely to give them all the year round. The mission's annual budget was £500, so they could not afford to redeem slaves, either, though they tried their best. Maori had often in the past been impulsively, homerically generous. Now they were learning the simple rules of trade: nothing for nothing; buy cheap and sell dear. The Maori were pushed irresistibly towards having slaves because though the free men of a tribe would always fight for their chief, in other ways they might well not obey him; they would certainly not till the soil for him. And slavery spread, because a runaway slave at once became the property of any man who could recapture him.

Maori killed quickly. A dead captive was the makings of a hearty meal of cooked meat; but if, on the other hand, you spared your prisoner's life, and put him to work, you thereby assured yourself of future hearty meals of vegetables. Curnonsky the gourmet claimed to have sat in on a cannibal meal in New Zealand: similar to pork, he remarked, but faintly flavoured with banana. The Maori had a preference for the flesh of their own folk, since European flesh, as they often complained, was too salty.

Even when fought with weapons of jasper and marble, their tribal wars had been gory. After battle, the warrior's practice was to drink the blood of the man he had killed, through his penis, then eat his body. The Maori victor would, however, preserve the dead man's head, scooping out his brains and moulding the skin in boiling water to a lifelike resemblance, then sticking up the dead man's image to taunt and mock. Heads of dear friends were also preserved with loving care, and a war canoe was provided with a pickled head fore and aft, to make sure it knew where it was going. On tribal raids, the other side's dried heads were trophies.

But this robustly savage life was rotting away. Since a native garment might take several months to weave, all that was given up, and the Maori went around in blankets. Muskets and powder had altered drastically the local balance of power. The tribe which hired out the most women, and sold most pork and potatoes, would have most muskets and make most conquests: thus the cycle of trade – or, if you prefer, the deadly contamination – spread inland.

By 1819, Thomas Kendall had made common cause with a far-sighted Maori chief called Hongi, whose ambition – not unlike Pomare's on Tahiti – was to become dominant along the profitable shore where the whalers called, and thus emerge as paramount chief. Though dozens of beachcombers had been murdered on the shores of New Zealand in the past few years for the clothes they stood up in, with Hongi as their friend the missionaries knew they were safe. Thomas Kendall expressed the view that to seek for converts yet was premature. A missionary, so he thought, should begin by mastering the language and customs of his native flock, and thereafter gently discourage such of their customary behaviour as was vicious or absurd. The fact was, Kendall had come to change the Maori, but they were changing him.

Hongi protected the missionaries because he intended to go on making use of them. By teaching young Maori to read and write and cipher, missionary schools could enable them, when they were trading, to see when they were swindled by gilded farthings. The new plants, animals and tools which Samuel Marsden sent to New Zealand had made Hongi more prosperous. But above all he needed weapons. In 1820, rumours reached Marsden that, in plain defiance of his instructions, Thomas Kendall had been trafficking in guns.

The Maori, according to their own legend, had come to New Zealand in long canoes twenty generations before, from a place which might well have been Hawaii – the languages were similar. Kendall's Maori grammar had thrown light on these similarities, and interested Professor Samuel Lee at Cambridge. Off went Kendall and Hongi, at the professor's invitation, to visit England. There, Kendall was ordained, and Hongi, with his hugely tattooed visage and dignified manner, cut a figure in London society. King George IV enjoyed his company, and loaded him with presents. The government in New South Wales had already sent dress swords to all the Maori chiefs, and a set of English regimentals. But George IV went one better, and presented Hongi with a helmet and coat of mail.

Hongi, though submitting to be pampered, was not the smiling pagan child that in London they all supposed. With the connivance of Thomas Kendall, he was buying up cases of English muskets and barrels of gunpowder, and loading them on board ship. In Sydney he gave the game away, by selling off some of the royal presents to buy more gunpowder. He got back to the Bay of Islands on 11 July 1821. Half the two thousand warriors who answered his call he could now arm with muskets, and nothing thereafter withstood them for long.

Before that year was out, Hongi was back in the Bay of Islands with 2000 prisoners, whom he put to work as slaves. On 22 February 1822 he beat the tribes at Waikato, going into battle in his suit of armour at the head of 3000 men. Two thousand of his enemy were killed and their corpses feasted upon; the prisoners were set to work. With his foreign weapons and his foreign wealth and his access to foreign knowledge, Hongi was invincible.

Until his death in 1828 he dominated the coast, and the missionaries worked busily in his shadow.

Samuel Marsden when his chance came was hard on Kendall, not the least of whose offences had been the taking of a Maori wife. Marsden compelled Kendall to go back to his lawful spouse, reporting to London that 'his mind had been greatly polluted, by studying the abominations of the heathen, and his ideas are very heathenish'. Thomas Kendall stayed with Hongi until 1825. He worked on a second edition of his Maori grammar, and at last went into the timber trade in New South Wales, and took to the bottle. Henry Clarence Kendall, the Australian poet, was his grandson.

Life was changing. During the thirteen years of Hongi's rule not a single missionary had come to harm, and drunkenness as a mode of debauch, so people said, was taking the place of cannibalism. Under the Reverend Henry Williams, a former naval officer, the mission station at Paihai became a refuge for girls who were sick of hiring out as prostitutes to whaler crews. One Sunday, the girls at the Bay of Islands who were still on the game went across to taunt these redeemed magdalens. While the good girls stood in rows singing a hymn, their fallen sisters did what they could to provoke their baser impulses with a lewd dance called ruru-ruru.

At last Williams took up his umbrella, and drove the bad girls away with hearty slaps on the rump. In a contemporary drawing, Henry Williams's mission looks comfortably shipshape: little bungalows with smoking chimneys inside neatly fenced gardens. Victoria would soon be queen.

In the eight years from 1823 to 1831 there were thirty baptisms at Paihai. Pagan Maori themselves had employed a rite similar to baptism, as well as revering an all-powerful spirit called Maui-pu, who sacrificed his son, as Abraham volunteered to sacrifice Isaac, though Maui-pu went further, not only sacrificing his son but eating him, thus providing Maori theology with a justification for cannibalism. There were just enough such resemblances, however, between Maori belief and the Christian sacraments, to ease the shift of allegiance from one religion to the other. At Paihai, seventy boys attended school in the mornings, forty girls in the afternoon. There was progress; the tide was turning.

In 1827 the Reverend William Yate arrived – a clever, cultivated Anglican parson, with a taste for science. He had previously served in Tonga, where the language was similar, so he picked up Maori quickly. Yate went to work at Waimate, in the interior. To reach the mission station there, a road had to be cut through virgin forest and the river Waitingi bridged. The Maori nearby lived in mud huts wattled with bulrushes. Though such work in common was new to them, Yate's Maori neighbours came in to help him. They sawed seven hundred thousand feet of timber and burned fifty thousand bricks. School and clinics were built, and chapels went up in nearby villages.

At the mission there were no locks on the doors; there was no theft, either. Girls as well as boys went to school, and twenty-five toddlers went to infant school. Yate broke the hard ground with a six-horse team, and put forty-eight acres under wheat and oats. He planted an orchard, and in the midst of all this work found time to begin translating extracts from the gospels into Maori.

In his own account of the new civilization that missionaries were fostering at Waimate, William Yate is perhaps too self-consciously the benign philosopher-king. He attends fifty patients daily, teaches school, preaches his sermons in Maori, redeems from bondage youths enslaved in the tribal wars. The Maori, so he discovers, can give names to over six hundred different insects, fishes and plants. Yate finds time to make an important collection of shells. Ten were new to science, of which one, *shell ovate, rather truncated behind, solid, brown with rather distant thin concentric laminae, which are higher behind and before, and waved*, bears his name, *Venus Yatei*. As he worked, pen in hand, Yate relished the subtleties of Maori, and its power of expressing fine shades of meaning. ('Translated, our Liturgy is most strikingly beautiful.')

In 1830 Yate brought a small press back from Sydney, and a fifteen-year-old boy, James Smith, from the *Sydney Gazette*, to help him print his work. In 1832 he went for eight months to Sydney, taking with him a young Maori, 'a native youth of

pleasing manners, whose conduct was such as to gain the esteem
and love of all who knew him'. There he printed his translations
from Bible, Prayerbook and Hymnal in an edition of 3300
copies. Publication had cost £500, but to buy a single copy of a
book, a Maori would gladly work for a month.

In 1834, having as a glorious gesture of farewell baptized
thirty-eight adults and sixteen children, William Yate left for
England. At a large meeting at Exeter Hall on 5 May 1835, his
account of the good work in New Zealand raised an evangelical
audience to a pitch of high enthusiasm. Yate brought out his
An Account of New Zealand (1835) just as politicians and businessmen alike were beginning to take an interest in that faraway
country. The book was a success. The British Museum gratefully
accepted Yate's collection of shells. He had an audience of the
King. William Yate was standing tiptoe on a pinnacle, and the
wobble hardly showed.

While being fêted in London, Yate, like Oscar Wilde sixty
years later, appears to have revelled in the giddy irony of his
imposture. Though in England the punishment for sodomy had
not long since been death by hanging, he dropped wilful and
risky hints. Some of the letters from Maori boys reprinted in his
book skate on thin ice. Others, devoid of innuendo, show poig-
nantly the conflict of every young Maori's mind between the
money ethos and the Christian faith.

'Sometimes I say within myself,' one boy writes, 'my thoughts
shall be fixed on God; then I think about sawing, and the payment
I am to have for sawing when I have finished my tree. This is the
way I am, this day and this day and this day. Mr Yate, what are
your thoughts?' This from a boy who, in another letter, signs
himself affectionately, 'Paru, whom you sometimes call Poke.'

Yate travelled back to the antipodes with his sister aboard
Prince Regent, and in Sydney on 12 June 1836 found himself cited
for 'gross immorality', with the *Prince Regent*'s third mate, one
John Morris. Old Samuel Marsden of course was his sworn enemy
from that day on. 'Trustworthy baptized natives', in Marsden's
own words, had been 'drawn in by the wretched man's persua-
sions and rewards without being conscious of the detestable
nature of the crime into which he was leading them'.

F

But Samuel Marsden, after laying down the law in Sydney for so long, had been thrown in the shade by the recent arrival there of his ecclesiastical superior, Bishop Broughton. To save Yate's neck, the Bishop at once indicted him in his own consistorial court for 'prevarication and falsehood', a breach of the seventy-fifth canon, implying that Yate's confession had not been explicit, but keeping him for the time being out of a civil court. Yate when aboard *Prince Regent* may even have been trapped, for John Morris spoke later of being bribed with 'a bucketful of ale' to sign a false accusation.

Early missionaries in the Pacific had often spoken in horror-struck tones of 'practices hinted at in *Romans I*'. The prevalence of sodomy in the islands had no doubt the same rationale as the prevalence of infanticide. The population on a small island, once Christian marriage had been instituted there, could very soon multiply (if epidemic diseases permitted) to the point of hunger. Less than fifty years after the *Bounty* mutineers landed on uninhabited Pitcairn Island, their overcrowded descendants were in such desperate straits that they asked the British authorities to move them to Norfolk Island.

The homosexual underground in Sydney was influential then as now, and with other men taking his part, Yate grew bolder. Declining a prudent offer by the Church Missionary Society to pay his fare back home, he put a brave face on it, and began threatening suits for libel.

Yate might even have got away with it but for Samuel Marsden, who was out for an exemplary punishment. Yate all the while he stayed in Sydney was in jeopardy – though he had been safe enough in New Zealand, since the islands were not yet annexed. The tough old clerical magistrate at once took ship in *Pyramus* for Waimate, so as to collect incriminating evidence on the spot. When the Crown Solicitor declared himself not satisfied by the first six affidavits from Yate's 'deluded victims', Marsden retorted that he could produce a hundred witnesses more.

Under Marsden's baleful and insistent eye, Yate's missionary colleagues proceeded to 'avert the wrath of an offended God' by keeping a 'day of fast and solemn humiliation'. They burnt every scrap of Yate's personal property, shot his horse, and abandoned the place where he had lived, naming it 'the Vale of Achan'. Shooting the horse gives their game away. They needed a scapegoat; they were out for blood.

'Tell the natives I mourn much for Mr Yate's conduct towards them,' was Samuel Marsden's parting message to the Maori converts. 'God will punish him in this life, and unless he repents and leads a new life, God will punish him in hell.' The Crown Solicitor had decided the charge could not be proven, so Marsden showered him with fifty more affidavits. On Saturday, 19 December 1836, Reverend William Yate and his sister got away in the brig *Ulysses* just in time.

'The new life' he had been told to lead was not made easy for William Yate. Six years later he was voted into a chaplaincy in a workhouse, but someone tipped off the Bishop of London, and he vetoed the appointment. At long last, in 1848, Yate found a billet in the seaman's church at Dover, where he was long remembered as having been 'very active in looking after ship-wrecked mariners'.

Is there any point in disinterring this old scandal? What with the loose women and the strong drink for which the Bay of Islands was notorious, there were plenty of others to choose from: missionaries in New Zealand were under stress. Yate did not introduce the vice he practised – it was flourishing there already. By any reckoning he did more good in New Zealand than harm, and the specific way he was hounded shows the moral relativism of those who had come out to instruct the Maori in Christian belief – in a faith, that is, based not on cruelty and taboo, the shooting of a horse to punish its master, but on for-giveness and loving-kindness. Samuel Marsden was obliged to be unforgiving because, though as a priest he served his God, as a magistrate he served the British Empire. And however good their private intentions, all the missionaries in New Zealand – as the Maori were beginning to suspect – had been placed in a similar false position.

As a Maori chief later put it to an Anglican bishop, when land-grabbing had brought their two peoples to the brink of war: 'We believe that there is a deep-laid conspiracy to destroy us. The English people first sent clergy here, to make us believe you were all a pious, God-fearing people – then by degrees the settlers follow – and now that they equal us in number, they instantly make a quarrel.' Or, as another Maori chief remarked sarcastically after much of his tribal land had been bartered away on terms that later he saw were derisory, 'Englishmen give us blankets, powder and iron pots. But we soon blow away the powder, the iron pot gets broken and the blanket wears out, but the land never blows away or wears out.'

Two words were enough to make any convict at the Bay of Islands feel an invisible noose constrict around his throat: *British annexation*. Across the Pacific Ocean there were fewer islands every year where convicts who fled their forced labour might be safe from the lash and the gibbet, and perhaps earn some kind of living in the service of a native chief, as trader, pimp or mercenary. As the threat of annexation loomed up in New Zealand, and talk began of sending a warship to round up the runaways, they made plans to seize some trading ship as she lay at anchor, and sail her east, perhaps to California.

When they had managed to make their way to more distant archipelagos, the scallywags would sometimes come ashore and claim to be missionaries. In the early 1820s, 'Old Tom Franklin' and 'Big-Legged Jimmy' launched a make-believe religion on Samoa – an impudent and fanciful religion of pleasure which did no great harm, and may even have helped emancipate a few Samoans from the obsessive burden of taboo.

Tom and Jimmy began their mission by abolishing all food prohibitions. All things that the Samoans found good to eat, so they preached, had been provided for them by the Great Spirit, and might be eaten freely. Food was a divine incarnation, and God could best be worshipped either by throwing a feast, or by giving plenty of food to his missionaries.

A man ashore from a passing whaler sold them a flute so they began their religious ceremony with *Old Tom Bowling* and ended it with *Black-Eyed Susan*. Samoan chiefs were so sacred that whatever their feet touched became at once their own property; therefore they had to be carried round pick-a-back. On the same principle, Old Tom Franklin and Big-Legged Jimmy had themselves carried round pick-a-back too.

Their Rabelaisian creed turned upside down the sexual attitudes the missionaries tried to implant. Polygamy was good, said Tom and Jimmy, so long as the missionary himself could have first go at any woman who took his fancy. Dancing and nakedness were good things, too.

Runaway convicts gave the Maori a picture of the outside world which contradicted all that the missionaries for their part would have them believe. Some of the beachcombers at the Bay of Islands had seen aborigines in New South Wales shot down as casually as kangaroos. Some may even have been ordered by their taskmasters to serve as beaters when the Tasmans were blotted out. Annexation – so all the convicts warned the Maori – would mean losing their land and being hunted to death.

Soon yet another contradictory picture of the world the Maori lived in came their way. The French were closely engaged in Tahiti; they also coveted New Zealand. A thirty-seven-year-old Marist priest, Jean Pompallier, had been appointed the Pope's Vicar-Apostolic in Western Oceania. In Tahiti he chartered a sixty-ton schooner, *Raiatea*, and set course for Australia; thence he sailed to Hokianga. Mass in New Zealand was first celebrated at Hokianga on Saturday, 13 January 1838.

Pompallier was an able, fearless and determined priest, though perhaps a little too apt, by modern standards, to identify the well-being of the church he served with the colonizing mission of France. This was a confusion of mind into which nearly all missionaries in those days fell, Catholic and Protestant alike.

Roman Catholic missions were quicker off the mark, as a rule, than Protestant, and cheaper to run, because their celibate priests were unencumbered with a family. No Catholic priest, therefore, was under invisible pressure to dabble in trade or buy land so as to provide for his children – and precisely for this reason of course, had Pope Gregory VII eight centuries before insisted upon clerical celibacy, at a time when church endowments had become a temptation to prince and priest alike.

The Roman Catholic missions launched in New Zealand by Pompallier appealed to many of the Maori because they were less forbidding; the Roman Catholic system too, here as else-where, accorded better with native customs. Some of the more sabbatarian among the Protestants had invented a taboo of their very own about Sunday work: you dare not even peel potatoes.

Religious medals became much sought-after, often being worn in the ear-lobe, and the Protestant missionaries, anxious to compete, found themselves being obliged to provide, at their own expense, real gold rings for wedding ceremonies. This ever-present competition between rival missionaries also helped to break the spell over the Maori mind. Catholic priests, for instance, were already warning their flock against inaccuracies in Yate's version of Holy Writ. Pompallier also made sure that the Maori got to hear about the nightmarishly puritanical kingdom which the British evangelicals had sponsored on Tahiti, as well as telling them that the French were the discoverers of New Zealand, and had as good a right to it as the British.

But the British were nearer and fiercer, and the guns in their ships of war, as the Maori knew, were terribly destructive. HMS *Alligator* had bombarded them at Taranaki as early as 1814, when rescuing Mrs Guard and her two children from the wreck of the whaler *Harriet*. Maori were also fearful of British soldiers, whom from their pipe-clayed equipment they called 'cross-belts'.

For the next fifty years, a Roman Catholic Maori was likely to be anti-British – though not necessarily pro-French. Even more intensely than other Maori, he distrusted land-grabbers, and if they happened to be Protestant clergymen, as they sometimes were, he despised them.

Maori land ownership was intricate. Tribal land was owned in common, so that conveyancing could take a long time, but once a proper bargain had been struck in accordance with traditional procedures, the buyer's title to his land was good. The Maori had been blarneyed – often by missionaries – into some very bad bargains. As late as 1848, a great tract of land, then unoccupied, on South Island – where few Maori chose to live, admirable though it was for sheep-farming – went for the equivalent of £2000, which to the Maori sounded like a fair price for waste land, though it works out at under a farthing an acre. Other land grabs were no less spectacular. Lieutenant Thomas McDonell, a vagabond son of the Earl of Antrim, who in 1835 managed to get himself appointed Additional British Resident, laid claim to the possession of twenty square miles, most of it valuable kauri forest. A man calling himself Baron de Thierry, who got his start selling grog on the beach at Hokianga, boasted of having acquired 40,000 acres on the Hokianga river for two dozen axe-heads. In fact, the axe-heads were only the earnest of the sale, the traditional deposit, and when this was at last brought home to him the Baron had to abandon the romantic plans he had made for re-establishing the feudal system on his estate in New Zealand.

Missionaries elsewhere in the Pacific had been deliberately encouraged to make money by trade. The large mission schooner *John Wesley*, for example, was sent back to England in 1851 'to be furnished with tanks to receive the coconut oil which the natives are beginning to contribute in considerable quantity'. The men themselves can hardly be blamed. They came out to spread the values of commercial, evangelical England. Unlike their rivals, they had never been required to take vows of poverty. For that matter, they had been bred up in a society where material prosperity was often considered a proof of God's favour, and poverty looked down on, as cousin to a crime.

At one time the largest single landowner on North Island was a Wesleyan missionary who came to Whangaroa in 1823. Reverend William White was an intensely emotional preacher, able to burst into tears at will. He very soon became a caricature of the missionary-trader. The beach opposite his chapel was 'covered with trade and barter of every description'. He shipped out cargoes of kauri pine, using converts as labourers. Victualling whalers was a paying game: White's going rate was one copy of the gospels (accurate translation or not) for fifteen baskets of potatoes or one live hog. White claimed to have bought the whole coastline from Mokau to Whanganui, including Crabhole Island, for one axe. For thirteen years, his acquisitiveness burned fiercer than any carnal lust.

William White of course overdid it. He had carefully not broken the Wesleyans' rule that missionaries must never buy land for themselves, only for their families. But he slipped from grace with a girl – 'attempted to commit a rape on the wife of a Christian native teacher' – and was dismissed, to become soon after 'a prey to intemperate and licentious habits'. For Maori and beachcomber alike, life was hard, but the strain of setting an example in a disintegrating society bore heaviest on the missionaries.

A woman's property in those days, unless cleverly secured, became her husband's on marriage, so one way for a poor but personable young man to launch himself in life was by running off with an heiress. The first time he tried it, when he was twenty, this scheme worked astonishingly well for Edward Gibbon Wakefield – his wife's family relented, and even found him a berth in the diplomatic corps. But when, as a widower of thirty, he tried to run away to Gretna Green with a schoolgirl, he found himself serving three years in Newgate.

To keep in good heart as he spooned up his skilly, Wakefield played at makebelieve imperial politics. In his *Letter from Sydney* – which readers were led to believe had been written, not in a London gaol, but from first-hand experience in Australia – Wakefield sternly criticized the lavish way that land grants were being doled out down-under. He had a more democratic and advantageous plan: to sell people in Britain small farms, sight unseen, and ship the purchasers out to the new colony with their own money.

Wakefield knew how to make a favourable impression on schoolgirls, and his persuasive manner worked with statesmen, too. He won over that fine piece of radical integrity, John Stuart Mill. He became Lord Durham's secretary – and the hand which wrote the famous Durham Report and determined the future of Canada was in all likelihood the ex-convict's. But the most promising place to apply Wakefield's land-settlement theories was obviously New Zealand, and quickly too, for the French king, Louis Philippe, was already deep in plans to launch *la Compagnie Nanto-Bordelaise* and establish French settlers there. So a charter was sought for a New Zealand Association to sell farms, ship in British settlers, and force the government into annexing.

At the time there were about 2000 British subjects in New

Zealand – most of them, said an official report, 'of bad or doubtful character'. Though phthisis and syphilis were killing the Maori off, there were still at least 100,000 of them, among whom Anglican and Wesleyan converts numbered about 5000; Roman Catholics were fewer. Many Maori by now had guns. They had so far sold off about 185 square miles of their best land to speculators, and land sales were making them uneasy.

The missionaries and their converts might be few, but they weighed in the balance, because the Colonial Secretary just then was a Clapham Sect son, Lord Glenelg: the New Zealand Association was dissolved. But alarming news soon arrived that the French had already put a settlement ashore at Akaroa on South Island, so yet another enterprise, the New Zealand Company, was launched with the intention of flooding the country with English settlers. Land was bought in New Zealand – or so the Company supposed – to the tune of £100,000. Out came the settlers, though with no official sanction, in a ship called *Tory*, most of them having sold all they possessed in Britain and paid over their money for farms in New Zealand on tracts of land the Company could not actually be sure it had bought. Angry Maori and angry Englishman, both with guns, would soon be facing each other down. If the object of *Tory*'s voyage were to force the British government's hand, it had succeeded.

London sent out an honest and level-headed naval officer, Captain Hobson, RN, who had spent much of his career fighting pirates and slavers in the West Indies. Marryat was once his shipmate, and he is reputedly the hero of Michael Scott's *Tom Cringle's Log*. Hobson had a dormant commission as Lieutenant-Governor in his pocket, and orders 'to establish a settled form of civil government'. Terms were offered in 1840 in the Treaty of Waitingi, which those Protestant missionaries and their friends who had been fighting so resolutely for the Maori interest in London considered to be as good as they could reasonably hope for. There were a few concealed trapdoors in the document they were asked to sign, but by and large the chiefs, though yielding up their sovereignty to Queen Victoria, were by treaty to keep their tribal lands intact and have all the rights of British subjects. Slowly all 400 chiefs came in and signed, since the real choice, as the Maori had the wit to discern, was between either British or French annexation – and the 'cross-belts' were nearer and more numerous.

Years of tribal warfare had disunited the Maori. They lacked, as yet, their own political spokesmen, and were therefore, more dependent than they might have wished on missionaries who spoke their language. And the missionaries, though they took risks and made great efforts for their Maori friends, were all linked to the British or French establishment by invisible strings.

Constitutionally, Queen Victoria was head of the Church of England, appointing its bishops on the advice of her government. Out to New Zealand, where Anglicanism was preponderant and the political situation tricky, the British government prevailed upon the Queen to send a hand-picked man.

George Augustus Selwyn was born at Hampstead in 1809, the great-grandson of Major-General Selwyn, a former governor of Jamaica, and the son and grandson of eminent barristers with court connections. George Augustus was a self-willed little boy, and his mother in her fits of depression would sometimes thrash him so excessively as to make the nursemaid fly to his defence. His father, an intelligent and good man, was fonder of him.

The boy grew up generous by nature, immensely intelligent, but ill at ease all his life at the thought of cruelty. He always drove himself hard. In his prep school at Ealing, Selwyn's chum was John Henry Newman, a religious genius who eventually became a Roman cardinal. At Eton, Selwyn was on intimate terms with William Ewart Gladstone, another brilliant son of a prosperous father – Newman's father was a banker, Gladstone's an opulent merchant. But Selwyn was also remembered as a boy who knew his Racing Calendar, and could dance the mazurka.

Selwyn, in the very first Boat Race, rowed for Cambridge. He swam every day, winter or summer, and once walked from Cambridge to London without stopping, in thirteen hours. But underneath all this highstrung muscular extroversion there was moral earnestness: the times were serious. Selwyn was one of a new generation of Anglicans who had begun to look upon the

Church of England as a legitimate heir to the values of Catholic Christendom. By Christian action these young men hoped, somehow, to cleanse England from the horrors into which uncurbed industrialism had plunged her.

George Selwyn took orders. Though a curate at Windsor and a private tutor at Eton, he was strongly against keeping the church as an upper-class reserve. 'Let the Church take root downwards,' he urged in 1836. 'Let every peasant have an interest in the Establishment, in the person of a son or brother or cousin. We have the best materials for the formation of a plebeian ministry that were ever possessed by any nation.'

At the age of thirty-four he married a splendid wife, who promised from the very start never to stand in the way of his duty, wherever it might lead her, and in 1841 their chance came. George Selwyn, not forgotten by his old friends now rising in politics, was consecrated Bishop of New Zealand.

Since faraway New Zealand was identified in the public mind with the blackest savagery, the news at first was treated as a joke. Only two years before, on 30 November 1839, John Williams, the most energetic missionary in Melanesia, which now was a part of Selwyn's enormous diocese, had been clubbed to death and eaten at a cannibal feast at Erromanga in the New Hebrides. 'It will make quite a revolution in the dinners of New Zealand,' urbanely observed Sydney Smith. '*Tête d'évèque* will be the most *récherché* dish, and your man will add, "And there is cold clergyman on the side table".'

During the long voyage out, George Selwyn not only learned Maori but mastered navigation. 'It's enough,' a seaman remarked later, as he watched Selwyn bring a ship through shoal water into harbour, 'to make a man a Christian, to see the bishop handle a vessel.'

Captain Hobson's reaction to the news had been sarcastic. 'What can a bishop do in New Zealand, where there are no roads for his coach?' Then on 29 May 1842 George Selwyn rowed himself ashore, and went on foot to pay his compliments to the lieutenant-governor. On his first Sunday he said prayers and preached in Maori. Six months later, George Selwyn was back in Auckland, having tramped 762 miles of a 2300 mile tour of inspection round his diocese; the rest was done on horseback or by boat; he had swum all the rivers.

Between land-hungry immigrants and suspicious Maori there had already been armed clashes, the Maori having done well enough in the fighting to lose much of their awe of British prowess. But for seven years after Selwyn's arrival the terms of the Treaty of Waitingi were pretty much respected. Henry Williams, the ex-sailor who ran the mission at Paihai, reported of Maori life after Waitingi, 'The whole fabric of native superstition is gone – their weapons laid by – their petty quarrels are settled by arbitration.' Slavery and cannibalism were things of the past. By 1853, thanks to the work of the three missionary churches, Wesleyan, Roman Catholic and Anglican, half the Maori were nominal Christians, and three-quarters of all adult Maori could read and write their own language, though the young men, so people said, were turning away from religion.

The New Zealand legislature in 1844 had decided to treat all religious denominations on equal terms, so the Anglican church there was no longer a state church. Selwyn did what he could to form an ecclesiastical endowment, by shrewdly buying land near growing towns, but his church was relatively poor, and this independence suited his plans.

The Treaty had given Maori the rights of British subjects; Selwyn behaved towards them accordingly. He would ordain no candidate for the priesthood not fluent in Maori, and told his English clergy bluntly that they were to 'go among the heathen as an equal and a brother'. St John's College, where Selwyn was training his men for the church, became under his influence an experiment in social living which in the Britain of those days was hardly possible. Settlers and Maori alike sent their sons there, and there was provision for the sick. The college income was derisory – £300 a year. But as Selwyn pointed out, St Paul had financed his own missionary journeys by working at his trade as a tent-maker.

Among educated men in Britain, work had long been derogatory – something they paid for – an inconvenient chore, which all those with no property were compelled to perform for others in return for wages, if they did not want to starve. 'The motive sanctifies the work,' Selwyn told his young men, as he set them to maintaining themselves and others by the labour of their hands.

Each student at St John's had one active job – on the college land, as farmer or forester – and one sedentary job, as weaver or carpenter or printer. Two hours a day on four days a week he was put to his studies. 'A boy of eighteen', Selwyn estimated, 'can maintain himself at college as a printer by working five hours a day.' From their work the students made a profit, which they applied – as in a mediaeval monastery – to supporting native schools and financing a hospital, where the bishop's wife worked as a nurse. Maori kept sheep, but did not know how to spin or weave; Selwyn shipped out disused spinning-wheels from Wales and his Maori students taught their kinsmen.

But there were snags. New Zealand, though very far away and still primitive, was in legal fact an outpost of that very capitalist Britain which had begun its modern existence by abhorring and destroying monasticism, and replacing it by individualistic free enterprise. In New Zealand, even a milder version of a monastery was an anomaly. The minds of the boys, Selwyn admitted, were much less lively after so much physical work than they had been in his day at Eton. The settlers were gravely disappointed in the bishop, for they had wanted their sons to receive a more genteel education. And though the principle upon which St John's had been founded was 'an equality of privileges and position', yet 'the disposition of the one to domineer over the other', as Selwyn put it, never quite faded: 'It seemed natural to every English man and boy to have a Maori for his fag.'

In 1849, Selwyn did a tour of the New Hebrides – a 400-mile chain of tropical islands north of New Zealand and east of Australia, where John Williams had so recently been killed and eaten. He threaded his way through the islands in a twenty-one-ton schooner, *Undine*, with the help of old Spanish charts, meanwhile drawing new ones of his own which were so excellent that they were taken by the Admiralty. 'Where a trader will go for gain,' said Selwyn, 'there the missionary ought to go for the merchandise of souls.'

Captain Cook in 1774 had found the islanders 'to excel in

honesty and friendliness of disposition', but as George Selwyn observed, 'three-quarters of a century, during which they have been left to receive and inflict every kind of outrage, have so entirely altered their original character for the worse that there are many places I should not think of risking the schooner or myself.'

The New Hebrides provided daring traders with sandalwood – sought after as incense for Chinese temples – and *bêche-de-mer*, the huge black sea-slug regarded by Chinese epicures as a delicacy. The trade was profitable. In a few years, sandalwood worth £70,000 – say a million dollars, at current values – had been shipped out of the small island of Erromanga alone. But as the islands were stripped of their sandalwood, another trade began: blackbirding.

When the supply of English convicts who might be set to work under duress as shepherds and herdsmen began to diminish in Australia, ships began visiting the New Hebrides to kidnap black men and put them, too, on the market, as forced labour, under the thin legal cover of indentures. The brig *Portaina* and the schooner *Velocity*, owned by Messrs Boyd of Sydney, were in the trade as early as 1848. Blackbirders as they sailed in would often take potshots with their swivel-guns at native huts, to frighten those they meant to kidnap.

Now it was the view of the natives of the New Hebrides that every man's death came by *nahak* – by sorcery. Therefore some other living person somewhere was accountable for every single human death. The men in ships were killers – and though they might have fascinating trade goods to offer, they were blatantly the guilty enemy, justly to be killed in their turn.

Selwyn's *Undine* – so low in the water it would be impossible to keep out boarders – would approach a New Hebridean island with no arms aboard, and no tobacco, either: the natives had learned about tobacco, craved for it, and used it as currency. Selwyn certainly took risks – but since the British government were concerned lest the French get a foothold in the New Hebrides, he was carefully looked after; his mission was also a show of force. In 1849, *Undine* was escorted round the New Hebrides by HMS *Havannah*, in 1850 by HMS *Fly*.

Not only did blackbirders sometimes fire their guns at random at the huts along the shore, from time to time so did warships. Even the little, naked, stone-age men of the New Hebrides had learned by experience how destructive naval gunnery could be. Some of the naval officers – Wilkes, commanding HMS *Vincennes* was one – thought the bishop was wasting his time and their own, and that the best way to civilize the islanders would be to blaze away at them with broadsides. Selwyn would have none of it.

Many dialects were spoken in the New Hebrides. On one island the size of the Isle of Wight there might well be three languages, all mutually incomprehensible. George Selwyn with his Etonian facility managed on each voyage to 'master the elements of a new language sufficiently to enter at once into communication more or less with the native people'.

While the intimidating warship kept off, in deep water, the little schooner would edge in close, and observe the crowd of almost naked islanders as they gathered on the shore, their bodies gaudily painted, their hair in a myriad of tiny plaits. Until traders began selling them muskets, their chief weapon had been the 'throwing-stone' – about the size of a whetstone. If women were to be seen among the men of the beach, they were possibly friendly.

The bishop would then row or swim ashore, often alone, and go towards the crowd of them, speaking aloud such words of their language as he might know or guess at, offering them gifts. Fish-hooks were very much sought after, but the islanders also had a particular liking for government red tape. Selwyn's intention was to persuade one of the chiefs to let him take away a son – not to forced labour, but as a pupil at St John's. The boy from the primitive New Hebrides would there learn his letters, and master a useful trade. He would learn a smattering of Christian notions, and bring what he had learned back home.

Although the presence of black-skinned boys in the school prompted some of the European settlers to withdraw their own sons, as from contamination, by 1850 Selwyn had thirteen lads from six islands at St John's. In five years he made seven voyages to Melanesia, and on his last voyage visited fifty islands. How very fond, people in Auckland would remark when they saw *Undine* put to sea, the bishop must be of yachting!

In 1851, gold was found at Bendigo and Ballarat. In three years, the population of Victoria trebled: the export of food from New Zealand to Australia suddenly became profitable. In 1853, New Zealand was granted a measure of self-government, including its own legislature. The Maori, though competent farmers by now, still owned land they did not cultivate. They had been told at Waitingi that 'no land would be taken from them which they were not willing to sell'. But they were well aware that the settlers and their political friends had begun to discuss ways and means of getting this land away from them. Many settlers were in favour of war.

The new legislature soon became the focus of settler resentment, one New Zealand legislator, a lawyer, going so far as to propose that Maori males should be sent over to Australia 'to serve as slaves for seven years', with Maori females meanwhile being 'carried away and dispersed as wives for the Chinese, and for well-conducted white convicts'. Such men as these had no use whatever for Bishop Selwyn, and soon they got a governor after their own heart, Colonel Gore-Browne, heavy-handed, unimaginative, a man ready to push things to the limit.

About 7000 Maori were armed – many with flintlock trade muskets, some with double-barrelled sporting-guns which agents of the New Zealand Company had given out in barter when buying up land. Since the settlers themselves could put only two or three thousand men into the field, they were outnumbered, but this did not quench their bravado. Over the horizon were British warships which, if only the right provocation could be given, would land 'cross-belts' anywhere along the coast. Once the fighting was over, land confiscations could begin. As the governor of Australia, Sir William Denison, pointed out to Gore-Browne, the governor of New Zealand, 'if backed up by England' he would 'in a short time annihilate the Maori race, and permit the occupation by the white man of the rich land yet in native hands.'

In years gone by, the prosperity of hundreds of native chiefs had been based on the slaves they captured in tribal war. But peace, Christianity and the legal abolition of slavery had under-

mined the chiefs' power and muted their rivalry. Traditional
local loyalties were losing ground. Out of yesterday's congeries
of warring cannibal tribes, an incipient Maori nation was emerging, literate and aware. The Maori mood of independence was
fomented by French Catholic priests, who used the image of an
egg to prove that the *pakeha* – the white interloper – held only
the coast of New Zealand: the shell. Why should not the living
chicken peck its way out?

In 1857, a Christian chief at Waikato, called Te Wherohero,
was elected King of New Zealand, as Potatau I. He chose for his
motto Faith: Love: Law. Next to the Union Jack he hoisted his
own flag: three stars and a cross. The British chose to regard this
as a deliberate challenge to their sovereignty, but in casting around
for a pretext to go to war, they at first chose badly.

In 1859, settlers tried to buy up land at the mouth of the
Waitara river, from a seller whose title to the land was defective,
and his tribe knew it. And so, as it turned out, did the government
commissioner, Parris, who was aware of the true facts but suppressed them. As the surveyors knocked in their pegs, old women
followed them around, pulling them out. One hard look at the
facts would have settled the matter, and undoubtedly in favour of
the Maori. But in February 1860 Governor Gore-Browne was
nudged into declaring martial law. Troops were shipped over
from Australia, to occupy by force the land of the Waikato tribe,
a predominantly Christian people and the most civilized of the
Maori, with their own churches and schools.

Bishop Selwyn still had the ear of his Etonian contemporaries
prominent in the House of Commons. 'The Governor is wrong
in making war upon a land question,' he wrote. Eventually the
more subtle George Grey was appointed governor, though the
main objective of British policy – to procure more land – remained
unchanged. Grey was an imaginative man – he had hopefully
introduced zebras to New Zealand, though no one could ride
them – and he bided his time, using the troops now stationed in
New Zealand to build a road to Waikato. To overawe the
'King movement', Waikato was garrisoned by a thousand soldiers, and dominated by forts. By 1863, when the *pakeha* were
ready for the war they had long had in mind, a force of 10,000

regular troops moved off against the brave but ill-armed Maori.
Only one in thirty Maori, according to Selwyn, went out to
meet them gun in hand, but they were supported according to
another good witness, by two-thirds of the entire Maori people.

In the long wait before the first shot was fired, George Selwyn
had argued the Maori case to the settlers until he became the
least popular man in New Zealand, a man to mob in the streets.
The motive of the war was greed for land, and the moral stance
of churchmen was not easy. The Anglican church in New Zealand
had managed by 1854 to acquire a landed estate of 14,000 acres.
Selwyn felt obliged, therefore, to take the line that he was
opposed only to illegal land sales – a purchase at a farthing an
acre not being reprehensible if the Maori, in their ignorance,
were willing sellers. But this was not what they wanted to hear;
he soon lost his authority over the Maori, too.

'Our influence as clergymen has waned', he wrote, 'ever since
the Maori king was set up.' Though no longer a state establishment,
the Anglicans had refused to add to their liturgy a prayer for
King Potatua I, while insisting that the Maori continue to pray
for Queen Victoria. The line of distinction between conciliation
and betrayal was becoming every day harder to trace.

Maori who once had welcomed Selwyn with delight would
not now permit him to cross their land; they treated him as a
spy. In one village they gave him a pigsty to sleep in. Nothing
daunted, the bishop rolled up his sleeves, mucked out the sty,
spread fresh litter, and had a good night's sleep. 'You can never
make this man less than a gentleman,' was the admiring Maori
comment.

Only one chaplain, a Roman Catholic, had arrived with the
ten thousand British troops, so Selwyn went into action with
them as their Anglican chaplain, and after the campaign accepted
a medal. Other clergymen were available, and would have done
as well as the bishop, but Selwyn had come to a dead stop.
Rejected by Maori and colonist alike, he sought the company
of his own kind. The young officers all admired him, and he went
out of his way to exhibit feats of cold courage, risking his life
to bring in Maori wounded as well as British. ('I ministered to
the fallen Maori *first*,' he explained, 'to give a practical answer

AMONG THE HEATHEN AS AN EQUAL 179

to their charge against me of forsaking and betraying them.')

The hardest fighting took place around a loopholed earthwork – or *pa* – which the Maori had built at Rangiriri. The 180 Maori inside the stockade beat off four successive assaults by regular troops with fixed bayonets: forty British soldiers were killed, eighty wounded. A hot fire was kept up all night, but at dawn the Maori, with all their powder gone, ran up a white flag.

'The soldiers instantly ran up and fraternized with the Maori, giving them biscuit,' noted Selwyn with satisfaction. 'If there must be war,' he wrote, 'our great effort ought to be at least to debrutalize it.' But at the same time, in a letter to his friend the Bishop of Auckland, he confessed, 'Our native work is a remnant in two senses: the remnant of a decaying people, and the remnant of a decaying faith.'

Soon began the confiscation of Maori lands. All the Maori king's land was seized, as a matter of course, but even chiefs who had stayed loyal to the British lost land. The more resolute Maori withdrew to 'King's Country' in the mountains, where the fighting dragged on in a desultory fashion until as late as 1879. As they saw it, the religion which had for so long been used to endorse – to sanctify – their treaty rights to land and equal citizenship had failed them. 'The only wonder is', observed Selwyn, 'that the whole people did not become Romanists.' But the Roman Catholic hierarchy too, though well aware that their priests had been encouraging the mood of independence among the Maori, were unnerved when the fighting came. Father Garavel, who carried messages for the insurgent Maori, was promptly shipped out of New Zealand by his bishop.

The Maori soon invented a composite religion of their own, in which at least two-thirds of them came to believe. The new cult was called Pai Marire – which may mean All Right, Very Good, or All Holy, depending on how you look at it. But the movement soon got the nickname Hau-Hau, from its ritual warcry, like an enormous gasp of despair, made by filling the lungs with air to the limit, then ejaculating with full force.

Pai Marire mingled ancient Maori paganism with notions taken from every other religious belief available – Wesleyanism, Judaism, Anglicanism, Catholicism, Spiritualism, Mormonism.

Pai Marire had begun when Maori warriors, reverting to the style of war practised by their forbears, killed Captain Lloyd of the 57th Regiment. To those who then drank his blood in ritual fashion, from the penis, the Angel Gabriel appeared. The faithful were assured that Gabriel and his legion of angels would soon drive the English from the land. Gabriel ordered the warriors to cut off the unfortunate captain's head, pickle it in the traditional manner, and carry it about the country as an oracle for communicating, by ventriloquism, with Jehovah. (There had been a minor anti-Christian cult thirty years before, called Papahurihia – 'of Satanic ingenuity and malignity' – which made its impression thanks to the ventriloquism and simple conjuring tricks which a sceptical Jewish ship's captain with a sense of humour taught a Maori in his crew, who later went ashore and set up as a prophet.)

Some of the Pai Marire rites had a note of collective sexual hysteria – for instance, running round and round an upright pole until the worshipper fell, cataleptic. Believers were assured that other men, better than the English, would soon come down from heaven and teach the Maori all European arts and sciences. There was no need to be strict any more about monogamy, or keeping the Sabbath. Sexual restraint was a thing of the past, and whatever Protestants might pretend to the contrary, the Virgin Mary was on their side. Pai Marire and its highly improper pagan sacrifices gave to those who were busy confiscating Maori land exactly the kind of moral justification they had so far lacked, but George Selwyn understood the truth of this new cult. 'The Hau-Hau superstition is simply an expression of an utter loss of faith in everything that is English, clergy and all alike.' Of the leaders of Pai Marire, one of the bravest and most intelligent, who met his death fighting, was Chief Henare Taratoa, in his youth a candidate for the priesthood at Selwyn's college, though never ordained.

By 1871, when the fighting petered out, the Maori had been reduced, mainly by disease, from about 160,000 – Yate's estimate, in 1830 – to less than 40,000.

The island of Tanna in the tropical archipelago of the New Hebrides is a flaming volcano – a landmark visible fifty miles off. Coconut palms climb the mountain slopes and creep down to the shore. In Selwyn's day, fever prevailed and the people on Tanna spent most of their time fighting one another.

Having lost their best missionary, John Williams, to cannibals on Erromanga, the London Missionary Society decided to leave the work of converting the New Hebrides and New Caledonia to native teachers from Raratonga and Samoa; brave men who were less conspicuous and less resented. By 1850, though slowly they had gained a foothold, forty of these teachers were dead of violence and disease.

In 1848, the Reverend John Geddie and his wife, single-minded Presbyterians from Nova Scotia, went to live on Aneiteum; the population there was 3500. Geddie and his wife translated the Bible into the local dialect most in use, and paid the printing bill by selling arrowroot to the value of £1200, but in an archipelago which lacked a common language, such efforts as these, though heroic, were of small practical effect. In June 1857, two more Nova Scotians, Reverend G. N. Gordon and his wife, got a footing on Erromanga, the island where Williams had been done to death. But two other missionaries, Turner and Nesbit, who tried to live on Tanna with its warring tribes and flaming volcano, were forced out by the incessant violence.

In 1858, a Scottish Presbyterian called John G. Paton, tough in mind and body both, and not long since ordained as a minister, landed on Tanna with his newly-wed Scots wife. They picked the wrong place to live, a fever spot, and she was dead soon after in childbirth. Next year George Selwyn called in at Tanna and, seeing the kind of desperate place it was, offered to take John Paton away with him, in HMS *Pelorus*. Paton refused ('and I like him all the better,' said the bishop). Paton disapproved of bishops on principle, but he made an exception of Selwyn.

He was then thirty-four, the son of a God-fearing stocking-maker near Dumfries. At twelve, John left school – which he had disliked, because his master beat him – to work alongside his father at the knitting-frame in the cottage. Their working day was from six in the morning to ten at night. With all the self-denying zeal of an ambitious Scot, Paton kept at his studies, slowly clambering up the Presbyterian ladder, first as church visitor, then as teacher, at last as a missioner in Glasgow.

Paton idealized the life he had known as a boy, of cottage industry and small peasant farming, and abhorred the industrial city. Pious Scots from rural homes like his own were being driven in hordes into the city's slums. For the Presbyterian church in Glasgow to survive, these immigrants had to be hunted out and organized; for ten years, in the ugly, exorbitant, vicious city, this had been John Paton's pastorate.

He found Tanna not much better. The natives he had come to convert were diabolical thieves. Except for a string of blue beads and a little blue and red paint, they ran about naked. Paton's nearest neighbour, a trader, gave a bad example. He scoffed at religion. To increase the sale of his second-hand flintlock muskets, he provoked small native wars, then sold gunpowder to both sides, at the rate of a wine-glass of powder to a live hog.

For the timber he needed to build a chapel, John Paton bartered fifty pairs of trousers which had been cut out, sewn and sent him by the girls of his Bible Class in Glasgow. Paton was strongly convinced that wearing trews was the first step towards being civilized, and the girls were glad to help.

Many of the views that missionary societies now professed – anti-slavery, education, race equality, human brotherhood – had been taken to heart as their own by large numbers of working people leading much harder lives than the prosperous committee-men who directed the societies' policy. Saving pennies – or *centimes* – for missionaries had by this time become a favourite pastime of the respectable poor. Those who by exercise of their own sober skill had thus far resisted being forced down into the slums looked upon a missionary box on the mantelpiece as a mark of decency. But the box was also, in its way, a romantic symbol of their inherited and repeatedly frustrated hope that the brutal world outside the four walls of the family home might also be redeemed and transformed.

As early as 1823, the Manchester Missionary Union counted on 1200 working-class supporters. The Church Missionary Society, which once had been financed by such rich men as Wilberforce and Thornton, now relied as well on Artisans' Missionary Unions. Members gave a penny a week and, sus-

tained by such mass support, CMS income never fell below
£40,000 a year. In a good year, the income of the London Missionary Society might rise above £100,000.

As well as trying at times to act up to some of the high principles
which encouraged their many working-class supporters, missionaries reporting home were from now on tempted to strike attitudes,
and to heighten the drama of their lives. They had a large
audience, ready to believe the best of them. They sometimes tried
so hard to appear what other men hoped they might really be as
to make themselves look silly. Direct, forthright John Paton on
Tanna was an exception.

The idea of those poor and desperately overworked but good
girls in Glasgow using up what little spare time they might be
granted in sewing trousers for naked cannibals may sound a
pleasantry, yet has its own pathos. In that unpaid work there was
more glamour than self-righteousness. The cannibal islands were
their dream world, a long way from the factory whistle and the
twelve-hour day. The cannibal islands in a sense were a simplifi-
cation of Glasgow. Why might not loving kindness one day rule
there, too, as well as here?

To judge by contemporary accounts, at least some of the sandalwood traders in the New Hebrides were honest and considerate
men. The trader who battened on Tanna's tribal wars was, of
course, a villain. But worst of all by far were the blackbirders,
come to kidnap forced labour for prospering Australia.

Not only did they run 'indentured labour' out of the islands
on terms hard to distinguish from chattel slavery, but certain
blackbirders had a vision of an even more profitable future ahead
of them, if only the islands could be stripped bare of humans as
some had been of sandalwood. They planned to achieve in the
New Hebrides what had already been sanctioned and accom-
plished with such total success in Tasmania. As the captain of
Blue Bell told John Paton on Tanna in 1860, 'Our watchword is,
sweep these creatures away, and let white men occupy the soil.'

Paton had witnessed this ruffian, two years before, run a
coffin ship aground off Tanna, for the insurance money. This
time *Blue Bell* was back with her hold full of natives collected

elsewhere in the Pacific, and all desperately ill with measles. To Europeans, measles was an illness left behind in childhood. To Melanesians, who had no resistance to the germ, measles was a killer.

Blue Bell's captain put sick men ashore in four different parts of Tanna, then kidnapped a local man, and locked him below until the infection had taken hold, before letting him go back among his own people. *Blue Bell* then sheered off to repeat the dose on the next island. But to clear the islands of natives was not enough. Inconvenient witnesses must also be got rid of. Sedulously, in all the native villages they came to, the blackbirders put the word about that the killing disease had been brought by the missionaries.

Some of Paton's flock on Tanna, with their disease hot upon them, would rush down and plunge into the sea, and so die almost at once. Others dug their own graves and lay down in them to await death. By this time Paton had about sixty converts on Tanna, of whom ten were chiefs: he had offered a red shirt to the first chief to learn his alphabet. But Paton as he nursed the sick now noted gloomily, 'They say we made the disease and we must be killed for it; that they never died in this way before the religion came among them.'

In May 1861, Reverend G. N. Gordon and his wife were chopped to bits on Erromanga by men persuaded that they had brought in the disease. A similar attempt to kill John Paton on Tanna failed, so a trader shipped in assassins from Erromanga, but that attempt failed, too.

On 18 January 1862, tribal war broke out on Tanna. To buy tobacco and ammunition, the warriors stripped Paton's mission to the bare walls (property, the Scots missionary noted grimly, worth six hundred pounds) and bartered off everything he had owned to the local trader, who in turn made a deal with the captain of *Blue Bell*, once again standing offshore: all Paton's possessions for gunpowder.

Glad to get rid of him at last, *Blue Bell's* captain cynically offered John Paton a passage to the island of Aneiteum, where other missionaries still hung on. Paton, down to his last shirt, was driven to accept the offer, his humiliation being the more complete since the captain and crew of *Blue Bell* were wearing his own clothes and flaunting his personal possessions.

Paton took a deck passage on yet another blackbirder from Aneiteum to Sydney. But if they thought that was the last they would see of John Paton, the blackbirders were wrong. Though in Paton's career as a Christian missionary there were lapses – he willingly acted as interpreter, for instance, when HMS *Curaçoa* bombarded Tanna – yet like all his colleagues he set his face sternly against making of the New Hebrides another Tasmania.

Paton began collecting money from Australian Presbyterians for a new mission ship – the brig *Dayspring* – and for a missionary counter-offensive in the archipelago. He raised £3000, much of it through children's collecting boxes. Soon the missionaries were back in the New Hebrides to stay, but *Dayspring*'s fate was ironical. Wrecked, her hull was sold by auction and bought by a French concern, who used the old missionary ship for blackbirding, until one fine day she broke her back on a reef.

John Coleridge Patteson had been consecrated Anglican bishop of Melanesia on 24 February 1861, when he was thirty-four. As an Eton boy he had heard Selwyn's last sermon before leaving for New Zealand, and it made its mark on his mind. In 1862, following Selwyn's example, Patteson collected into his school over fifty lads from the islands, and eventually mastered over thirty of the islands' multifarious dialects, reducing them to writing. Bishop Patteson's was a voice which could easily carry from the New Hebrides to Britain, and in January 1871 he made a solemn public protest against the blackbirders, who were reducing his diocese to savagery. But Patteson took a further step yet, condemning also the random punitive bombardments from warships which John Paton had condoned, and which appealed so much, as a cure-all, to some of the civilizing powers.

'I desire to protest by anticipation', he made clear, 'against any punishment being inflicted upon natives of these islands who may cut off vessels or kill boat's crews, until it is clearly shown that these acts are not done in the way of retribution for outrages first committed by white men.' By Patteson's day the population of the New Hebrides had shrunk, in two decades, from an estimated 240,000 to 70,000 – a third of the inhabitants having been wiped out by measles. But Christianity was taking root among the survivors; by 1887 there were 12,000 converts.

In September of the year when he had spoken out so decisively against blackbirding and bombardment, John Coleridge Patteson landed from the missionary ship *Southern Cross* on Nukapu, a small island in the Santa Cruz group, northward of the New Hebrides. His ship's boat lay in wait off the reef, and the bishop went ashore in one of the native canoes which paddled out to meet him. No one aboard *Southern Cross* was aware that a blackbirder had just kidnapped five men from Nukapu.

Next day, 21 September 1871, an unmanned canoe drifted out to sea. Stretched out in the bottom was the bishop's dead body. He had been clubbed to death, then pierced through with five wounds, to symbolize the five men kidnapped. A palm branch with five knots had been placed on his breast.

In London, the next Queen's Speech to Parliament, in 1872, announced measures to make illegal the kidnapping of forced labour. But for years to come, the blackbirders eluded all such attempts to check them by legislation. The falling population of the nearby Ellice islands, Samoan-speaking, from which blackbirders went on shipping men and selling them into forced labour in the coffee plantations of Central America, the copper mines of Peru, and the sugar plantations of Queensland, is a measure of how blackbirding continued to thrive. In 1850, the Ellice Islands were reputed to have a population of 20,000. There were only 3000 human beings living there by 1895.

8   A Few Perishing Souls

'All men tremble at punishment, all men fear death;
remember that you are like unto them, and do not kill,
or cause slaughter.' *The Dhammapada*

'The system of religion here has no power over the heart.'
Adoniram Judson, on Buddhism in Burma

In 1811, a young American of twenty-two called
Adoniram Judson, the son of a minister, was taking passage in
wartime from Massachusetts to London when his ship, *Packet*,
was taken by a privateer out of Bayonne, called *L'Invincible
Napoléon*. Judson was small and delicate, with a round and rosy
young face and a very loud, clear voice. He was the lineal descendant of a Yorkshire Puritan who had reached New England
in 1634.

Before deciding to cross the Atlantic in the midst of a war,
Judson had never known hardship – at home, he was his father's
favourite – though he had already seen a little more of the world
than most theological students. He had gone through a personal
crisis two years before, losing his belief in God. ('French infidelity',
as he afterwards explained, 'was sweeping over the land like a
flood.') He had then become stage-struck, keeping company
with actors and even spending six weeks with them in wicked
New York. But the faith of his fathers had by now been restored
him.

The French put Adoniram Judson down in the hold with
their other prisoners, where he was 'excessively seasick', but
prayer brought him round. He was lucky enough to have in his
pocket a Hebrew Bible, so he 'amused himself with translating
mentally from the Hebrew to the Latin'. Judson was marched
through the streets of Bayonne to a very uncomfortable prison,

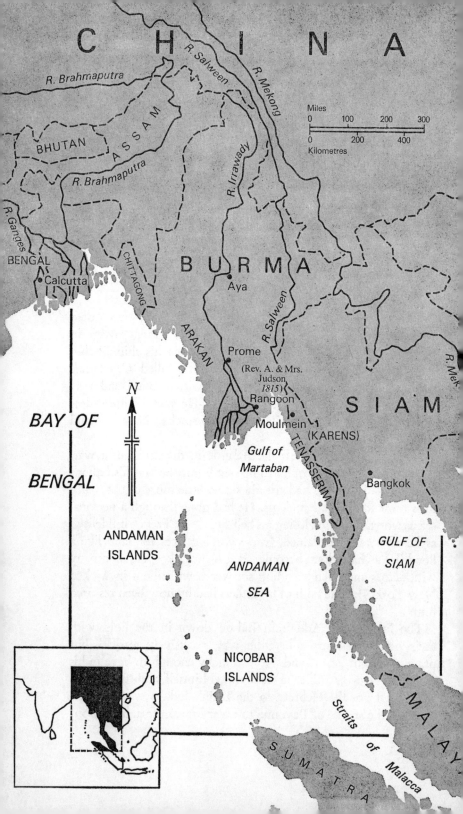

but a fellow-American from Philadelphia, no doubt a blockade-runner, was told of his plight, and bribed the guards to let the young man escape.

Adoniram Judson when he reached London still had in his pocket the letter of introduction to the Reverend George Burder, of the London Missionary Society – the man who had once nursed hopes of finding Welsh-speaking Indians out there on the Mississippi among the Choctaws. British evangelicals were by now sending missionaries all round the world, from South Africa to Tahiti, but their American counterparts could not but admit that the hopes raised long ago by John Eliot had been disappointed: 'Attempts to evangelize the aboriginal tribes of the American wilderness have been attended with so many discouragements' that 'for the pagans on this continent, very little can immediately be done.' Adoniram Judson, however, was determined to go abroad as a missionary, even if it meant offering his services to the British. And they would have been glad enough to employ him. But while Judson was coming to terms with the London society, Mrs John Norris, a merchant's widow from Salem, Massachusetts, left a legacy of $30,000 to finance American foreign missions. Merchants from New England were already trading profitably in the Orient; American missions there were a practical possibility. Presbyterians and Congregationalists united to form the Board of Commissioners for Foreign Missions, and began to look out for promising young men, so Adoniram Judson went home again.

In short order he was ordained, married, promised a salary, and sent on board the brig *Caravan*, bound for Calcutta. Though Judson himself was in fact to stay in the Far East for thirty-three years before seeing Boston again, the average life expectation of a missionary out there was then five years. The one misgiving the Board had of this young pioneer they were sending forth was on account of Judson's 'excessive self-reliance': they read his character shrewdly.

On the long and tedious voyage round the Horn, Judson studied his New Testament so intently as to come at last to the conclusion that there was 'no authority for infant baptism'. This meant cutting himself loose from those who had sent him out. In Massachusetts there had long been a sectarian hostility between Baptists and Congregationalists and it was still acrimonious, even if Baptists trying to enter the state were no longer tried and flogged, as had been the case in years gone by. Judson once he got to India announced himself a Baptist, and the Board dismissed him; luckily, he had a little money of his own.

Adoniram Judson landed at Calcutta, planning to join the group of English Baptists who lived in the nearby Danish enclave of Serampore, where the East India Company could not interfere with them. Forbidden to enter British India, these English pioneers spent much of their time on Biblical translation. Six years before, their American co-religionists had supported their work to the tune of $6000. No Christian missionary was yet allowed to work in the vast provinces of India which the Company controlled, though in London politically influential members of the Clapham Sect were pushing the East India Company hard on the issue. The argument was that if the Company sanctioned the preaching of Christianity to the Hindus, they might well be incited to rebellion – as the Indian Mutiny later showed, they were not far wrong.

Ten days after Judson's arrival in Calcutta, the East India Company ordered him back to America. Since he would never be allowed to work in India itself, the English Baptists in Serampore advised Judson and his wife to launch a mission elsewhere, perhaps on the island of Amboina in the Moluccas ('fifty thousand souls are there perishing'). Two months later Judson was still waiting in Calcutta for a passage when he was put under house arrest, and ordered back to England, as a prisoner in an Indiaman. With the connivance of a friendly ship's captain, he and his wife got away in *Belle Créole* to the island of Mauritius. After many such adventurous comings and goings he at last made his way to Rangoon, in Burma – the port at the mouth of the Irrawaddy river. The American Baptists themselves had meanwhile formed their own missionary organization, and were advancing him a modest salary.

An English Baptist missionary, Felix Carey, had reached Burma before Judson, but he married a Burmese girl, gave up the ministry and became an official at the king's court. Judson therefore had the field to himself, and was so remote from his committee's control that for years to come he could act very much as he himself thought best. He was confident and gifted. He was in earnest. And what could a Christian missionary of his talents and strength of character expect to achieve in a politically independent nation like Burma, which was also overwhelmingly Buddhist?

Between the Roman Empire and ancient India there had been regular seaborne trade, thanks to the monsoon. Some Roman trading ships made their landfall on the south-west coast, and there, at Malabar, early Christianity struck root, the apostolic missionary who planted the faith being St Thomas according to legendary tradition.

When the first Jesuit missionaries reached south India in the seventeenth century, churches of the Syrian rite were still surviving. The Jesuits had initially in India a missionary success almost as great as they were to have in China and Japan, and the church they established managed to survive both the dissolution of the Society of Jesus and the conquest of India by a Protestant power which at first would allow no missionaries whatever to enter. In 1936, in the autumn of the British raj, there were still 3,334,938 Roman Catholics there, according to census.

Once pressure had successfully been brought to bear in London upon the East India Company, so that Christian missionaries, both Protestant and Catholic, could enter, the Protestant missionaries enjoyed the apparent advantage, but the long-term handicap, of being too closely identified in Hindu and Muslim eyes with the rule of an alien power. Here as elsewhere, converts from Islam were few, in proportion to the effort made. People on the margin of the Indian society – untouchables, aboriginal hill folk – were less difficult to win over. Missions offered western education and modern medicine, and so made gradual headway. By 1936 there were probably six million nominal Protestants in India, but even before 1914, and certainly by 1936, recent missionary effort was breaking into spray on the rock of a nationalist sentiment with which both Hindu pantheism and the militant monotheism of Islam were in different ways identified. For what was to happen later that century in the enormous Indian sub-continent, Adoniram Judson's lonely and obstinate experience in nearby Burma was as it were a laboratory instance.

The Burmese were a Mongol folk which years before had migrated from West China and Tibet, down the great rivers Irrawaddy and Salween, to this mountainous, forested, tropical land facing the Indian Ocean. Not only were they staunchly Buddhist, but passionately hostile to the British raj in India, which jostled them along their north-western border. They would first need to be convinced that a man who spoke English yet called himself 'American' was not a British spy.

The King of Burma – like the Emperor of China – nominally owned all the land in his kingdom. He ruled despotically. Bribery was universal, aggressive border wars frequent; the wealth of a man who had been executed reverted to the king. Non-Burmese minorities had a thin time of it, and royal government in Judson's day was little more than a well-policed system of squeezing the peasants for all they were worth. The unfortunate Burmese peasants found their consolation in Buddhism.

The Buddhist church in Burma was distinct from the state. Almost every village had its Buddhist monk, who had taken vows of poverty and chastity, and taught the village children to read; almost every Burmese boy passed some time in a Buddhist monastery. A monk never touched money, but begged his bowl of rice. He taught respect for all forms of life – since any living creature, however insignificant, might be a transmigrating soul. The monks tried to instil indifference to suffering. Accepting their doctrine would blot out awareness of the arbitrary violence – indeed, the deliberate relish for cruelty – of everyday official life in Burma.

Judson defined the essence of his own confrontation with Buddhism as follows. A Christian, he considered, is morally responsible for the consequences of his own deliberate acts – he has, therefore, a social conscience – whereas the Burmese were being taught indifference to the evils of their everyday life, which they regarded merely as a probationary state, after which, through detachment, the bliss of nirvana might at last be attained. The evils of pain, instability and change could, in the Buddhist view, be avoided only by detachment.

Now Buddhism, as Judson saw it, included no doctrine of atonement or redemption, and could not therefore hold out, as did evangelical Christianity, any way of escape from the continuous accumulation of guilt which may so easily drag down those who live, as did the Buddhists, merely by virtue of a moral code – a set of commandments. 'The system of religion here', he noticed early on, 'has no power over the heart'.

All miseries, social as well as individual, were in Judson's opinion the consequences of sin – 'the alienation of our moral affections from God'. Only the incarnation and the atonement – the vicarious taking upon himself of the burden of human sin by Jesus Christ the son of God – could restore to the Burmese the affections of the heart. Then, 'the radical moral evil of the soul being corrected, there will flow from it, by necessity, the fruits of justice and charity'. The emotional religious conviction – intense though perhaps narrow – which inspired the evangelical missionaries of his time could hardly have been put more lucidly. Adoniram Judson was clear in his own mind from the very start: he had come to Burma as the servant of his master, the Atoning Christ, to offer to the guilt-ridden Burmese redemption from sin – and from this high view of his task he scarcely wavered.

When Judson first settled in Rangoon, except for seamen ashore from their trading-ships, there were almost no Protestants in the place. The King of Burma had, however, a number of Catholic subjects – descendants of Portuguese who had married Burmese wives. Roman Catholic priests could minister to these Burmese, but were forbidden to make converts, and after their first Burmese convert was pounded to death with an iron maul the Portuguese priests accepted the situation with patient prudence. Judson hardly counted them as Christians.

A son – the second of Judson's many children, few of whom survived life in Burma – was born in Rangoon on 11 September 1815 and died eight months after. By August 1816 Judson had finished his Burmese grammar. A printing press with Burmese types was shipped in from Serampore, and another missionary arrived from America, luckily a discreet man. Judson and he agreed 'to put all our money in a common fund' and 'not to engage in business', for, as Judson sensibly observed, 'one wrong-

G

headed, conscientiously obstinate fellow would ruin us.' The king's police were everywhere. Yet despite the risks, the religious tracts they were printing in Burmese began to circulate from hand to hand. By 1823, the Burmese New Testament was ready. Five thousand copies would cost $5000 – but the Baptists in America, four times as numerous as their energetic British counterparts, were no less prosperous, and funds came in fast. Two more American missionaries had arrived by ship. Both were consumptive, one went mad and jumped overboard. Just after, there was an outbreak of cholera.

Adoniram Judson had made up his mind from the first to use what he described as the apostolic missionary method. He would expound and spread his Christian beliefs not, for example, by teaching children – they were being taught already by Buddhist monks – but by engaging the interest of serious-minded adults as individuals, by talking over religion with them earnestly, face to face. As recruits to his church he looked only to those who had undergone a moral transformation. On 4 April 1819, six years after his arrival in Rangoon, he took the calculated risk of beginning public worship. On 27 June, his first Burmese convert was baptized.

But even this cautious advance was dangerous. Except for a few Burmese of a heroic cast of mind, those who had studied his tracts and offered Judson a chance to speak his mind to them on Christianity, though profoundly attracted to this religion which claimed the power to cancel sin, were living also in continual fear of the King of Burma. 'The lord of land and water' or 'the owner of the sword' – the king was always named in a roundabout way – might suddenly decide to cut off the head of anyone who had taken to this new foreign religion. When persecution threatened, Judson decided to go boldly upriver to the royal capital Ava, near present-day Mandalay, and there confront the king himself.

'His dress was rich but not distinctive,' Judson reported from the court, 'and he carried in his hand the gold-sheathed sword' – symbol of his royal power to decapitate. The King of Burma graciously took the tract which Judson offered him, read a few words, then sat down on a cushion and began listening to music. The king was in a particularly confident mood – he had come back victorious from one border war, and was now planning another, against Siam.

The royal physician, a Portuguese Catholic priest, was candid with Judson. There was no chance whatever of the king's officially tolerating a Christian mission – least of all in the interior – though Judson was racking his wits to find a way of going to work further inland. So back he went to Rangoon.

In 1824, his wife went on a visit to the United States, Adoniram pledging himself meanwhile to 'restrain natural appetites within the bounds of temperance and purity'. There were by this time twenty-four church members in Rangoon. On her return, after a rapturous reunion, Judson decided once again to go upriver to the royal capital, this time taking his wife. He could hardly have chosen a worse moment. The royal capital, Ava, was becoming a refuge for Sikhs and Brahmins who, having fled East India Company rule, were busily making the Burmese better aware that the British in India were their predestined enemies.

They had an eager audience among the aggressive Burmese. As one royal prince expressed it, 'The British are inhabitants of a small and remote island. What business have they to come in ships from so great a distance to dethrone kings and take possession of countries they have no right to? They have never yet fought with so strong and brave a people as the Burmans, skilled in the use of sword and spear.'

A Burmese army set off, cock-a-hoop with confidence, to attack the contested border with the British, at Chittagong. On his way up to Ava, Adoniram Judson ran into Burma's most famous general, Bandula, amid his army of spearmen and golden war-boats: the British were the declared enemy.

Now Judson, as ill-luck would have it, had been drawing his money by orders on Bengal, through the British resident in Ava. This convinced the Burmese that he must be a spy, not that it made much difference – soon after he arrived there all Europeans whatever in Ava except Mrs Judson were summarily arrested. She was pregnant and near her time, yet at great risk devoted herself to helping the prisoners. Attached by three sets of fetters to a long pole, Adoniram Judson lingered out long months in the 'death prison', where captive foreigners had been crammed in a hundred to a room. He survived because Mrs Judson even during the twenty days of her confinement bribed and cajoled his captors, bringing in food, smuggling medicine to sick prisoners, even managing to hide Judson's precious Biblical translations for him in a pillow.

The gaolers in the 'death prison' had themselves been common convicts, some branded for their crimes, others with ears or nose lopped off, now all given free rein to extort or terrorize the political prisoners. These gaolers, known as 'children of the prison', were social pariahs, intermarrying only among themselves, and compensating for their own bygone humiliations by tormenting those now given into their power.

The prison governor, nicknamed Tiger Cat, though a convicted and branded murderer, was a psychopath with a special sense of humour. He would make good-natured jokes to prisoners while manacling them, and caress them while he tormented them, calling the prisoners his beloved children. To a deputy whom he overheard expressing the opinion that nothing more could be squeezed out of a certain prisoner, Tiger Cat answered, 'My son, be sure you have never wrung a rag so dry but that another twist will bring another drop.' But Tiger Cat took Mrs Judson's bribes, and that saved Judson's life.

The rains ended in October, but the British were stuck fast in the mud of Rangoon. Then on 15 December they defeated Bandula in a pitched fight outside the city, and advanced up the river Irrawaddy to Prome. This plunged the Burmese from over-confidence into superstitious gloom. One of the British flags bore the image of a lion, so into Judson's prison they dragged a live lion in a small cage, and there the beast was starved to death.

The European prisoners were tied up, strappado-fashion, with a thin cord, and dragged barefoot across eight miles of sand and gravel to a place where it was rumoured that they were to be burned alive. Some died on the way. As he stumbled and limped his way across a stream, Adoniram Judson admitted later that he 'ardently longed to throw himself into the water to be free of misery. But the sin attaching to such an act alone prevented.' His wife meanwhile had borne her third child, Maria.

While her father was being taken off to what all predicted would be his funeral pyre, little Maria caught smallpox, and her mother went down, first with dysentery, then with spotted fever. As Mrs Judson lay there, with shaven head and blistered feet, undergoing the desperate remedies of the time, the girl who looked after little Maria for her caught smallpox, too. What kept Mrs Judson, so she said, from 'sinking under my accumulated sufferings' was, in her own words, 'an assured conviction that every additional trial was ordered by love and mercy'.

Suddenly, Adoniram Judson was released, his mind clear but his nerves permanently shaken. He was led off to the Burmese army camp, to act as adviser and interpreter. On their march towards the capital, the British had demanded an indemnity of ten million rupees, and the release of Mr and Mrs Judson, and little Maria. But they are not British, said the King of Burma, so why should we?

Judson, as the only scholar available with a perfect knowledge of both Burmese and English, had become irreplaceable. He was willing enough to serve the Burmese, and did not wish them 'to receive an impression that he was in the interest of the English'. The King of Burma offered him riches if only he would enter his service – though he would not tolerate Judson as a missionary. The British too were keen to use him – there were terms of truce to arrange, and a treaty to be drawn – and at least in their camp his wife and child would be safe.

Twist and turn though he might – and well aware of the trap they were all nudging him towards – Adoniram Judson after having for so long preserved his independence was ineluctably drawn from now onwards into the machinery of imperialism. He gave the British a hand with the terms of peace, and then withdrew with them to one of the two great tracts of Burma – Arakan and Tenasserim – which they had occupied after their victory, yet knew very well as he went with them that he was jeopardizing his mission. Mrs Judson's last words to him – she died of remittent fever on 24 November 1826 – were 'an earnest entreaty not to enter the service of the British government'.

The British then lured Judson into helping them with their commercial treaty by holding out to him the hope – doomed in the event to disappointment – of making the Burmese include in it a clause guaranteeing religious toleration, so that foreign missionaries would be free to enter and work. But the Burmese now looked upon Christian missionaries as the precursors of merchants and fleets and armies, and were no longer willing to allow Judson even the limited scope he had enjoyed before the war in Rangoon.

The British paid him a handsome fee for his services; Judson passed it on at once to his missionary society. He sought earnestly to come out of all this with clean hands. But with the kingdom of Burma denied him, where else could he continue his mission but under the protection of British bayonets? So he settled at Moulmein, in Tenasserim, on the mouth of the Salween river. His little Burmese church was already broken up: four of Judson's converts joined him at Moulmein, three stayed on at Rangoon.

The publicly successful years of the American Baptists' mission in Burma were about to begin.

In 1826, four converts were baptized, of whom three were British soldiers of the 45th Regiment, stationed in Burma. This small fact measures the growing political strength of evangeli-calism in Britain even before the Reform Act. Not very long before, on 11 July 1803, in Gibraltar, five soldiers, two of them corporals, were sentenced by their colonel to 500 lashes each for attending a Methodist meeting, and the corporals were also reduced to the ranks. But those intolerant days were past.

From 1829 to 1831, the missionaries based on Moulmein baptized 209 converts – the greater number of them Karens, a primitive people living in the jungle between Burma and Siam. The Karens had been conquered by the Burmese – whom they detested – only a generation before. Many thousands of the Karens had been carried off by the Burmese to forced labour – there were by now only 13,000 Karens left.

The Karens were slovenly, hated towns, loved alcohol. In the jungle they lived by the slash-and-burn agriculture of neolithic times, but the primitive society they had inherited was trembling on the brink of collapse, so they were attracted by the consolation of any religion, so long as it was not the Buddhism to which lipservice was paid by their oppressors.

Judson's fellow-Americans were content to minister in comparative safety to the British garrison, and to evangelize the Karens, but Judson himself insisted on going back to Rangoon: 'an experiment we are making with fear and trembling'. He found when he got to Rangoon that the poor people there were being screwed down hard by the king, to make them pay their share of the huge indemnity the British had demanded: 'Poverty, distress and terror', Judson reported, 'are the order of the day.' His old acquaintances shunned him. 'People here view me', he was driven to admit, 'with an evil eye.' For the Burmese, he had become a 'suspicious character ever since I deserted them at the end of the war, and went over to the British.'

Judson made a few converts, but the little church met in secret, and when the Burmese government eventually forced him out, he too decided to minister to the Karens. There in the jungle Adoniram Judson underwent a spiritual crisis, in some way connected with the fear of death which had been imprinted on his nervous system during his imprisonment. He went out of his way to nurse those Karens who were suffering from the more revolting of their diseases. He lived in a bamboo hermitage on the edge of the forest, eating only rice, and often fasting. He read Fénelon and A'Kempis, discovering in this personal extremity that the religious writers who meant most to him were Catholic. He slept beside his own new-dug grave. At last, to face death down, Judson wandered for forty days in a jungle overrun with tigers, carrying nothing but his Bible, and emerging, they said, with 'unusual self-possession'.

But all this was separating him from the earnest and eager young men who had begun to flock out from New England to the famous and now flourishing mission station at Moulmein, in British territory, where the morbid cruelties of the Burmese had become a thing of the past. His fellow-Americans began to whisper that Adoniram Judson was arbitrary and eccentric. Not being able to evangelize in Burma, Judson consoled himself from now on by enormous labours on his Burmese Bible, going deeper than other Biblical translators of the time into the Hebrew and Greek originals, and taking careful account of the latest German textual scholarship, which soon was to overturn the traditional view of what the Protestant Bible meant. He read widely in Burmese poetry, and spent much time cross-questioning ordinary Burmese, pursuing the idiomatic phrase which might give him an exact rendering. The work of revision alone took him six years; the quarto Burmese Bible appeared on 21 October 1840, and was a brilliant exception to the common run of missionary translations.

In 1834, Adoniram Judson married the widow of another pioneer missionary. 'Very affectionate and pious' with her 'soft blue eyes, her lovely face and elegant form', she too was fluent in Burmese, and had translated *Pilgrim's Progress*. By 1837 (when Judson was forty-nine, and the first two of their eight children had been born), after a mission lasting a quarter of a century, only 207 Burmese had been converted, but 729 Karens were already baptized.

Mrs Judson, a victim all her married life of chronic dysentery, had her eight children by Adoniram Judson in ten years, and lost three of them. Judson, deeply enamoured, once wrote to her, 'If such exquisite delights as we have enjoyed with those now in paradise, and with one another, are allowed to sinful creatures on earth, what must the joys of heaven be?' The uxorious missionary goes on to hazard a guess: 'Surely there is not a single lawful pleasure the loss of which we shall have to regret there. What high and transporting intercommunion of souls we may therefore anticipate, and that to all eternity!' Judson in his fervour had begun to picture to himself a heaven only one short step from the Muslim paradise; but Mrs Judson's bliss was not unalloyed. Her health began to break up, so they took a convalescent voyage in the merchantman *Ramsay*, of Greenock.

Ramsay's captain was a godly man. He and sixteen of his crew had signed a resolution in the ship's Bible, to serve the Lord. They agreed with Judson that adult baptism was scriptural, so when at anchor in Moulmein, the captain, his mate and two seamen, 'together with a Burmese female', were baptized by total immersion. Not only was there a Sunday service aboard

Ramsay, but a prayer-meeting every Wednesday: in early industrial society, some of the British working class were marked as
indelibly by evangelicalism as others, elsewhere in the world,
have since been by Marxism.

Judson's sermons brought tears to the seamen's eyes; he converted three who were as yet unregenerate, and though Mauritius,
where they dropped anchor, was notoriously 'a very wicked
place', Judson was able to report of his sea-going congregation
that, 'though they have been exposed to some temptation since
their arrival in port, I do not hear that a single one has fallen off.'

In 1845, the second Mrs Judson died. The philoprogenitive
missionary, then fifty-seven, took the surviving children back
to Boston, and a few months later married again, taking his
third wife ('Emily, who, as you know, is rather delicate') straight
back to Rangoon. Hostility there to foreign missionaries was
greater than ever as Burma drifted, or was diplomatically edged,
into yet another war with British India, but Adoniram Judson
had decided to run the risk.

He was supposed to minister only to the religious needs of
foreigners in the port of Rangoon, but slowly, cautiously, he
began collecting up his Burmese converts again. The third Mrs
Judson, straight out from Boston, must have found the place
a living nightmare. The house where they lived, in the Muslim
quarter, was infested with bats: Judson killed 250. All their movements were dogged by the police. Emily was pregnant (and yet,
remarked her husband indelicately, 'as thin as the shad that went
up Niagara'). They had no choice but to observe the Buddhist
Lent, which lasts four months – and Mrs Judson loathed rice.
However, a neighbourly Muslim smuggled them in some
fowls.

On any day a service was to be held, the Burmese Christians
would come in one by one at intervals from morning to night,
pretending to be tradesmen, or kirtling up their clothes so as to
be taken for coolies. Ten Burmese, one Karen and two foreigners
arrived at one time for communion; since the import of alcohol
was forbidden, Judson had concocted his sacramental wine from
raisins. Though he risked certain prison and likely death for
changing his religion, one brave new Burmese convert was

made. He was baptized by total immersion, furtively after dark in a tank behind some bushes.

Rangoon was then administered, said Judson, by 'the most ferocious bloodthirsty monster I have ever known in Burma . . . his house and courtyard resound day and night with the screams of people under torture.' Judson had no choice but to report that 'while the present monster is in power I shall not be able to convene the disciples for worship as hitherto . . . I hope to do something yet, in private, to help a few perishing souls . . . not even a tract can be given out publicly.' Yet the final blow, when it fell upon him, came not from the 'monster' but from Judson's fellow ministers in Moulmein and New England.

Adoniram Judson was by this time America's most celebrated Protestant missionary – but nothing spectacular in the way of conversions or translations could be expected from him if he stayed risking his life with this tiny clandestine church. The heroic days were over. Spectacular progress, which could be measured in numbers and which therefore pleased the subscribers, was being made among the Karens. His committee would rather have a Burmese dictionary out of Adoniram Judson than a martyrdom.

The mission was slowly ossifying into an establishment; only exceptional men were eager to go upcountry. In 1847, of the twenty-nine Baptist missionaries who were Judson's colleagues, twenty-four were snug in Moulmein, and Judson had hardly made himself popular with them by asserting that this was wrong. Mission work had by now become fashionable in America too. By 1846, the American Board of Foreign Missions was spending a third of a million dollars a year; by 1848 there were a thousand American Protestant missionaries at work around the globe. Judson was a figure from the past.

He had always been frugal with money, giving back much of his salary and, in times of need, making the missionary committee free of any money he might have by him of his own. But to make sure that Judson would be obliged to leave his dangerous, self-sought task in Burma, and return to Moulmein, and there go to work on his dictionary, those set in authority over him in New England 'cut off funds' for Rangoon. Since Judson was unlikely to leave of his own accord they would starve him out.

'All through our troubles I was comforted by the thought', said Judson wryly, 'that my brethren in Moulmein and in America were praying for us, and they have never once thought of us.'

In the lifetime remaining him, Adoniram Judson kept at a certain distance from the church he had pioneered, attending to the spiritual needs of the 150 Burmese living in Moulmein and, at the age of sixty-one, yet again admitting, 'If only I could get a little foothold in Burma, I would be off at once.'

Emily had become frail, and he devoted himself to her, but she outlived him. 'It is the opinion of the mission', she told Judson when he fell ill, 'that you will not recover.' 'A few years would not be missed', he argued with his wife, and with himself, 'from my eternity of bliss, and I could well afford to spare them, both for your sake and the sake of the poor Burmans . . . otherwise I am willing and glad to die.' He was buried not long after, at sea, in a strong plank coffin, with several buckets of sand poured in to make sure it sank.

9   On to the Golden Age

'The world is rolling on to the golden age. The inmates
of our workhouses have more comfort than rich chieftains
in Africa have; they have soap, clean linen, glass windows
and chimneys.' *David Livingstone*

The Dutch had maintained a station at the Cape of
Good Hope since 1652 for their East Indiamen, and this the British
took over in 1795, after the Low Countries had been occupied
by a revolutionary French army. There were by this time 21,000
people living at the Cape, of Dutch or Huguenot descent, most
of them farmers providing victuals for passing ships: they were
the Boers.

Marriages at the Cape between white and black had been
acceptable in the seventeenth century, provided that both
partners were church members. But by this time, half the people
living in Cape Town were slaves, and almost all children born
there to slave women were illegitimate. Fear bred prejudice,
and prejudice fear: the penalty accorded by the Dutch code to a
slave who raised a hand against his master was death by slow
strangulation, impalement, or breaking on a wheel.

In 1798 a transport, *Hillsborough*, which the British government had chartered to take convicts out to Port Jackson, Australia, consented to land some evangelical missionaries at Cape
Town as it called by. The most remarkable man among them
was a fifty-one-year-old Presbyterian minister called Johannes
Vanderkemp, who was also qualified as a physician, and had for
sixteen years of his life been a Dutch cavalry officer. Years before,
Vanderkemp had in fact refused an offer from the Dutch East
India Company to go out to the Cape as their military commander;
now he was going there as a missionary.

He was a carelessly dressed man with deep-set eyes and a
huge, domed forehead, and his life so far had been marked by
an extreme independence of mind. In his teens, Vanderkemp

had defied his respectable family – his father was a professor of theology – and run off with a peruke-maker's wife, older than himself, who bore him a daughter and then left him. Vanderkemp brought up the little girl himself. When she was five – and he had been promoted captain of horse – he outraged propriety in Holland still further by this time proposing to marry a girl ten years younger than himself – a poor cotton-spinner. 'I took such a pleasure,' he writes, in his manuscript autobiography, 'in the lower circle in which she moved that I was inclined to exchange my manner of living for that of a common mechanic or journeyman.' Vanderkemp's family did their best to buy the girl off, but they married and were happy, though William V of Orange not long after caught this officer of his guard fetching buckets of water so his wife could scrub down her step, and gave him a solemn wigging.

Vanderkemp resigned his commission soon after, and turned to medicine. By this time, though bred up a strict Calvinist, he had become a pantheist, with a private cult of the erotic. Vanderkemp was too much of a scientist for Christ's miracles not to perplex him, and but for his wife and child would have given up his church membership. But they were drowned suddenly, in a boating accident, and he was overwhelmed by a violent religious emotion – the 'conversion' which, to serious-minded men in the eighteenth century, was a sign from above to begin an altogether new life. Vanderkemp went to London, and after being ordained there as a minister in the Church of Scotland – theologically close to his own church at home – he offered his services as a missionary. He turned down a chance to go to Tahiti – where his strong and eccentric personality, as soldier, physician and amorist, might have written a different tale. Everyone began to suggest that he was the right man for South Africa. While waiting for his passage, Vanderkemp took a job in a Hoxton brickyard, having decided that nothing would be more useful to a missionary in a savage land than knowing how to make bricks.

With Tahitian experience in mind, the Society had laid down the law in earnest to the missionaries going out in *Hillsborough*. 'It is utterly improbable that you should propagate the Gospel

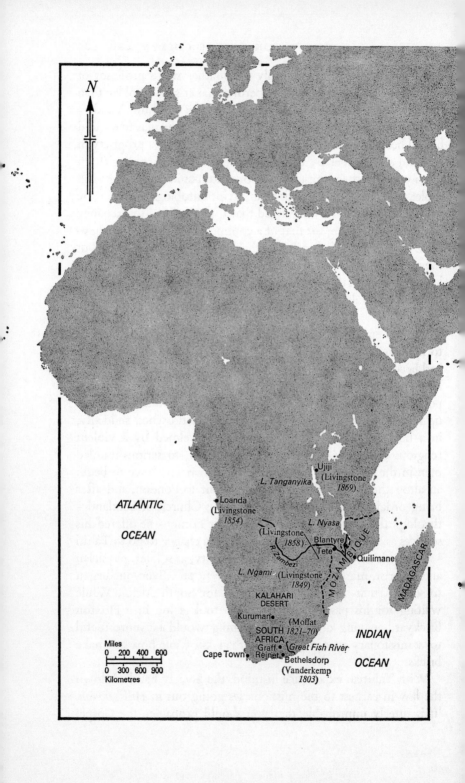

N

ATLANTIC
OCEAN

Ujiji
(Livingstone
1869)

L. Tanganyika

Loanda
(Livingstone
1854)

L. Nyasa

(Livingstone
1858)
R. Zambezi
Blantyre
Tete
Quilimane

MOZAMBIQUE

MADAGASCAR

L. Ngami
(Livingstone
1849)

KALAHARI
DESERT

Kuruman

(Moffat
1821–70)

SOUTH
AFRICA
Graff
Reinet

Great Fish River

INDIAN

Cape Town

Bethelsdorp
(Vanderkemp
1803)

OCEAN

Miles
0   200   400   600

0   300   600   900
Kilometres

among the Heathen in greater purity that you experience and practise it yourselves,' ran their instructions. 'Ever beware of your own corrupt inclinations. Avoid to the utmost every temptation of the Native women.'

In *Hillsborough* there were 300 convicts in chains, on the orlop deck at the wet bottom of the ship, below the waterline. They were hiding in their midst a naval deserter – almost certainly a mutineer from the *Nore* – and sympathizers in the crew passed them down knives, files and saws. The convicts, as Vanderkemp came on board, were busy making desperate plans for filing off their irons and capturing *Hillsborough*, or else drilling holes in her bottom and, as she sank, taking to the boats. They managed to overawe a cutter full of armed marines, and when a young naval officer was sent down to the orlop deck, to ferret out the deserter, they manhandled and stabbed him.

When *Hillsborough* sailed, sentries with loaded muskets were standing at every gangway, and the transport proceeded under the guns of an escorting frigate, HMS *Amphion*. Away went the missionaries in a ship which was an eloquent embodiment of their own troubled times – a civilized society in the captain's cabin, proceeding with wine and conversation as it always had, and a mass of violence, resentment and rebellion seething underfoot on the lowest deck of all.

As they got under way, the one man the convicts would allow down into their midst was bald-headed old Vanderkemp, and the sickness on the orlop deck kept him busy. After a three-day storm, five feet of water rose in the hold. By the time they reached Table Bay, after a thirteen week voyage, thirty-six convicts had already gone over the side, fifteen more were at death's door, and such was the influence gained by Vanderkemp over these defiant criminals that, at his tactful urging, those convicts still alive who previously had sawn through their chains consented once again to be fettered.

Once in South Africa, would Vanderkemp continue to act on the pattern which so far had been followed by the evangelicals in the turbulent industrial cities of the time – as a moral police-man? His first sight of slavery, in Cape Town, shocked him out of his wits. 'Marriage among these unfortunate people is not only unknown,' he reported, 'but even declared to be unlawful by those European barbarians who rule over this land.' He saw human beings 'sold as beasts, and separated from their children by monsters who call themselves Christians'.

Out in the country, most slaves were Hottentots, kidnapped young and put to forced labour as cattlemen. As well as trying either to enslave or else to wipe out the Hottentots – the black people who were occupying South Africa when they themselves arrived there – the Boers were also obliged to carry on a running warfare with tribes of cattle-raising Bantu, whom they called Kaffirs, and who pressed down on them from the north-west. Kaffirs and Boers competed along the disputed border for water and grazing. After being told that these Kaffirs were 'very cruel and intractable', Vanderkemp wondered if this might not be the right place for a missionary, so he set off for the Great Fish River with Bruntjie, a famous Hottentot elephant hunter, as his guide.

Gaika, the Kaffir king, had already attracted to his camp a motley group of renegades and refugees. Vanderkemp found there deserters from the British army, making common cause with the Kaffirs. Among other fugitives from Cape law was the intellectual leader of the Dutch Jacobins – and this chance acquaintance was to give Vanderkemp an undeserved bad name with the British authorities, though in point of fact he had no love for Jacobins in general or the French Revolution either, but simply liked this particular man. The Boers, too, were watching Vanderkemp closely, and tried to make sure that the Kaffir king would do their dirty work for them, by warning Gaika that Vanderkemp and his companion – who carried the sacrament with them – were 'spies and assassins, armed with enchanted wine'.

Gaika's sister, Hoby, fell in love with Vanderkemp. When she tried to get into his tent at night, he nobly rebuffed her, but possibly this infatuation saved his neck. What most upset Vanderkemp was his discovery that the Kaffirs too, though black men themselves, had Hottentot slaves. The Kaffirs ignored his talk of redemption and salvation, but the Hottentots were eager to listen. The God of their adoration hitherto had been called

Thuuikee – *He who induces pain.* What Vanderkemp had to offer sounded better. On the last day of the year he left Kaffirland at the head of a little procession of thirty Hottentot followers, among them Sarah, a widow with two children and his first convert.

Vanderkemp was offered a church at Graaf Reinet, but the church members there found his black converts more than they were prepared to tolerate. Another Calvinist church nearby pasted on its door a notice, *Hottentots and Dogs Forbidden to Enter.* The obstinate missionary quitted his church, in company with his black converts, and the moment he was gone the pulpit he had used at Graaf Reinet was publicly scrubbed down, to cleanse it from contamination.

Vanderkemp had a small private income – £137 16s 6d per annum, enough in those days to live on decently – so that, though often defying established authority, he could not easily be starved out. By 7 September 1801 he had brought sixty-two Hottentots together in a school. Some were runaways from servitude, but he did not propose sending them back, telling the British authorities bluntly that 'the Hottentots should be perfectly free, upon an equal footing in every respect with the Colonists, and by no sort of compulsion brought under a necessity to enter into their service, but to have a piece of ground given to them by Government as their own.' At the end of June 1801, three hundred Boers inspanned their wagons to converge on his school and destroy it – but cooled off when they saw that Vanderkemp had British dragoons within call. On 23 October the Boers came once more to Vanderkemp's school, set the building afire, shot at him, and made slaves of all the mission Hottentots they could catch.

From 1803 to 1806, in accordance with the Treaty of Amiens, the Dutch once again ruled at the Cape. Their governor, Lieutenant-General Jan Willem Janssens, was an old comrade-in-arms of Vanderkemp's, and to begin with (though his patience eventually wore away) Janssens decided to help Vanderkemp. The Hottentots were given a large tract of land near the Kaffir border – ten miles in circumference, but with brackish water and a sick soil which grew nothing but scrub. Vanderkemp called the place Bethelsdorp. When the local Boers all stuck together and

refused to sell Vanderkemp seed-corn, his old comrade the governor sent him seventy sacks. By 1804, there were 320 to feed at
Bethelsdorp, of whom 43 were church members. Their first and
second year's crops failed, and they were scratching the barest
living by pasturing sheep and goats on the scrub. Hottentots and
missionaries alike lived in fifty or so little beehive-shaped reed
huts. Vanderkemp's hut was eight feet square. They all ate together, and he was discovering, so he told a visitor, 'how little
was necessary to support life'.

James Read, who had gone as a missionary to Tahiti on *Duff*'s
second voyage and been captured by a French privateer, fetched
up at the Cape as Vanderkemp's assistant at Bethelsdorp. Read
very soon 'fixed his choice', as the London Missionary Society
was civilly informed, 'on a young Hottentot girl, the inventory
of whose possessions is two sheepskins and a string of beads to
ornament her body'. Vanderkemp married the incongruous lovers
without turning a hair.

To the shocked young prig who is our eyewitness of Bethelsdorp at this time, Vanderkemp's personal appearance was almost
as reprehensible as Read's private marital arrangements. He wore,
we are told, no hat or stockings, no shirt and no neckcloth, only
a threadbare black coat and Hottentot sandals on his bare feet.
Soldier, physician and parson, the organizer of Bethelsdorp was
reported as being 'mild, placable, and ingenuous, hospitable' but
not as a type to get on in the world, 'lavish of his present stores,
and careless of making provision for the future'. But Vanderkemp,
in fact, while spending his own money freely to keep Bethelsdorp
going, had also begun putting his wits to work to increase its
prosperity. He soon had Hottentots burning lime and boiling
soap. The women made baskets and the girls learned how to
knit socks – much in demand with the soldiers of the nearby
British garrison. Vanderkemp even turned the brackish water
supply to advantage by damming a salt pan four miles by two,
and selling 10,000 bushels of salt for £400 in five months.

Maltreated Hottentots knew they could always find a refuge
at Bethelsdorp. What they principally learned there was to live
and work in common, to share and share alike. Thus, instead of
helping to keep the Hottentots quiet, as Governor Janssens had

hoped, Bethelsdorp in a rural society depending on forced labour was becoming a menace. In 1805 the governor, after forbidding the missionaries at Bethelsdorp to teach the Hottentots to read and write, recalled them to Cape Town, where they were kept under surveillance as 'pro-English'. The Cape was expecting invasion.

In 1806, a fleet of sixty-three ships landed an expeditionary force. Sir David Baird won the battle of Blueberg, and the Cape was thereafter British. For Vanderkemp this meant that from now on, in a crisis, he could go over the heads of local officials and appeal directly to his influential friends at Clapham and in Parliament. While compelled to stay in Cape Town, Vanderkemp had not wasted his time. He ministered to the slaves there. He wrote one book on *The Theodicy of St Paul* and another, a practical handbook much needed in remote farms, on midwifery. He was already printer and publisher, in 1802, of South Africa's first book – a spelling-book with 3138 monosyllables. But he also fell in love.

From the remnants of his little fortune he raised £670 to buy out of slavery a Malagasy woman and four of her children, fathers unknown. Vanderkemp, by then fifty-eight, had his eye on her seventeen-year-old daughter. This time James Read performed the ceremony, and of Vanderkemp's second marriage three sons and a daughter were born. Decent society at the time was horrified, and missionary historians have been uneasy ever since.

The British allowed Vanderkemp to go back to his work at Bethelsdorp – by 1809 there were 979 living there. Now there was no one to stop the Hottentots from learning to read and write, so that, next to the smithy and the carpenter's shop at Bethelsdorp, there was soon a library. Then the Hottentots ran into trouble. The law passed in the British Parliament in 1807 making the trade in slaves illegal was applied also in South Africa. This meant that Boer farmers could no longer recruit their herdsmen by the cheap and expeditious method of kidnapping them. But Hottentots must somehow be compelled to go to work on Boer farms, so the Pass Laws were invented. When moving from place to place, a Hottentot not carrying an official certificate could at once be put to forced labour. Another proclamation, in 1812, allowed a farmer to claim, at the age of eight, any Hottentot child 'born on his premises' and use him 'as an apprentice' for ten years thereafter. Hottentot labour was also winkled out of Bethelsdorp by sending the men there to work without pay on the roads, or for the army. In 1814 a tax was levied, called the *opgaef*, cleverly gauged to take two-thirds of the earnings of any Hottentot who took refuge in Bethelsdorp.

'Vanderkemp is a worthy man,' exclaimed Britain's Colonial Secretary, Lord Liverpool, when appealed to in 1811, 'but an enthusiast!' Asked point blank by a Cape magistrate if he 'did not consider it his duty to compel Hottentots to labour', Vanderkemp had replied, 'No, sir. The Hottentots are recognized to be a free people, and the colonists have no more right to force them into labour in the way you propose than you have to sell them as slaves.' The tale was sedulously put about that Bethelsdorp was a hotbed of venereal disease. When Kaffirs, the traditional enemies of the Boers, began also seeking sanctuary in Bethelsdorp, Vanderkemp was officially ordered to keep them out. His answer was a defiance. 'God has sent me, not to put chains upon the legs of Hottentots and Kaffirs, but to preach liberty to the captives.'

Yet this continual harassment was wearing Vanderkemp down. He died of apoplexy on 19 December 1811, and on his deathbed he was planning a new mission somewhere else – in Madagascar, where his wife and her mother and their children might all feel more at home.

Neil Livingston was a tenant farmer on a small island off Mull. In 1791, like many other poor and hard-working Highland Scots in those times when the textile trades were booming, he was evicted to make way for a sheep-run. Livingston went to Glasgow, and eight miles outside the city, at Blantyre, he found work in a cotton mill. He managed to apprentice his son as a tailor, and thus got him out of the mill, but his grandson David, born in 1813, was sent to work when he was ten years old, as a cotton piecer, from six in the morning until eight at night, on six days a week.

David Livingston's father and mother and their five children lived in one tenement room, fourteen feet by ten. Of the workers in the Blantyre Mills, three-quarters were children. So hard did they work that during five of the least prosperous years the cotton trade had so far known, James Monteith, the owner, managed to amass a personal fortune of £80,000.

The mill was steam-heated to over 80° Fahrenheit. Each cotton spinner had three piecers – children like David – who ran under the machinery to knot broken ends together. If a child's attention flagged, the spinner applied the strap, or doused him with cold water. Thus, at ten years old, Livingston was already walking to and fro, with bent back, in a tropical atmosphere, a daily distance of twenty miles. This was his training as an explorer.

When he finished work at eight o'clock, Livingston trotted off to night school until ten. Often, in their one small room, his mother had to snatch the book from him at midnight, and put the light out. After six hours' sleep, the boy would go back to the mill. In this cruelly obstinate way, he began his intellectual training as a medical missionary.

A cotton mill was a licentious place, but David's father was an earnest Presbyterian. As well as taking refuge every night in books, the boy could look forward to the tranquillity of Sunday, when they all wore their best clothes and lived their religion. At eleven, David Livingston began to learn Latin. At twelve, with the living hell of a *laissez-faire* cotton mill crowding up daily against his boyish senses, he began to be afraid of being damned. He was about seventeen when a radical revival stirred up the less prosperous, more plebeian members of the Scots kirk – coinciding with a wave of political dissent as the campaign for the Reform Act agitated Scotland – and this revival gave emphasis less to old-fashioned Calvinist damnation than to doctrines of atonement. Predestination which divided the world of men into a minority of saved, and a mass who were hopelessly doomed, began at last to be discredited. Even a young factory worker on the hellish margin of society, like David Livingston, might – so these evangelically inclined kirk ministers implied – be saved by grace.

The same men went on to attack the link, in Scotland, between kirk and state, and they condemned slavery. Science was becoming a word of authority, and the philanthropic idea of foreign missions was in the air: someone else was more wretched than you were; you might save him.

Livingston's father dismissed science out of hand as ungodly, but at nineteen, David came across an eccentric Scots astronomer called Thomas Dick, who in *The Philosophy of a Future State* claimed to have reconciled science and religion. Young Livingston went to see him, and the scientific attitude – accurate, methodical, based on measurement and drained of feeling – henceforth took on importance in his way of looking at the world.

For a Scot trapped in a mill there were several ways out, all depending on thrift, will, energy and self-reliance, and the forswearing of debilitating sins like drink and women. Self-education was one such, emigration to America another. David Livingston tried in vain to persuade his parents to emigrate. He then made up his mind to try for medicine, but his father would consent only if he put medicine to the service of God. Luckily, a call came for medical missionaries to go to China, where less religiously inclined Scots were just then making large and notorious fortunes in the opium trade. Young Livingston decided for China.

To arrive in Glasgow in time for his first medical lecture, he had to rise at five and walk for three hours, often through snow. In his college vacations, Livingston went back to work as a spinner in the mill. Surgery in those days was without anaesthetic, dissection was in its infancy, and little was known of tropical medicine; David Livingston, when he qualified at the age of twenty-seven, knew more medicine than an African witch-doctor, but not all that much more. At least, he had shaken off the rigid and fearful Calvinistic theology which haunted his childhood. He went to theological college in England, and managed to scrape through, despite his inaudible sermons, harsh features and lack of scholarly polish. He was ordained at a Congregational church in Finsbury on 20 November 1840, and offered his services to the London Missionary Society. The first Opium War had blocked access to China, so David Livingston was sent to Africa.

Christian missionaries, Nestorian or Catholic, had gone down the long overland trade route from the Mediterranean to China both in classical antiquity and again in the fourteenth century, and managed to make some headway there. But the Chinese churches they then set going hardly survived the persecutions begun by the Ming dynasty after 1386.

When the Manchu came to power in 1644, they needed expert help in astronomy for fixing the calendar, and in other techniques such as gunfounding, and they turned to the Jesuits, thus giving the Society of Jesus their great missionary opportunity in China. By the beginning of the nineteenth century, when the Jesuits were dispersed, and the Manchu also had begun to persecute, Chinese Roman Catholics numbered about 200,000 though by this time Christianity was illegal.

The Manchu were doing their best to limit China's contact with the world outside to one trading station at Canton, and an annual overland caravan into Russia. So the Protestant missionaries arriving by sea could make their way inland only when China had been 'opened up' as a market. Thus mainland China in modern times was made accessible to Christian doctrines, paradoxically enough, chiefly because of military victories won between 1830 and 1860 by Britain and France in the two Opium Wars. An immense missionary effort was made thereafter, particularly by America. But by the men who in our own day were to unite and modernize China, Christian converts were viewed with suspicion, and persecution in recent years has again been severe.

David Livingston had first been won over to the idea of work as a medical missionary in China by the persuasiveness of Dr Gutzlaff, a missionary of ambiguous antecedents who in the first Opium War had served Britain as an intelligence agent. Had he gone to China, as first planned, David Livingston whether he liked it or not would have been the beneficiary of a government drawing large revenues from the opium trade, and this could not but have compromised him. In Africa, he was to have a freer hand.

Seven thousand Boers had trekked north from the Cape since Vanderkemp's time, to escape British legislation against slavery.

They settled in two small, land-locked republics, the Orange
Free State and the Transvaal. Missionaries, too, had gone deeper
inland, skirting the barren western flanks of these republics, to
Griqualand and beyond. The Boers still wanted the blacks in
servitude as cattlemen; the missionaries still maintained Vanderkemp's splendid tradition of defending them.

Kuruman, in sun-baked Bechuanaland, was a far outpost, run
since 1821 by another self-educated Scot, Robert Moffat, once a
gardener. His isolated little community was regarded as a famous
missionary enterprise, but Livingston, who had taken two
months to reach Kuruman by ox-cart from the coast, found it
disappointing. Publicity in England had painted Moffat's mission
in more glowingly idealistic colours than the humdrum reality.
The place was so small as almost to seem futile – only about
a thousand people lived within a ten-mile radius of Kuruman.
Robert Moffat, six feet tall, his long beard streaked with grey,
played the familiar role of philosopher-king, though a dour one.
Moffat was of the same generation as the artisan-missionaries on
Tahiti, and shared most of their preconceptions. When he retired,
in 1870, Moffat boasted, 'In former times the natives could not be
prevailed upon to buy anything from traders in the shape of
merchandise, not even so much as a pocket handkerchief. . . .
Now, no less a sum than sixty thousand pounds' worth of British
manufactures pass yearly into the hands of the native tribes in
and about Kuruman.'

To introduce his people by easy stages to this world of money,
Moffat had built stone houses, irrigated orchards, made soap and
clothes. He had opened a school and was translating the Bible,
but the lack of challenge in this well-established missionary
settlement irked Livingston. Three hundred and fifty attended
service, there were forty communicants, but most of the locals
had not yet succumbed, contending that the new religion was only
a trick to get them to give up their wives. The stumbling block
here, too, was polygamy. Wives were a measure of a man's
importance; they did his donkey-work. To undermine polygamy
was to break up the inherited structure of the tribe. But Moffat
saw polygamy as sensual self-indulgence, and rebuked their
'ignorance, their degradation and their wallowing in wickedness'.

Livingston was not a man to relish life very much in the shadow of another, older, somewhat less intelligent and already celebrated missionary. 'I shall preach the gospel beyond every other man's line of things,' he soon announced. He founded a new mission station 200 miles to the north, near the Limpopo river, buying a tract of land there a mile long and half a mile wide for some beads and a gun worth £4. Eventually, in 1846, he settled further north with the Bechuana, under their chief, Sechele.

They raised cattle and grew maize, but drought was an affliction. Livingston got them digging irrigation ditches, paying them in tea, sugar and beads. When he knelt down to pray, they thought he was talking to God underground. As he gained insight into the way their thoughts and habits corresponded with the harsh needs of their everyday life, Livingston slowly became uneasy about the glib dogmas which in London roused such enthusiasm among rich evangelicals and encouraged them to dig deep into their pockets. He began to see that every tribal practice, however bizarre, might have a rational function. 'Those who have gone to circumcision together', he pointed out, as an example, 'are bound in a cohort under one of the chief's sons or brothers for ever after.'

All the virtues recommended by prospering folk in early industrial society as respectable – thrift, hard work, buying cheap and selling dear, personal ambition, monogamous marriage – were held in Bechuanaland to be vices. Generosity was the prime virtue. Anyone who tried to sell a surplus of food at a profit would have been cut dead. Notions of sin and salvation were well-nigh inconceivable. The resurrection of the dead was thought in Bechuanaland to be a particularly distressing idea – were the enemies they had gone to such pains to kill in battle one day to rise from their graves again, spear in hand?

To a man with Livingston's insight into the African's mind, Moffat's translation of the Bible into Sichuana must have been galling. Moffat had felt obliged to translate 'holiness' by the word used with hearty approval to praise the fatness of a cow. 'Sin' was the word more commonly used for cow dung. There was only one expression in Sichuana for 'love', and it signified the carnal act with no overtone whatever of agape, so the 'love of God', in Moffat's translation, signified a hearty carnal embrace.

The word chosen to render 'soul' was the word in use for steam coming out of a pot.

Bred up in the precocious sexual hothouse of a cotton mill, Livingston for all his strength of will had a personal problem, too. Some missionaries in Griqualand had continued Vanderkemp's example and taken black wives – or mistresses – but to Livingston black women were never appetizing: 'I cannot conceive of any European being so far captivated with them as to covet criminal intercourse.' And how Moffat would have condemned such a lapse! Moreover, Moffat had a twenty-three-year-old daughter, Mary, 'a little, thick, black haired girl, sturdy'.

'The daughters of missionaries', Livingston sardonically noted, 'have miserable contracted minds.' Not long after he had made his marriage of convenience, he was writing another and more pathetic note: 'I should like to commence being more of a Jesuit – O, that I could begin again!' By then it was too late for regrets, and soon David Livingston was dragging sturdy little Mary Moffat north across the appalling desert, pregnant, to his mission station, where ticks and lice abounded, and for much of the year the water failed.

The chief there, Sechele, was intelligent. He had learned the entire alphabet in one day. Cleanliness was another new discovery. He would stand in a tub for his wives to soap him down, and he liked wearing European clothes, particularly a suit of formal cut made up for him from leopard skins. When Livingston first arrived, Sechele offered to tell his head men to fetch their whips and flog the entire tribe into a belief in Christianity.

For Sechele, giving up his wives was the obstacle. Could he be counted as a Christian, he wanted to know, if he 'acted justly, fairly avoided fighting, treated both his own people and strangers kindly, killed witches and prayed to God?' There were well-intentioned misunderstandings on both sides. Livingston managed to persuade Sechele that rain-making was superstitious, and then had to bear the blame for the long drought which followed.

Sechele wanted to use the missionaries as a counterweight to his mortal enemies, the Boers, who regarded his people as 'black property' and raided into their tribal lands, from their republic across the Vaal river. The Boers needed child 'apprentices' to run their cattle for them, the younger the better, since a boy 'apprentice' so young that his memories of home could be driven out of his mind was more biddable.

The worst Boer raid against Sechele's people robbed them of 3000 cattle and 200 women and children. The Boer commandant in the Transvaal wrote warning Livingston that no further missionary advance might be made without his permission. The Boers also dropped an amiable hint that, in future, the missionaries might do better trying to convert the baboons.

What the Boers feared most was that, with missionary connivance, the threatened tribes might procure guns to defend themselves. The direct accusation was made that Livingston had provided Sechele's people with firearms, and to a Cape newspaper he wrote a denial which was so carefully phrased that it might just as well mean its opposite: 'If you can prove that I either *lent* or *sold* or *gave* a gun to Sechele, I shall willingly leave the country.' Yet in February 1846 David Livingston is confiding to his father-in-law, Moffat, that 'Sechele is greatly in love with your rifles'. He had also managed to lay hands on a stock of gunpowder left behind by a big-game hunter. To Joseph Sturge, a Quaker politically influential in England, Livingston wrote to justify arming the Africans. Already Livingston was moving away from the specifically religious activities of which his missionary society approved – the counting up of baptisms and conversions – towards a kind of moralized individualist politics.

The heat at the mission was appalling: a thermometer buried three inches in the soil measured 132° Fahrenheit at midday. Mary Livingston had five children by her husband in six years – 'crowds of flies continually settled on the eyes of our poor little brats' – and in what spare time she might snatch from her own family his wife ran an infant school for eighty other children. Livingston's own day was an incessant round of work, intellectual and manual – 'my hands have the same aching sensation I had when spinning.'

The black Africans took no heed for the morrow – but was that unchristian? 'There is no pressing necessity apparent to those', Livingston noted, 'whose wants are few, they take the world easy.' Africans found it 'extremely difficult' to accept the usefulness of machinery or money. And so, too, with education: 'The Art of writing is very curious, but of what use is it to those who can send all their messages viva voce?' The Africans among whom he lived, admitted Livingston, showed 'more intelligence than is to be met with in our own uneducated peasantry'. He was on a treadmill of mission work and family life, with more than one ironic echo of the Blantyre Mills he had struggled so valiantly to escape. He had grave inner doubts as to the real usefulness of what was expected of him by the London Missionary Society, and he took scientific notes of the fauna and flora, as an anodyne for his troubled state of mind.

Then came a chance of release. In 1849, Livingston met William Cotton Oswell, a well-to-do public-school man, who after ten years in the Indian Civil Service had come here to Africa for his own amusement. Oswell wanted to explore, taking Livingston with him as guide, interpreter and companion; he was willing to pay. So they crossed the Kalahari desert, travelling only in the evening and early morning, their eighty oxen sometimes plodding seventy miles at a stretch between one waterhole and the next. Together they found and mapped Lake Ngami.

The Royal Geographical Society gave Livingston a prize for his share in this discovery. The missionary movement fed on publicity, so his employers, the London Missionary Society, were by no means displeased. Livingston had tasted fame, and wanted more. Only why share the credit, next time?

In 1850, he dragged his pregnant wife and young family north to Ngami. When the children were mosquito-bitten and caught malaria, he wrote coldly to Moffat, 'It is an interesting fever. I should like to have a hospital here, to study it.' The new baby was born, and died. 'Just as likely to happen', said David Livingston, 'if we had remained at home, and now we have one of our number in heaven.' The ordeals undergone by the wives and families of certain missionaries began to sound, at last, like quiet arguments for clerical celibacy.

Livingston, as he pushed northward to the upper reaches of the Zambezi river, was coming towards an inland country where tribal life had been devastated over the years by slavers based in the Portuguese colonies of Mozambique and Angola, and even by Arab slave raiders moving down from the north. Despite the British naval blockade, 50,000 Africans were being shipped across the Atlantic every year, to Brazil, Cuba and the southern United States, where slavery was still legal.

Though the French had formally abolished slavery in 1848, slaves for the French sugar island of Réunion continued to be bought, surreptitiously, until about 1861, under a 'Free Labour Emigration Scheme'. Slaves were bought on the African coast, 'freed', then shipped to the plantations, where they worked for five years under 'supervision'. One Marseilles house supplied 25,000 blacks under contract to Réunion in two years. There might technically be no 'slavery' in French Réunion, any more than there was in Australia, but a consequence of this method was that the slave trade flourished in the heart of Africa.

As Livingston soon discerned, the African chiefs who went to war for captives they could then sell to the slave dealers, did so because their material needs were growing – they wanted guns, tools, beads, cloth – yet all that tribal society produced was human beings. But the violent incursion of the professional slaver broke up the structure of the tribe, which had been the Africans' psychological citadel, bringing fear, anxiety, insecurity. They were therefore becoming all the more ready to accept what consolation a Christian missionary might have to offer.

Now suppose – reasoned Livingston – that the great River Zambezi, which reached the sea in Portuguese territory yet penetrated deep into Africa, could be used as a highway for peaceful trade? If only trade could be developed here in central Africa in some other product besides human beings, then the economic needs of the tribe could be met without bloodshed, war and suffering. It must be borne in mind that when such ideas as these began to germinate in Livingston's mind, the whole interior of Africa from Timbuctu to the Zambezi was a blank on the map.

A similar idea had been tried out in 1841, on the west coast, by the Society for the Extinction of the Slave Trade and for the Civilization of Africa. They sent three steamers, *Albert, Sudan* and *Wilberforce*, up the Niger, Samuel Crowther going with them as interpreter. Livingston himself, when a medical student, had heard Thomas Fowell Buxton, Wilberforce's successor, explain to an enthusiastic meeting in Exeter Hall that year that 'it is the Bible and the plough that must regenerate Africa'. The British government invested nearly £80,000 in the venture. The Quakers gave the expedition £4,000 for a model farm.

But 'a fever of a most malignant character' broke out in *Albert*, which none the less got 300 miles upriver and set the model farm ashore. *Sudan* and *Wilberforce* had meanwhile turned back; 130 of the 145 Europeans contracted malaria; forty died. The model farm managed to grow a little cotton, then collapsed; the enterprise up the Niger had been a dismal failure. But if a similar expedition up the Zambezi should do better, commerce and Christianity together might cut the ground from under the slave-traders' feet. Livingston himself saw 'the advance of ruthless colonists' as a 'terrible necessity'. But British businessmen – many of them his co-religionists – he looked upon hopefully, despite his boyhood experiences at Blantyre Mills, as being, in comparison with businessmen elsewhere, 'the most upright and benevolent in the world'. The Africans were feckless as Highland clansmen had once been, but Livingston had every reason to think that they would attain his own pitch of civilization 'by a long contin- ued discipline and contact with superior races by commerce'. Had not the same cruel but salutary process fetched his family off their lonely croft, and got him by the scruff of the neck out of the cotton mill – made him a physician and a minister of religion? 'I might have been a common soldier, a day labourer, a factory operative or a mechanic,' he once observed, 'instead of a missionary.'

In 1852, Livingston, intent upon his new enterprise, took his long-suffering wife and children down to the Cape – a six- months' journey – and put them on a ship for England. Though perfectly fluent in the native tongue, his children could hardly speak English, and they were so unnerved by the first stairs they met that they came down backwards. Livingston, who had in mind a feat of exploration which might make him famous and listened to, instructed his children henceforth to regard Jesus as their father. ('I have given you back to Him, and you are in His care.') Mary, once in England, vagabonded from one set of furnished lodgings to another, and took to the consolation of the bottle. Her husband, as if to mark a point of departure in his own life, adopted the poetic whimsy from this time on of spelling his name with a final 'e': *Livingstone* – a living stone.

In 1852, David Livingstone, having shed the encumbrance of his family, headed inland from the Cape. He left Linyote on the Chobe, a Zambezi tributary, on 11 November 1853, travelling with twenty-seven Africans of the Makolo tribe, and he reached the Atlantic coast at Loanda, half-starved, dysenteric, feverish, on 31 May 1854. Though this was a great feat in itself, Livingstone then turned about and crossed the continent once again, in the other direction, from west to east. He traced much of the course of the Zambezi as it flowed towards the Indian Ocean, and in 1856 reached civilization, among the slave-traders of Mozambique. Since leaving his family at the Cape he had travelled 6000 miles, on an exploration which had filled in accurately an enormous blank space on the map. He had set up a great landmark in African exploration.

Livingstone's purpose had been not only to bring back scientific and geographical information, but above all to find a commercial route into the heart of Africa which might undermine the slave trade there and blaze a way for missions. He had financed this enormous journey on his £100 a year from the London Missionary Society – which, having just then a £13,000 overdraft, had formed the opinion that whether Livingstone succeeded or died in the attempt, the publicity might well do them good.

'I am serving Christ when shooting a buffalo for my men,' Livingstone argued, 'or taking an astronomical observation.' In three years he had suffered twenty-seven attacks of fever, which he treated with a ferocious laxative of his own concoction, afterwards sold commercially as 'Livingstone's Rousers'. He derided those who were 'unmanned' by fever: 'If God has accepted my service then my life is charmed until my work is done.'

Livingstone's faithful horse Sinbad had gone with him 1500 miles of the way, before succumbing to the tsetse fly. Livingstone had carried with him a magic lantern, showing slides of Biblical events, to astound and divert the natives. He had kept meticulously a journal of 800 quarto pages, recording the fauna, flora, meteorology and topography of his route. In the interior he had gone across highlands that were fertile, healthy, and suitable for European settlement.

Missionary Travels and Researches in South Africa appeared just after the shameful disasters of the Crimea, the Indian Mutiny and the second Opium War, when the British were badly in need of a hero who corresponded better with their own view of themselves: a man who could be idealized. The book was a runaway success, selling 70,000 copies, and here in London was David Livingstone, cotton-spinner turned missionary, exploring scientifically in the name of Christ yet opening Africa to commerce. The Royal Geographical Society this time gave him their gold medal. Livingstone was modest, picturesque, rather inarticulate, self-made, the wise and simple doctor loved by his black followers – and behind him, echoing his pronouncements, stood the huge and powerful political constituency of evangelicalism, a force to be reckoned with, particularly in the manufacturing centres of Britain.

The government of the day hastened to agree with Dr David Livingstone that the Zambezi might well be the African commercial highway which everyone for the past half-century had been seeking. Lord John Russell, in his enthusiasm, even went so far as to order the Admiralty to transmit the prescription of Livingstone's Rousers – a formidable mixture of jalap, calomel, rhubarb and quinine – to all of Her Majesty's ships in tropical waters, as a remedy against malaria, until the Royal College of Physicians interposed to hint that if diarrhoea accompanied the fever, the remedy Livingstone habitually used on himself might well be lethal.

The Zambezi Expedition left Liverpool on 10 March 1858, with Dr Livingstone in overall command, in the 160-foot Colonial Office steamer, HMS *Pearl*. Livingstone had quietly parted company with the London Missionary Society on his appointment as HM Consul in Quilimane in Portuguese Mozambique, with £500 a year, and from now until his death he made a point of wearing his peaked, yellow-banded consular cap. Mary was obliged to wait behind in England, pregnant once again, but comforted with a 5000 guinea nest-egg: the royalties from Living-stone's best seller.

The Zambezi flows to the sea through many shallow, mosquito-infested mouths: *Pearl* spent a frustrating fortnight trying to find a channel deep enough to float her in. Livingstone had chosen not to emphasize in his book the acute discomforts of the Zambezi's feverish lower reaches – he had hoped to get his expedition upriver quickly. But soon *Pearl* was stuck, and the exploring party were obliged to transfer to the eighty-foot river launch *Ma-Robert* – the native name for Mary – soon to be nicknamed 'Old Asthmatic'.

Though *Ma-Robert* was designed to draw only three feet of water, they found that even 150 miles upstream the Zambezi was still only two feet deep. The brunt of navigating these shallows fell on Commander Norman Bedingfield, RN, a testy naval officer who had earlier been dismissed his ship for 'contemptuous and quarrelsome conduct towards a superior officer'.

Besides David Livingstone there were six other Europeans living cheek by jowl aboard Old Asthmatic – including his brother, Charles, a recently ordained minister of religion, but a bully and a sneak who had joined the expedition for no good reason, so far as the others could see. They complained that he had 'the manners of a cotton spinner', and he once outraged his shipmates by kicking an African, Glasgow-fashion, with his hob-nailed boots. 'Nothing but the high personal regard for Dr Livingstone averted bloodshed,' said a witness. 'The spear was poised.'

Of recent years Livingstone had gone exploring in the exclusive company of adoring Africans. He was ill-at-ease with men of different professions and social classes, all watching him – as commanders are invariably watched – to see if his conduct came up to his reputation. John Kirk, a twenty-seven-year-old Scots surgeon and a Crimean veteran, a judicious rather than a vindictive man who later was appointed consul in Zanzibar, several times relieved his feelings in his diary at Livingstone's expense: 'He knows how to come round niggers very well, but if his digestive system don't go all right he loses his diplomatic powers wonderfully.' Kirk saw Livingstone as apt to take 'small intense hatreds

H

. . . very narrow, I should think mean . . . ever ready to nurse suspicions'. In Livingstone they evidently had a cold, hard, touchy leader. His iron will drive them past obstacles, but he was prone to long, brooding silences, and like other heroic solitaries he was morbidly sensitive to slights.

Nor was *Ma-Robert* quite as comfortable as a gentleman's club. Crowded, feverish, overrun with cockroaches, the launch grunted its way up the Zambezi through driving rain, in a temperature of over 100° Fahrenheit, going aground time after time on sandbanks and having to be winched off. Though needing to be fuelled with several tons of hardwood a day, *Ma-Robert*'s engine was 'made to grind coffee in a shop'. Their average rate upstream was fifty miles a month. When after half a year of unending exasperation they got as far as Tete, the Portuguese settlement furthest inland, the steel plates of *Ma-Robert*'s hull were already rusting through; soon she wore thirty-five patches covering a hundred holes. Yet worse was to come.

Livingstone, when describing in print how he crossed Africa from west to east, had never made it unequivocally clear that he was not, in fact, personally familiar with the entire course of the Zambezi. Everyone in Tete had heard tell of the Kebrabasa Rapids, only sixty miles to the north-west. But Livingstone, perhaps from obstinacy, had not in the last stages of his enormous journey made the detour necessary to verify if the rapids were passable. If the Kebrabasa Rapids were as bad as they said, all his effort this far was in vain.

As *Ma-Robert*, under-powered and slowly rusting away, got closer to Kebrabasa, Livingstone began to talk boldly of crossing the rapids at high water, after heavy rain, or even blowing a way through them, with explosive. But his shipmates in *Ma-Robert* could soon see for themselves that the first cataract had an eight-foot fall in thirty yards, while just beyond was a thirty-foot fall over which water streamed at an angle of 30°. As a commercial route, the Zambezi was hardly what Livingstone had hoped or claimed, and the horrid fact could no longer be concealed. As Lord John Russell observed, when the news of Livingstone's fiasco reached his office: 'He must not be allowed to tempt us to form colonies only to be reached by forcing steamers up cataracts.'

Though as a waterway penetrating far inland the Zambezi was useless, its large tributary, the Shire, which flows eventually into Lake Nyasa, was navigable at least as far as the Murchison Falls. And thereabouts, in days yet to come, in the healthy highlands south of the lake, around a settlement to be called Blantyre in memory of Livingstone, very nearly all that he had predicted as a possible future for a central Africa freed of the slave trade was to come to pass, under the energetic philanthropic impulse of Scottish businessmen who had taken his book to heart. But this lay ahead, in the future, and was of no help to Livingstone's fading reputation in London, where the Zambezi Expedition, which had cost £50,000 and half a dozen lives, was loudly being written off. 'We were promised trade,' snorted *The Times* on 20 January 1862, 'and there is no trade. We were promised converts, and not one has been made.'

The Oxford and Cambridge Mission, led by Bishop Mackenzie – 'a jolly, rollicking set of fellows, with a great deal of the soldier in their character' – soon followed Livingstone's track into the Shire Highlands. Mackenzie had been a missionary in Natal, among the Zulus. He marched across country with a bag of seeds on his back, his crozier in one hand, and a double-barrelled shotgun in the other. Livingstone sold the jolly, rollicking young men a second-hand cotton gin: the American Civil War was making cotton desperately hard to come by. Livingstone had already hinted in his book that cotton might be procured hereabouts, but the young men found that here, too, the promise was greater than the performance: 'You cannot get as much cotton as would fill your bag if you travel for days'. Moreover, Bishop Mackenzie's mission was soon at odds with the local slave-traders.

The Portuguese at Tete had warned Livingstone not to interfere with slave caravans – which, as far as they were concerned, were legal. But the bishop had but to clap eyes on one – eighty-four newly enslaved villagers, many of them women and children, linked hands and neck in a living chain to forked slave-sticks – and his blood began to boil. Both Livingstone and Mackenzie, despite the cloth they wore, had been at different times provoked into opening fire on the region's most notorious slave-dealer, Ajawa, and Livingstone's volley killed six.

Mackenzie died not long after of malaria, so that by the time the shooting became common knowledge Livingstone, who was taking a great deal of other blame already, was left alone to bear the odium of this too. Early in 1863, a crowded meeting in the Sheldonian agreed with the saintly Dr Pusey that, rather than kill his enemies with a gun, a missionary should accept martyrdom. Neither as a leader of men nor as an exponent of his faith had Dr Livingstone measured up to the highflown picture which he had allowed others to create for him, for their own ends. When he got back to London at last, Livingstone found himself cold-shouldered.

But he was still a uniquely experienced African traveller, and the Royal Geographical Society offered him £500 to go and investigate the problem of the central African watershed. Rivers flowed outwards from that great chain of African lakes – Tanganyika, Kivu, Victoria, Mweru, Nyasa. Might one or other of them be a source of the Nile? Of the Congo perhaps? Lord John Russell offered Livingstone a solatium of £500 and an honorary consulship with neither pay nor pension. James Young, the inventor of paraffin, once Livingstone's fellow-student at Glasgow and now a rich man, advanced him £1000 to help him on his way. Mary was dead, and Livingstone's nest-egg was to vanish in a bank collapse. His entire life of cruel effort had so far been predicated upon success. Now, mercifully, he was being offered one last chance.

African lakes were often used as convenient routes by Arab slave traders, who shipped their victims across in dhows before marching them in long files down to the coast. The best known East African slave mart was on the offshore island of Zanzibar; by 1845, the Sultan was making £20,000 a year from his percentage. Livingstone might therefore reasonably hope that while he busied himself elucidating the geography of Africa's rift valley, his mission of some day replacing slavery by trade under a Christian aegis might never be lost from sight.

The source of the Nile had been a problem since antiquity. Livingstone was ambitious to solve it chiefly as 'a means of opening my mouth with power among men'. Sir Richard Burton, who since Speke died had put himself forward as the authority on the headwaters of the Nile, detested Livingstone both as a rival explorer and as a missionary who defied the advanced thought of the time by sentimentally treating black men as human equals.

Burton was a widely travelled man, intensely curious of native customs, and well able to cut a figure at the time in the Anthropological Society. He is now best remembered for the lewdly informative footnotes he added to his translation of *The Arabian Nights* – a set of books our forebears kept carefully locked away from the children in a glass-fronted bookcase. Burton had travelled from the coast up to the African lakes in style, with never less than 130 bearers, and a harem of black beauties. A cruel, swaggering man, he liked Arabs, and would amuse himself by advancing ironic arguments in favour of slavery, but he treated missionaries as a joke, and openly despised black Africans as 'unprogressive and unfit for social change'. There was a shady side to the character of this adventure-seeking pornographer ('systematically wicked, impure and untruthful' in Livingstone's opinion). Livingstone and Burton were Jekyll and Hyde; in the eyes of their contemporaries, if one were right the other must be wrong.

In 1866, the *Anthropological Review* dubbed Livingstone's well-advertised sympathy for Africans as the opinion of a 'poor naked mind bedaubed with the chalk and red ochre of Scotch theology, and with a threadbare tattered waistcoat of education hanging round him'. Livingstone, the first time he was given a chance, riposted about his black friends thus: 'Anyone who lives among them forgets they are black, and feels they are just fellow men. If a comparison were instituted, and Manyuema, taken at random, placed opposite say the members of the Anthropological Society of London, clad like them in kilts of grass cloth, I should like to take my place among the Manyuema, on the principle of preferring the company of my betters.' Both men claimed to represent the scientific attitude, and perhaps neither did; the difference in attitude dividing them goes back to Las Casas and Sepúlveda – or even beyond, to Aristotle and St Augustine.

Travellers in East Africa had to buy their way, paying local chiefs a wayleave of cloth or beads, for the right to plod the narrow footpaths linking villages. A string of beads bought an egg; ten strings a chicken. A caravan was made up of a proportion of armed men, and the bearers, each carrying between forty and seventy pounds weight of necessities or trade goods. The pace was slow: about a hundred miles a month. Livingstone and his handful of followers, in his famous journey across the continent, had travelled further to the south, where conditions were different. This time, moreover, he was not very generously financed, so he went up from the East African coast short of trade goods and with dangerously few men – twenty-three porters and thirteen sepoys. Soon he dismissed his sepoys, as if to make it abundantly clear that this time he had no intention of relying on violence.

Livingstone's iron physique was no longer what it had been. He was suffering the consequence of dosing himself for years with strong aperients, thus no doubt exasperating a temperament naturally irritable, and when back in Britain he had neglected to undergo a necessary operation for piles. Some of his porters tried to bribe the Somali guide, ben Ali, to go astray on purpose and lead the party back to the coast. On 20 January 1867 the man who carried the medicine chest ran off with it, and Livingstone wrote, 'I felt as if I had now received the sentence of death.' One by one they deserted, excusing their own cowardice when back in Zanzibar by reporting Livingstone dead. He had only a loyal handful of followers, and almost no trade goods to pay his way. Other Europeans used to keep the caravan together with whip, gun and slave-chain. Livingstone held the view that since his porters were not slaves, they should be allowed to go off when they chose.

Along trails between Zanzibar and the inland lakes he passed through burnt-out and abandoned villages, and was often haunted by the sight of corpses – captives, who in the march down to the coast had straggled and been killed out of hand for it, as an example to the others. His physical difficulties multiplied and Livingstone drifted into a silent dream, in which his boyhood reading at the cotton mill came back to him with particular vividness. He was obsessed by a need to reconcile his researches with the accounts of the Nile's sources provided by Ptolemy and Herodotus. He did not look too intently in directions where discoveries might have been made which, though geographically accurate, might contradict Herodotus who, following an

Egyptian legend, had placed the great river's source in marshy land, inhabited by pigmies, near a great river infested by crocodiles, and flowing from west to east. Moses also loomed large in his mind: 'An eager desire to discover any evidence of the great Moses' having visited these parts spellbound me.' To his other and more humdrum motives had been added a yearning 'to confirm the Sacred Oracles'.

The Arab-organized traffic in slaves was efficiently combined with a trade in East Africa's other valuable and portable commodity, ivory. Linked by the forked slave-stick to his neighbour, a captive was also a pack-animal capable of carrying a tusk of ivory, which at Zanzibar would fetch about £25. As pianos and billiard tables multiplied in suburban villas, the demand for ivory in Europe had become insatiable.

Though obliged to live off goat's milk – having by this time no teeth, and no digestion any more for solid food – Livingstone went on doggedly with his scientific investigations, discovering Lake Bangweulu, and coming at last, beyond Lake Tanganyika, upon a great river flowing north, which the natives called the Lualaba. Livingstone mistook the Lualaba for an upper reach of the Nile. Further downstream, however, the Lualaba swings west, not north, and eventually reaches the Atlantic; the Lualaba was in fact the Congo.

On 14 March 1869 Livingstone at last reached Ujiji, 'a ruckle of bones'. Arab slavers had lived there for thirty years. With its flat-roofed, Mediterranean-looking houses and cool courtyards, its white-robed, dignified inhabitants and its irrigated agriculture, worked by slave labour, Ujiji though in the heart of primitive Africa had a misleading air of calm and civilized organization. The supplies which Livingstone expected to find sent up for him to Ujiji had been pillaged. He was at the end of his resources.

Arab slave-traders were often cultivated men, intent in their religion, and considered the Islamic culture which they themselves had established at Ujiji and elsewhere as exactly the type of civilization most suitable for Africa: the view still obtains. Having Livingstone dependent on their goodwill suited them very well. They respected his eccentric single-mindedness, but they took him for a British spy, since they knew that the Sultan of

Zanzibar, who controlled their outlet to the sea, was under pressure these days from the British. The doctor was their hostage; they made the best of it.

Their commercial activities made Livingstone's flesh creep. Yet they treated him better than they might have done, and one of them, Mohammed Bogharib, the 'gentleman slaver', gave him proofs of friendship. But in their promises to convey Livingstone's letters to Consul Kirk in Zanzibar, they were disingenuous. Of the forty-four letters which Livingstone wrote, only one arrived. It took a year, and asked above all else for stimulants: fifty pounds of coffee, six bottles of port wine, and the ingredients, jalap, calomel, quinine, necessary to concoct Livingstone's Rousers.

The last thing Livingstone wished was to go back home, broken in health, penniless, and with his geographical mission incomplete – for then, who would ever listen to him again? To continue his journeys of investigation he must pay his way with trade goods. Three followers still stuck by him. But the Arabs at Ujiji – the representatives of all he most detested – had broken his line of communication to the coast, up which Kirk might have sent supplies. The slave-traders held him in thrall; the 'great doctor' was both their guest and their prisoner.

From the very start, the abolitionist movement in Britain had experimented cleverly with the devices of the modern public-relations man. The missionary societies which later stepped into their shoes were no less adroit at publicity. Records of 'conversions' submitted to headquarters from missionary stations all over the globe were scrutinized and publicized as if they were cricket results. And whenever a missionary could be turned into a living legend, or a martyr, money flowed in freely.

By the 1870s, old-style evangelical support for foreign missions, based on confidence in Britain as the workshop of the world, had begun to ebb. Germany, France and the United States had set up industries of their own which, technically, were often more up-to-date. The frenzied search was soon to begin for African colonies which might become both sources of raw materials and markets from which competitors could be excluded. This new epoch – the brief, giddy heyday of world-wide imperialism – very much needed to find its tone of voice, its particular moral justification and its hero. And here, for Britain, was Livingstone – physician, explorer, man of the people and man of science, yet man of God, but also heartily in favour (and for the most exalted reasons) of the spread of modern commerce. Alive or dead, Dr David Livingstone was a missionary hero easily adaptable to the propaganda needs of the immediate future, even though the image the publicists were setting themselves to create might only approximately resemble the man himself.

Deserters from Livingstone's caravan had saved face on reaching the coast by reporting him dead, but they were not quite believed. In London there were obituaries, but also an intriguing rumour that Livingstone had gone native at last, and married an African princess. In fact, after being stuck at Ujiji for nearly two years, Livingstone had managed in 1871 to get away from the Arab traders who were keeping an eye on him, and attack once more the great geographical problem set by the rivers near Lake Tanganyika. Was the Lualaba the Nile? Or might the sources described by Herodotus be further south, in the Katanga country?

Livingstone was in an African market-place called Nyangwe, on the banks of the Lualaba river, in March 1871 when Arab raiders arrived. The place was crowded, and a horrifyingly deliberate massacre of womenfolk began. Here under Livingstone's very eyes was a sample of the terror used to stupefy the Arabs' unhappy captives, and send them stumbling away, heart-broken and submissive, on the long march to the coast, as merchandise. 'Men', reflected Livingstone as he watched, 'are worse than beasts of prey.' He 'had the impression he was in hell'.

Livingstone got back to Ujiji in October. On the 28th in marched a magnificently equipped caravan, led by a man with a heavy moustache. He was ready for anything, his porters even carried a folding boat; he was an American reporter called H. M. Stanley. Whether his greeting, 'Doctor Livingstone, I presume,' was a journalistic witticism thought up in advance, or a measure of the diffidence with which the two men first began to sound each other out, may only be surmised. Stanley travelled in a style hardly displayed before in East Africa, even by Sir Richard Burton, and his motives were a travesty of Livingstone's, yet the two men were not long in discovering an emotional link of common experience.

Stanley had whipped his 192 porters up from the coast with such brutal effectiveness that they marched the 500 miles in only three months. He left nothing whatever to chance: his men carried six tons of stores, including twenty miles of cloth, a million beads, forty guns. What these two exiled men, one by origin Scottish, one born in Wales, found that they principally shared was the devastated childhood so often characteristic of the early industrial age – Livingstone suffering in a cotton mill, Stanley in that other prison for the unlucky poor, a Victorian workhouse. Both were self-educated, both in their different ways were self-made men; thus far, personal experience might unite them. Yet the gap dividing them was greater than the lapse in time between one generation and the next. For the great newspaper-reading public, Stanley might avidly sentimentalize and mythicize everything that Livingstone hoped he stood for, but, at heart, Stanley was an imperialist of the new generation.

Stanley in his subsequent career gave no sign of loving his neighbour whether black or white, nor indeed did he so much as hint at a private religious belief which might have articulated such a love. Like most of those who henceforth were to transform the map of Africa – Cecil Rhodes, Carl Peters, Frederick Lugard – he knew well enough how to make use of black men to his own greatest advantage. He might not enslave, but he knew how to exploit. He had a cruel streak, but there was a reason.

Stanley had been locked up in the workhouse at St Asaph when he was five. At the age of fifteen, he knocked down the brutal workhouse-master – a man later declared insane – and escaped. He shipped out of Liverpool to New Orleans as a cabin boy and, at twenty-one, joined the Confederate army. Livingstone's eldest son Robert, too, had run away to America, and after enlisting in the civil war had died in a Confederate prison. Livingstone was soon speaking of Stanley, emotionally, as 'braving death and danger to serve me as a son might have done'.

After the war, Stanley had turned with great success to journalism, giving his paper, the *New York Herald*, a world scoop when he was war correspondent in Abyssinia. As a circulation-raising stunt, his proprietor had sent him off to find that legendary wanderer, David Livingstone.

The two incongruous friends lived four months together. The Franco-Prussian war – the first of the modern, scientific wars to smash at the fabric of European civilization – was all news to Livingstone. Through Stanley's newspaper he informed the world of the Nyangwe massacre – but Livingstone, though glad to be helped, did not particularly want to be rescued. What he asked for were porters and supplies, to continue his exploration.

Stanley reported sensationally to the outside world on the practices of Arab slave-traders, and this was useful ammunition for the British abolitionists, who were just then beginning to agitate in earnest against Arab slavery. By 1872 the political pressure they had brought to bear obliged the British government to send Sir Bartle Frere to Zanzibar. Much of the working capital in the Zanzibar slave trade was provided by British subjects there of Indian extraction; none the less, Sir Bartle managed to browbeat the Sultan into closing his slave market. An Anglican cathedral was afterwards built on the site, with the communion table where the whipping-post had been.

For the benefit of his readers, H. M. Stanley continued to embellish the Livingstone myth which other publicists before him, religious and secular, had begun to sketch out for their own purposes. Those who elaborate such myths are usually the first to be misled by them. After living on such close terms with the man himself, Stanley too became a little disillusioned: 'He was not of such an angelic temper as I believed him to be during my first month.' A chronically sick man, warped by an inhuman effort of will in childhood and youth, and worn out by journeying over rough country with little more than obstinacy and blind faith to sustain him, David Livingstone was hardly likely to be sweet-tempered. Any picture of a missionary which makes a plaster saint of him clearly does both the man and his faith no service, those who mould plaster saints for the rest of us to admire having motives of their own.

Stanley sent Livingstone fifty-seven porters from the coast –

236 AN OPEN PATH

and a slave chain, in case they should grow mutinous, which shows how much he mistook his man. In a waking dream Livingstone once more headed out of Ujiji for Lake Tanganyika and the Katanga country, in search of the source of the Nile; the rains were due. Antiquity was a dream of long ago, a boyhood escape, an alternative world about which one had read while spinning cotton, from an open book propped against the loom. 'It is not all pleasure, this exploration,' Livingstone noted in the swamps of Bangweolo when, weakened by anal bleeding, he was at the same time attacked by leeches and red ants. While the merciless ants bit into his flesh, Livingstone made scientific observations of their behaviour: the advantage of the scientific attitude for a boy who had once so dreaded hellfire was that it drained the world of feeling.

His porters found him, one morning not long after, dead as he knelt by his camp bed. In his lower intestine was a clot of blood the size of a fist. Those men who knew the best and worst of Livingstone – his African porters – were in loving awe of him. They removed his intestines, pickled his flesh in salt, soaked his features in brandy, wrapped the corpse first in calico then in sailcloth, and carried it to the coast. Their long journey took them from May 1873 to February 1874, and as they plodded onward with the long tarpaulin bundle on their shoulders, they sang a dirge: 'Today the Englishman is dead/who has different hair from ours.'

Livingstone's desiccated remains were shipped back to South-ampton, and taken by train to a London which in those days heartily relished a solemn funeral. On 18 April 1874 the boy from the cotton mill was buried in state in Westminster Abbey, in the presence of the Prime Minister and the Prince of Wales.

Livingstone had long ago ceased to represent a missionary society. But ambitious though he was, his work as scientist and explorer was coloured to the last by the missionary motive. His deepest concern was to help redeem other human beings from the cruelties of blind economic process. The newspaper apotheosis contrived for him after his death was used to give a moralistic tinge to policies of colonial expansion based on sentiments of racial superiority which would have been repugnant to him.

The deprivations of his childhood had given him a keener savour than most for the taste of success. His vision of an Africa transformed by commerce and Christianity could easily be misrepresented, and very soon was, by those more interested in trade and annexation than religion. But even today, many who busy themselves with the economic development of the Third World have scarcely caught up with his insights, particularly his knack of treating those brought up in a different culture as essentially his equals.

In 1874, H. M. Stanley took a line of his own. To Tipu Tib, the greatest name among the Arab slavers, he paid a fee of £1000 to escort him six days' journey down the mysterious river which Livingstone had discovered, the Lualaba. Tipu Tib was a sophisticated Muslim with an African mother and ambitious to found his own Central African principality in the heartland between the Lualaba and the Lomani rivers – his mother's country – based on slave labour kidnapped in the jungles of the Congo. To those who criticized his methods, Tipu Tib would answer suavely, 'I have heard that a few years ago in a great country called Russia, slavery existed under another name. In fact, what difference is there between a slave and a servant? My slaves do not want to leave me; they are content with their lot.' Stanley was prepared to use Tipu Tib, and even, later on, to praise and defend him.

Stanley found himself afloat and going westward on the current of a great river which was navigable for a thousand miles. The Congo was the world's second-largest river, but explorers trying to work up from its mouth on the Atlantic coast had soon found their route blocked by impassable falls. Now Stanley had found a way to enter the Congo by the back door.

In August 1877, Stanley reached Boma, on the Atlantic coast. His hair had gone completely white, but he had found a way of access to an enormous river basin, as big as Western Europe and almost unexploited. He had filled in another great blank on the map of Africa. H. M. Stanley was not yet, as he was soon to become, an explorer slowly sullying his great reputation by acting as colonial agent to King Leopold of the Belgians. He was the man who had created a legend at Ujiji; he lived for the time being in the glow of Livingstone's aura. With such respect was Stanley listened to that a few phrases in his despatch to the *Daily Telegraph* electrified the missionary societies in London. Stanley had said that the Kabaka of the Baganda – in what is now Uganda – would welcome Christian instruction. Marvellous things might be done, might they not, for the Christian religion, in that landlocked, scarcely discovered black kingdom on the shores of Lake Victoria?

10 An Essay in Colonization

'They strengthen our hold over the country; they spread the use of the English language . . . in fact, each Mission Station is an essay in colonization. *H. H. Johnston to Cecil Rhodes, 17 August 1890*

'If Augustine had landed in Kent with Maxim guns, the members representing the Church Missionary Society who are going to support this vote would have been Pagans now.' *Sir Charles Dilke in the Parliamentary debate on Uganda, 1 June 1894*

'Love the poor pagans; be kind to them; heal their wounds. They will give you their affection first, then their confidence, then at last their souls.' *Cardinal Lavigerie, 1869, to the White Fathers*

On the morning of 15 November 1875, a man's hand reached through a chained front door in a middle-class residential road in Headingley, Leeds, to fetch inside a loaf of bread, a bottle of milk, and the *Daily Telegraph*. The letter-box was then emptied and most of the letters – begging letters – pitched into the fireplace, but some were important communications, from explorers and geographers.

The floors of the house were bare, and piled high with books. The owner was Robert Arthington, an immensely rich man, who had discovered that he could keep himself alive by spending half-a-crown a week on bread and milk. He would dine on a piece of bread and a red herring, and was known all over Leeds as the Miser of Headingley. Had Arthington changed his clothes five times a day, and gambled away his unearned increment in the casino at Monte Carlo, as a rich man properly should, his neighbours might have been easier in their minds.

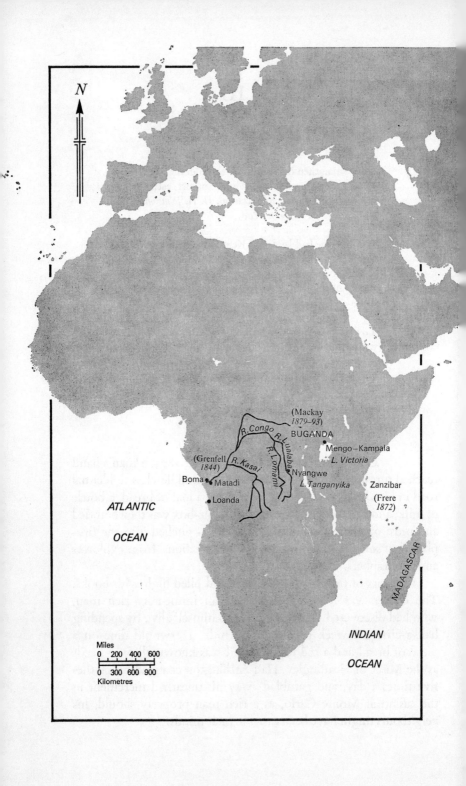

Arthington had his private reasons for choosing to live like a hermit of the middle ages. Though his material circumstances might be sordid, his religious imagination was aflame: he had made up his mind that when the gospel was preached in every corner of the world, we could all expect the Second Coming. That morning in the *Daily Telegraph*, Arthington read H. M. Stanley's appeal for missionaries to go to Buganda, and soon was deep in books on African geography, confirming facts, appraising possibilities, corresponding about the problem with experienced travellers.

Once both Livingstone and Stanley had crossed Africa from coast to coast, blazing a trail, the next need as Arthington saw it was for a chain of mission stations linking the continent from east to west. In the newspaper, Stanley had written his account of this realm in Central Africa where the black king, though a pagan, would welcome Christian missionaries. Arthington sent a cheque for £5000 to the Church Missionary Society – on clearly defined conditions – to finance a mission in Uganda. In 1877, another of his cheques went to the Baptist Missionary Society, to encourage them to work their way up the Congo, 'a part of Africa on which I have long had my eye', wrote Arthington, assuring them that, to him, it would be 'a high and sacred pleasure if the Baptist Missionary Society will undertake at once to visit these benighted interesting people with the blessed light of the Gospel. I hope we shall soon have a steamer on the Congo.'

Prefabricated in 1880 by Thorneycrofts, and again financed by Robert Arthington, this Congo steamer, called *Peace*, was a triumph of design. Seventy feet long, but only drawing eighteen inches when fully laden, *Peace* if attacked by dangerous cannibals could raise steam from cold water in ten minutes, and move off at twelve miles an hour, the crew being protected by steel-netting screens, of a mesh fine enough to stop breech-loader slugs and poisoned arrows.

By 1880, when the steamer he had planned was launched, Robert Arthington was fifty-seven, and set in his eccentric ways. He had gone to Cambridge, collected coins and shells, made a little name for himself by writing monographs on fertilizers and preventable diseases. His parents were Leeds Quakers, and when he was twenty-seven they had, from conscientious scruples, closed down the family brewery. Then they died, leaving him a very rich young man.

The girl he loved jilted him; Arthington started a more bizarre collection, of spectacles and umbrellas. But gripped at last by the futility of a rich man's life, he invented for himself an existence of deliberate poverty, as if trying to take the curse off the money he had inherited (which multiplied every year, at compound interest) and which he spent in imaginative ways – on famine relief, on African missions – to lessen misery and ensure Christ's Second Coming. Despite his enormous donations, Arthington was still embarrassed by over a million sterling – £1,119,848 – when he died at the age of seventy-seven. After providing £100,000 for his relations, he left £839,000 to missionary societies.

The party from the Church Missionary Society which Arthington had financed was led 800 unexplored miles inland, to the shores of Lake Victoria, by Lieutenant George Shirgold Smith, RN, who had been invalided out after his service in the Ashanti war ('I love the African and want to preach Christ to him'). But for the next fourteen years, the most effective man in this pioneering mission was to be a Scots engineer called Alexander Mackay, then twenty-six, the son of a Free Church minister in Aberdeenshire, who had been employed in a locomotive works in Berlin when his imagination was set alight, as Arthington's had been, by the Livingstone legend. Mackay decided to become 'an engineer missionary'. 'If you can send me', he told the Church Missionary Society, 'to any of those regions which Livingstone and Stanley have found to be groaning under the curse of the slave hunter, I shall be very glad.'

The capital of Mtesa, king of Buganda, was a sprawling township, six miles long and two miles wide, built across four hills, around the royal enclosure on Mengo Hill. In the centre of the enclosure was Mtesa's beehive-shaped reception-house, huge and elegant, built on high wooden posts, with a reedwork roof. Huddled around Mengo Hill lived the kingdom's great noblemen, in handsome houses, sometimes eighty feet high, constructed of poles, reeds and straw. Their sons served in the court, as royal pages. Banana plantations interspersed the houses, and women worked the fields. The kingdom thrived on slave labour. The Baganda were a warrior race, who regularly went off to war with neighbouring peoples, armed with two stabbing spears and a long, pointed shield, their faces striped white and red; every year, thousands of their neighbours became their slaves.

Mtesa, six foot high, a shrewd if superstitious man, and given to generous impulses, ruled a couple of million people living across a stretch of land greater in area than England. His court, full of intrigue and ceremonial, sharp wits and sudden punishments, was not unlike that of a pagan Anglo-Saxon kingdom, except for an extravagant delight in inflicting pain: 'the terrible Baganda grin of pleasure in cruelty', as Mackay recorded glumly in his journal. The usual capital punishment was burning alive, after torture. On waking, the king was apt to celebrate a significant dream by human sacrifice. One fine morning after he had happened to dream of his father, five hundred slaves were sacrificed. Should he ever dream of any man living, that warned him of treachery, and the man in the dream was killed out of hand.

Though flirting with Islam, for political reasons, and even building mosques (which usually faced the wrong way) Mtesa had recently burned to death two hundred of his subjects who had actually become Muslim, on a charge of 'refusing to eat the king's beef', having first tricked them by offering them in hospitality beef which had not been ritually slaughtered. Mtesa had asked H. M. Stanley to send in Christian missionaries mainly because he hoped to play them off against the Arabs.

The Egyptians, as they pushed towards the headwaters of the Nile, were pressing on his kingdom to the north, and Arab slave-traders, patronized by the Sultan of Zanzibar, were thrusting deeper inland from the coast. But by this time the English down on the coast were bringing the Sultan to heel. Mtesa therefore looked upon the men sent him by the Church Missionary Society as a political as well as a religious counterweight to the emissaries of Islam. 'Now my heart is good,' he said, as he welcomed them, 'England is my friend.'

Alexander Mackay and his companions soon discovered that

Mtesa had 'a larger collection of wives than any human being of whom we have record'. He offered to seal his new friendship by adding an English royal princess to their number, but he was suffering at the time from a venereal disease, which might not have recommended him as a son-in-law to Queen Victoria.

These first Protestant missionaries, self-reliant and idealistic eccentrics, found that they were obliged to dance attendance more than they might have wished at Mtesa's court. But they began to make converts there, chiefly among the aristocratic warriors of the royal bodyguard. The most picturesque of these early missionaries, Dr E. J. Baxter, down in Mwapwa, was still serving in 1910. Dr Baxter won a name for himself in East Africa by fitting the donkey he rode with two pairs of trousers, as a precaution against the tsetse fly. He also borrowed, from Australia's cork-hatted swaggies, the interesting device of keeping flies at a distance by dangling champagne corks on strings from the brim of his solar topee. A milder but no less amiable eccentric was Reverend Robert Ashe, who brought in the first bicycle. The Baganda were at first suspicious, in case the bicycle should turn out to be a machine-gun. They knew about machine-guns, because the Germans were using them on rebellious Arabs down in Tanganyika. But they soon arrived at the happier conclusion that the bicycle was an iron donkey.

Ashe had come up from the coast in a caravan led by Henry Stokes – always called 'Charlie' – a Baptist who gave up being a missionary on Lake Tanganyika when his wife died and he earned the disapproval of the Baptist Missionary Society by marrying a black girl; since the more tolerant days of Vanderkemp, values had altered. So Charlie Stokes adopted long white Muslim robes, grew a patriarchal beard, discreetly added to his harem, and set up in business as an ivory dealer and gun-runner. One head-load of half a dozen ten-pound gunpowder kegs might very likely fetch him a profit upcountry of £250 in ivory.

Charlie bore no resentment, and was always glad to do his old friends, the missionaries, a good turn. His gun-running made him popular, too, with successive kings of Buganda, for a new weapon, the breech-loading rifle, deadly accurate and with twenty times the range of a flintlock musket, had recently

AN ESSAY IN COLONIZATION 245

made all Africa's muzzle-loaders obsolete. 'The Monarch of Central Africa', so the saying went, 'is King Rifle.' The Arab traders who menaced Mtesa's kingdom from the coast had Sniders; the Sudanese soldiers to the north were armed with Remington Repeaters. Charlie Stokes not only ran in guns and took out ivory. He carried up from the coast, in sections, a steel boat, and with his boat and his rifles was soon dominating the dug-out canoe traffic on Lake Victoria.

The most effective of all these odd characters, however, was the dour, earnest young Scots engineer, Alexander Mackay. 'I hope to connect Christianity', Mackay had declared at the start, 'with modern civilization'. Mackay had less affection than some of his companions for the black people he had come out to evangelize. 'Lies, lust, cruelty, murder,' was his succinct summing-up of life in Buganda. A small man, with calm blue eyes and a large brown beard, always in clean linen, and sporting a grey Tyrolese hat, Mackay set up his workshop in 1879, and quickly established a reputation at court by repairing two broken royal trumpets. Mackay stayed in Central Africa fourteen years, never taking a furlough, and his workshop was a portent. The Muslims had already gained prestige in Buganda by bringing in several useful techniques: they could make soap, and run pig-iron, and braze metals. But as a practical engineer of the Victorian epoch, Mackay was omnicompetent; he put the Arabs in the shade.

On a native loom, only four pieces of cloth two yards by three could be made in a year. Mackay made a modern loom, and even a spinning jenny. He worked as a gunsmith. He set up a printing press. He caught fever and died just as he was working on the boiler of an engine to drive a steamboat up and down the lake. He was also the first of the missionaries to master Luganda – in the kingdom of Buganda live the Baganda who speak Luganda: they now inhabit Uganda. Mackay began a translation into Luganda of St Matthew.

But Mackay's masterpiece was King Mtesa's coffin – it cost him a month's work. He beat out brass trays, copper sheathing and tin packing-case linings to produce a gleaming and ornate outer coffin-case. The king's dead body was placed in the wooden interior, and swathed in thousands of yards of thin calico, to the value of £15,000; Mackay buried him thirty feet deep.

Prominent members of the royal entourage were already turning to Christianity. Some had become Protestants, some were Roman Catholics. When Mtesa died, on 9 October 1884, for the first time in Buganda on the death of a king there was no human sacrifice – though when he first fell ill, in 1880, hundreds had been slaughtered in ritual expiation.

When he came to the throne, Mtesa had as a matter of course put to death his brothers. But times had changed: he spared his sons.

In June of 1878, half a dozen Europeans, in red caps not unlike Arab skullcaps, and wearing white robes similar to a burnous, rode into Mtesa's capital on donkeys. Their caravan had taken a year and three months to cover the 800 miles from Zanzibar to Buganda, since they had lingered by the way to set up small missions along the caravan routes.

These new arrivals were Roman Catholic missionaries – the White Fathers, organized by the famous and formidable Cardinal Lavigerie, Archbishop of Algiers and Apostolic Delegate of the Sahara, and led to Buganda by Father Livinhac. Their sartorial resemblance to Arabs was no accident.

From 1800 to 1870, Islamic influence had crept southward across the Sahara and the Sudan (Arabic: Bilad-es Sudan = land of the blacks) into the heart of Africa. Not all Muslims by any means were slave-traders, and though they had as yet no formal missionary organization, African converts to Islam could by this time be counted in millions. The appeal of Islam to Africans emerging from tribal society was powerful. Islam tolerated polygamy, so that the status an African enjoyed on account of his womenfolk, whose endless hard work sustained the tribe, would not be in jeopardy. By treating the acceptance of Allah as submission to fate, a Muslim convert's exercise of free will might be lacking him, but his life, if morally undramatic, even passive, was less fearful and perplexed than it had been under paganism. He had chosen a man's religion.

And however persistent its efforts, no Christian mission had so far made any impression worth noting on the followers of Islam.

As a critic sardonically pointed out in *The Times* in 1887, the average cost to the Church Missionary Society of the conversion of one Muslim was £11,000. Nor did Cardinal Lavigerie, in sending forth his White Fathers, expect to make Christian converts of Muslims until after a lapse of time which he measured by centuries. Not only were the White Fathers he sponsored to dress like Muslims, they were in every material respect to share their life. When speaking to their Muslim neighbours they were to avoid controversy and any hint of preaching, or even religious conversation. They were – so said the great Cardinal – to win the affection and confidence of those about them simply by loving behaviour. By 1887 there were 125 White Fathers at work, in and around the Sahara. By 1888, eleven White Fathers had been martyred; fifty had died.

Those White Fathers sent to Mtesa's kingdom in Buganda had been instructed not to set up a mission nearer than ten kilometres to any other Christian mission. But when they found themselves in the hectic atmosphere of Mtesa's court, this rule had soon been broken.

The closeness of a dwelling to the royal enclosure on Mengo Hill was a measure of the owner's prestige. The land Mtesa gave these Catholic newcomers to build on was nearer the palace than the Protestants were living, though it was also closer to the Protestants' own mission than the White Fathers' rules allowed. But they stayed where they had been put. Mtesa presented the White Fathers with an acre of banana-plantation for their subsistence, and thirty head of cattle. In return, they gave him some French dress-uniforms – gorgeous with gold epaulettes – which they had bought second-hand in a Paris slop-shop. (As gifts to chiefs, the Baptists preferred brass bedsteads, which they had sent out to them from the Army and Navy Stores.)

Alexander Mackay, an unflinchingly anti-papist Scot, did his best to turn Mtesa against these newcomers by warning the king that they worshipped a woman called Mary; the White Fathers riposted by not kneeling down when Mackay began to pray. 'And has every white man', Mtesa had asked sardonically, 'a different religion?' He was glad to have the rival Christian sects at odds.

Yet except for diehards on both sides – men like Mackay – relations between Protestant and Catholic in the early years in Buganda appear to have shifted from wary respect to a discreet measure of brotherly affection. In their mission work at court they had about equal success, particularly in converting the black aristocrats of the king's guard, who saw the Arabs as the chief menace to their personal rule out in the provinces. By Mtesa's death it was being reckoned, as a rough measure of Christian influence, that Protestant and Catholic alike could each put a thousand armed men into the field, whereas the Muslims could call out only three hundred. As if there were no lessons to be learned from Europe's wars of religion, the rival versions of Christianity in Buganda were becoming parties in the state.

Until the years of crisis after 1883 – when the Mahdi destroyed a British-officered army in the Egyptian Sudan, thus raising Islamic hopes all over North Africa – the White Fathers managed to get on surprisingly well with the Arab slave-traders around Lake Victoria (whom, of course, in their hearts, they abhorred). In Africa the usual missionary technique of the Roman Catholics was to gather up a tribal society's human debris – orphans, the sick and old and useless. These victims they would bring together in a rural settlement, meant to be for them, so to speak, a Christian oasis, where slowly they would come under the influence not so much of preaching and Bible study as of a pervasive atmosphere emotionally hard to resist, of affection, consideration and security. The Protestant appeal – except insofar as it might be directed at a listener's obscure sense of guilt – was usually more intellectual. The Roman Catholics, for their part, tried to create a milieu with a friendlier emotional tone than that of the cruel world outside. In Buganda, both had their successes.

At their halts along the caravan trails, the Arab slavers would often find the White Fathers waiting for them, and willing to give them handfuls of beads, or a few metres of cotton cloth, in exchange for the slave caravan's human refuse – cripples, old folk, motherless children, who otherwise, according to the rules of the trade, would have to be knocked on the head, to save the expense of their rations, and so as to terrorize their companions. Outside the royal capital, these poor people were the raw material of the Roman Catholic missions, but on Mengo Hill they won over courtiers. Then, after Mtesa's death, prophetic Islamic nationalism began to preponderate in the Sudan. The political tensions began to pull all ways, until the fairly friendly relations hitherto possible among Muslim, Protestant and Catholic would no longer take much strain.

King Mtesa had been nicknamed the 'Causer of Tears'. An eighteen-year-old of the blood royal, called Mwanga, was picked out as his heir. Mwanga's nickname was the 'Mild One'.

The Arabs at court had nobbled Mwanga early, playing on his temperamental weakness, and teaching him the novel pleasures of sodomy and smoking *bhang*. Mwanga had also been sent to take instruction from missionaries, both Catholic and Protestant. He could recite his Paternoster, but Robert Ashe, who had the chore of trying to teach Mwanga his alphabet, found him 'flighty'.

Mwanga was pulled first one way, then another, by the three foreign religions which now formed three contending parties at his court. He was sometimes tempted to kick out all three, and restore paganism. But having once accepted the poisoned gift of guns, cloth, literacy and foreign technical knowledge, to go back to the simpler, self-sufficient life was not really possible.

At the beginning of the young king's reign, having established themselves at court by pandering to Mwanga's pleasure, the Arabs were in the ascendant.

For the Christians of Buganda, 1885 was a year of terror. In January, three boys, Serwanga, Kakumba and Lugalama, who had been learning their catechism from Mackay and Ashe, were arbitrarily taken out, on Mwanga's orders, and put to death. Before throwing them on the usual slow fire, the executioner cut their arms off. Mockingly the onlookers bade their victims pray to Isa Masiza – Jesus Christ – to be saved. 'The dear lads clung to the faith,' records Mackay's journal, with an uncommon flicker of emotion, 'and in the fire they sang.' That night one of the public executioners 'impressed by the behaviour of our dear boys under fire and knife,' came in secret to the Protestant missionaries 'to learn to pray also'. Mackay sagaciously formed a council of the most trustworthy among his Baganda converts, to guide the church if the foreign missionaries should be killed in their turn, or else expelled.

The next martyrdom, in June of the same year, involved both Protestants and Catholics at once, and was on a much larger scale. One day Mwanga had the whim of wishing to sodomize some of his pages, but he picked on boys who happened to regard this particular service as incompatible with their Christian belief. After the king's advances were rebuffed, thirty-four Christian pages – twenty-two of them Catholic, the rest Protestant – were dragged sixteen miles out of the royal capital, to Namungongo. There they were laid in a row, on a huge funeral pyre built up from faggots of dried reeds. The young victims were held in place by the *kaligo* – the forked slave-stick, designed to hold a captive helpless. A slow fire was lit under the reeds nearest their feet, in the belief that a gradually intensifying pain might prompt at least one of them to give way. But all held firm; and as they slowly burned to death, they too were taunted, 'Now let your God come and take you out of the flames.'

Other Christians were picked out, to be speared, beheaded, shorn of their limbs, castrated. Mwanga and his men put it around that the resistance the Christians were making could be accounted for only by witchcraft: a spell had been laid upon them, making life indifferent to them, and death attractive.

Mackay began quickly printing off hymn sheets and prayer-book services for a church which might soon go underground. He and Ashe were surprised at the number of serious enquirers who came to them during the persecution; at the same time, ninety-seven new converts were baptized by Father Lourdel of the White Fathers.

In October, Bishop Hannington was due to arrive. An energetic man, not long consecrated, with a blunt nose in a cheerful, bearded face, he might well have been a tower of strength to the Anglican mission in Buganda. At the border he was stopped by Mwanga's guards. On the very day that Mackay finished his translation of St Matthew into Luganda, orders came from Mwanga to spear the captive bishop and fifty of his party to death. Once Mwanga knew for sure that the bishop was dead, he called Alexander Mackay to his reception house. Sitting there on his leopard skin – in Buganda, only the king was allowed to sit on a leopard skin – he taunted the Scots engineer for three hours, threatening to put him to death, too. 'What if I kill you – what could Queenie do? What could all Europe do?'

The White Fathers were withdrawn, and at last even obstinate Mackay was edged out. In London there was prudent, craven talk of abandoning the mission field in Buganda. To this suggestion, Mackay replied scathingly, 'Tell me, ye faint hearts, *to whom* ye mean to give up the Mission? Is it to murderous raiders, like Mwanga, or to slave dealers from Zanzibar, or to English and Belgian dealers in rifles and powder, or German spirit sellers? All are in the field.'

If the missionaries in Buganda had slowly become the catspaws of political forces stronger than they could reckon with, it had not been for lack on their own part of courage and good intentions. But by now, there were two other strong contenders – besides those Mackay had named – for the broad and fertile territory later named Uganda, though their names had not yet come to the fore: the Queen of England, and the German Emperor.

Sir William Mackinnon had started life as a poor boy in Lanarkshire. His character was stiffened by the radical moral influence of the Free Church of Scotland, then he went to work as a grocer and a haberdasher. In 1847, at the age of twenty-five, he went out to India, to seek his fortune. Seven years later, he had contrived to buy his first steamship. In 1862, he launched the British India Steam Navigation Company, and eventually made a pile of half a million. Mackinnon became interested in East Africa through Sir Bartle Frere, who in 1872 had compelled the Sultan of Zanzibar to close his slave market. To keep British influence paramount there, Sir Bartle wanted a line of British mail steamers to ply between Bombay and Zanzibar, and Mackinnon set them going.

William Mackinnon was 'a dapper little upright man, with sidewhiskers, a pouting mouth and a strutting manner'. As with other self-made men of his time, his imagination had been captured by Macaulay's *Essays:* why should not he himself play in East Africa the role of another, more moral Warren Hastings? Why should he not be the man to bring to a businesslike fulfilment Livingstone's great dream, by adding East Africa to the British Empire, as Warren Hastings a century before had added province after Indian province to the raj?

In 1887, Mackinnon procured a concession from the Sultan of Zanzibar: in 1889 he obtained from Queen Victoria a charter founding the Imperial British East Africa Company – a small-scale East India Company, as it were, which was virtually under his personal control.

Mackinnon had some good names on his company's letter-heading: Lord Brassey, son of the eminent and wealthy railway pioneer; Sir Thomas Fowell Buxton, grandson of the paladin of anti-slavery, and treasurer of the Church Missionary Society; James Hutton, Manchester merchant, president of the Chamber of Commerce there, and Member of Parliament; Burdett Coutts, the philanthropical banker; and Colonel Francis de Winton, soon to be knighted – a soldier of fortune with a romantic name and good connections who at the beginning was cast for the role of East Africa's Robert Clive.

As it turned out, the role of Clive there was to be played by another English soldier of fortune, a thirty-year-old half-pay officer called Frederick Lugard, small, ruthless, with hollow, sunken eyes, who had got into a mess in India with a woman. In 1888, Lugard took a deck passage down the coast of Africa, in search of profitable adventure. His father had been an army chaplain in India, and his mother a missionary there, so he was well aware how to handle missionaries. Privately, he had not much use for them: not single-minded enough about the Empire. Like many of his generation – the strong, silent men of middle-class origin being sent abroad in their thousands from the newly created Victorian public schools – nothing gratified Lugard more than making a speech, or writing a newspaper article.

Education in England had at last been made universally compulsory, and the press was the great new power. Lugard soon learned the knack of manipulating publicity, yet though in his day he had a great newspaper following, he has never quite managed to impose himself on history as a legend. He was perhaps too purposeful, too functional, never quite able to veil what he was up to in glamour.

Lugard was, however, an extremely competent professional officer. He had recently seen service as a transport officer in campaigns in Abyssinia and Burma, where modern weapons had been used with crushing effect against enemies wielding sword and spear. As Lugard on half-pay drifted down the East African coastline, with his faith both in women and religion impaired, and his imagination toying, like Clive's, with the idea of suicide, he was recruited by the Livingstonia Company to command their irregulars in Nyasaland.

Mackinnon was a leading spirit in the Livingstonia Company too. They were Scots businessmen, who in a practical way were trying to fulfil David Livingstone's vision of establishing a civilized community along the shores of Lake Nyasa. They had their wits about them. For instance, they bought ivory at a higher price than an Arab trader could afford. Therefore, it no longer paid him to enslave an African to carry his tusk to the coast. This was a blow at the slave trade, but of course earned them Arab hostility.

In Glasgow a Nyasa Anti-Slavery and Defence Fund was soon organized, to buy and arm the black Presbyterians of Nyasaland with King Rifle. Lugard told his Livingstonia Company that he also wanted a mountain gun shipped out, to Quilimane on the mouth of the Zambezi. If the Germans, up the coast in Tanganyika, had just used machine-guns against rebellious Arabs with terrifying effect, in Nyasaland, thought Frederick Lugard, field artillery should do the trick.

When Lugard did in fact prise his mountain gun loose from the unwilling Portuguese customs authorities, and bring it up to bombard the Arabs' stockaded fort, the little campaign flourished, though not for long. The Arabs remained a threat in Nyasaland until Harry Johnston finished them off in the 1890s.

Lugard went up the coast, nursing a wound, and with a useful newspaper reputation as a British regular soldier who had actually fought Arab slavers, if not with great success. In Zanzibar, de Winton took him on the Imperial British East Africa Company's payroll, to go upcountry with some askaris, cope with Mwanga, and if at all possible to make a treaty with him before the colonizing Germans could arrive in Uganda.

In 1888 Mwanga, twisting and turning under the lash of his appetites and fears, had decided to resist the pressures put upon his kingdom by Arabs, Germans and British alike, by launching a pagan revival. His simple-minded plan was to kidnap all the whites and all the Arabs in Buganda, and maroon them on an island in Lake Victoria until they starved to death. But the plot was discovered. Brought together in this common peril, the three monotheistic parties, Muslims, Protestants and Catholics, joined their forces to expel Mwanga and enthrone his younger brother, Kikewa.

The new king took on a Roman Catholic prime minister – importance at court meant prosperity for other members of the ruling sect, out in the provinces. But the real power in the land turned out to be the Muslim leader Ali Bey – a man so fat that he had to ride everywhere on a donkey. Ali Bey went to work on Kikewa, playing on his fears until he had persuaded the new king that the Christians meant to depose him.

Christian chiefs were driven out of the capital, and the mission stations plundered. For a year, the Muslims controlled Buganda. The Arabs soon made themselves unpopular by trying to carry out forcible circumcisions – an indelible mark of allegiance. Kikewa himself refused downright to be circumcised, so another brother called Karema, who no doubt thought the operation a small price to pay for a kingdom, was placed on the royal leopardskin: Karema soon put Kikewa to death.

In 1889, all Buganda's native Christians, both Protestant and Catholic, had had enough, and were ready to sink their differences and restore even the bloody-minded Mwanga to the throne, as the lesser evil. But the foreign missionaries, when consulted, were half-hearted. Charlie Stokes, having no such scruples, began running in guns to arm those of either creed who were ready to fight for Mwanga. He took his payment in ivory. For a year, the fighting between the little Christian and Muslim armies swayed back and forth, until a decisive Christian victory at Bulwanyi, in February 1890, brought Mwanga back to his palace on Mengo

Hill. The uneasy alliance of Protestants and Catholics had won Mwanga's kingdom back for him, but was soon to fall apart.

Mackinnon's Imperial British East Africa Company offered to take Mwanga under protection. Then the formidable Dr Carl Peters arrived at Mwanga's palace, and in the name of Germany made him an offer which the Catholic fathers thought so much better that they urged him to accept. Catholic and Protestant, against their better intentions, and almost against their will, were now openly the spokesmen for two rival foreign powers.

But over the heads of Mwanga and Peters and Mackinnon, statesmen in Europe were striking bargains, exchanging Heligoland for Zanzibar, and drawing arbitrary lines across the map of Africa. On 1 July 1890, four months after Mwanga had beaten the Arabs, the Treaty of Berlin placed Buganda in a British sphere of influence. The Imperial British East Africa Company had only to play its cards in the right order – take power locally, then sway public opinion in Britain to agree to a protectorate – and the countries later named Uganda and Kenya were ripe fruit to be plucked.

But the Company by this time was running out of both money and enthusiasm. Mackinnon was no longer so keen on East Africa. Trade with a hinterland where goods had to be carried to market on human heads at a cost of two or three hundred pounds a ton was not tempting. In proportion to the traffic it might hope to carry, a railway to Buganda would be enormously expensive. Mackinnon's attention was divided; he had also been lured by King Leopold II of the Belgians into his project for exploiting the Congo basin – a proposition which sounded both easier and more profitable, and was said to be philanthropic, too.

Mwanga was clear in his mind by this time that the Protestants represented Britain – the chief rival for his kingdom – so he turned Catholic; though when the principal Catholic chiefs at court, disapproving of his sodomy, put several of his favourite boys to death, he wobbled in his faith. But in Buganda the Catholics were now – marginally – the patriots.

Armed to the teeth by Charlie Stokes, the Catholics were ready, if need be, for civil war. On their hill, near the palace, the Catho-

lic missionaries built themselves a brick blockhouse, loopholed
for defence, and not far from their half-finished cathedral. The
new Anglican bishop, Alfred Tucker, arriving in the capital that
Christmas a fortnight after Lugard, was astonished to find how
many of the Protestant Christians who came to hear him brought
their rifles with them to church. Protestants and Catholics if it
came to war could by now each put about 2500 men in the field.

In had marched Frederick Lugard, the Company's accredited
agent, with a caravan of 270 armed porters, led by a hundred
soldiers, fifty of them Sudanese in tarbooshes. Those tarbooshes
provoked a gasp of fear. The Baganda dreaded the Sudanese,
who at that moment were harrying their northern provinces.

Lugard, though well aware that his hundred infantrymen
would hardly tip the scales if war broke out, began to act with
calculated arrogance, as if he already controlled the situation. He
put a peremptory stop to Charlie Stokes's gun-running. He set
up his headquarters on Kampala Hill, within gunshot of Mwanga's
royal enclosure, and there ran up the Company's flag: a rising
sun, with the words *Light and Liberty*, and a little Union Jack
in the corner. And word spread that Lugard had brought upcountry with him two of these terrible new weapons which not
many years later were to cut short the lives of thousands of young
Englishmen in Flanders: machine-guns.

The effective range of a smooth-bore, muzzle-loading musket –
the commonest firearm in Buganda – was 100 yards. Mwanga's
royal guard were by now armed with both Sniders and Remington Repeaters. The Sniders were good up to 2000 yards, the
Remingtons having a shorter range but a more rapid rate of fire.
But Lugard's two Maxims fired faster than you could count, and
their cone of fire, outranging a rifle, could sometimes deal with
a human target three miles off.

Leaving a token force in the capital to sustain his bluff, Lugard
swung upcountry, and there crushed what was left of the Muslims
in a masterly little encounter – the Maxim gun helping greatly –
in which 300 Muslims were killed for the loss of only 15 in
Lugard's force. He then marched back with 100 more Sudanese
recruits, so as to be prepared, when the Christians fought each
other, to intervene at the right moment and decide the outcome.

'Destructive riffraff' was how Ashe describes Lugard's Sudanese.

But before use could be made of them, the Imperial British East Africa Company, deep in financial difficulty, sent Lugard an order, telling him to evacuate Buganda.

Lugard did what his great exemplar, Clive, might have done, and coldly ignored the order; luckily, a few days later it was countermanded.

Lord Salisbury's Conservative government had failed to get a subsidy for Mackinnon's Company through Parliament. The possibility of building a railway up from the coast was receding. To keep Lugard in Buganda would cost £40,000 a year, and where was the money to come from? Sir William Mackinnon arranged to meet Bishop Tucker, now back in England, on board his steam yacht off Balmacara in sight of the island of Skye. The luxurious surroundings, the romantic scenery, Mackinnon's glib tongue, all did their part. Mackinnon said he would pay a quarter of the £40,000 out of his own pocket, and collect £15,000 from his friends, if only the Church Missionary Society would find the balance. Of course, Mackinnon would be glad to handle someone else's money as well as his own, but more important still, he wanted the Church Missionary Society, with its enormous influence, to act as his political accomplice. An emotional speech from Bishop Tucker to the Gleaners' Union – the organization of Anglican children which collected pennies to support such men as Ashe and Mackay – quickly raised £16,000. In this roundabout way, the pennies of the faithful may have been used, for all they knew, to replenish the ammunition belts on Lugard's Maxim guns.

Lugard had discreetly stiffened the Protestant party with 350 muzzleloaders and 150 Sniders, so they would be more of a match for the Catholics, previously armed by Charlie Stokes. Tension grew between the rival Christian armies, until on 24 January 1891 civil war broke out in the capital. The Protestants began by taking Rubaga Hill and setting the Catholic cathedral there on fire. Meanwhile the Catholic fathers, taking it for granted that their last moment had come, gave each other absolution. The triumphant Protestants then moved off to attack the royal

I

enclosure on Mengo Hill, over which Mwanga's flag still flew: two stabbing spears and a pointed shield, in white, on a red ground.

The Catholics rallied, and they streamed out to attack the Protestants in the rear. Frederick Lugard, overlooking the battle-field from his headquarters on Kampala Hill, saw that the decisive moment had come. At long range, he opened fire on the Catholics with the dreaded Maxim gun. 'My calculation and my sighting were correct,' he recorded with all due modesty, 'and my shots went in among the enemy, even at this extreme range. I had broken up their charge, and dispersed and terrified them.'

As the Catholics wavered, Lugard 'seized the critical moment' and threw in his professional soldiers. 'I covered the advance with the gun. There was no holding our Sudanese and Zanzibaris! Down the hill they went with a rush, full of excitement and mad for a fight.' Thanks to their help, the Protestants won. After the battle, thousands of defeated black Catholics – 50,000, so some witnesses claimed – were enslaved. Certainly not 50,000, pro-claimed the winners indignantly. Hardly more than 5000, and many of those were eventually let go. Suppose the winners are taken at their word: the irony is complete. The enemies of slavery have made slaves of their enemies.

Accompanied by six Catholic fathers and their bishop, Mwanga fled to an off-shore island called Bulingngwe. Lugard sent his second-in-command, Captain Williams, with a hundred men and a Maxim to winkle them out. Fifteen canoes crammed with riflemen made a night landing, while from the shore, 400 yards off, Williams played the Maxim gun on all the native huts he could see, particularly upon the one where Mwanga was supposed to be asleep. Hundreds were later massacred by Lugard's Sudanese.

The Roman Catholic bishop, Monsignor Hirth, led such followers as remained with him helter-skelter towards the out-lying province of Buddu near the German border, the inhabitant's of which, in Mtesa's time, had been enslaved by the conquering Baganda. 'A new fatherland for us, for an immense migration has followed us for several days,' he wrote. 'The whole of Buddu has become a Catholic province,' adding, with an uncharitable but perhaps understandable glee, 'The Protestants though ten times more numerous have been driven out.' 'The race for converts,' the British Consul was to report, from Zanzibar, 'now being carried on by the Romish and Protestant missionaries in Uganda, is synonymous with a race for political power.'

But, for the time being, the reins of power were in the hands of Frederick Lugard. Returning to his diocese in December 1892, Bishop Tucker found that the freethinking soldier of fortune had made a religious as well as a political settlement to suit himself, handing out the country's provinces, six to the Protestants, Buddu to the Catholics, three small provinces to the Muslims. Later, in 1892, the Muslims were so hot-headed as to rebel, so two of their three provinces, whatever the religious predilections of their inhabitants may have been, were taken away from them, one being handed over to the Protestants, one to the Catholics.

As well as determining the religious faith to be followed in the various provinces of Buganda, the Maxim gun had other achievements to its credit. Natives on the island of Uvuma controlled much of the lake traffic. With no provocation, so far as the missionaries could judge, the Maxim arrived and chopped them down. Muslim Baganda went in with the expeditionary force, and enslaved the survivors. The final triumph of the Maxim was to overawe – as nothing else would have done – the mutinous and violent Sudanese, who now that Buganda was reduced to submission had served their purpose.

Lugard, with his laurels fresh upon him, went back to London and wrote long-winded but well-informed letters to *The Times*, and the Imperial British East Africa Company orchestrated a publicity campaign with exemplary skill. Few were better than Lugard, as it turned out, at explaining the business advantages of a colony in Uganda to provincial Chambers of Commerce. Cecil Rhodes, the South African diamond multimillionaire – in those days, on the Stock Exchange, a name to conjure with – offered to build a telegraph from Nyasaland to Uganda at his own expense. H. M. Stanley, the famous explorer, warned against 'a cowardly and disgraceful scuttle'.

The Church Missionary Society, believing that only a British protectorate would maintain the advantage Protestantism had gained by Lugard's division of the provinces, was already committed up to the hilt, and led in behind them the Anti-Slavery Society, the Ladies' Negro Friend Society, and the Young Men's Christian Association. The Scottish Presbyterians were heart and soul for a British Uganda. At the Church Congress, at Folke-stone, E. W. Benson, then Archbishop of Canterbury, prayed publicly that 'our country's course may be so shaped that the Christian converts of Uganda may not be abandoned to imminent destruction'. The political pressure in this way generated at last became irresistible. Mackinnon's Imperial British East Africa Company was bought out, no doubt to the relief of the eminent shareholders, who had parted with large sums in administering Uganda, with no sign as yet of profits to come. On 13 June 1895, Uganda and Kenya were added to the Empire, at a cost to the tax-payer of less than £220,000.

In the decade when Uganda became a British protectorate, the missionary movement was conditioned by the economic reality of the time. Colonies which would serve as markets and sources of raw materials were held to be economically essential for industrialized countries; those who argued against imperialism on moral grounds were therefore often stigmatized as old-fashioned religious reactionaries. Yet at about the same time in the Congo, imperialist and missionary were at loggerheads.

Leopold, Duke of Brabant, was heir-apparent to that uncle of Queen Victoria's whom, in 1831, the European powers had rather arbitrarily lodged on the throne of a small modern nation their diplomacy had created: Belgium.

A foxy-faced man with a straggling beard, Leopold was rich and extremely clever, as well as heir to a kingdom. Before and after he came to the throne, he pursued a hobby which grew in course of time to an obsession: colonies. The Belgians, a stay-at-home people, were not particularly interested, but their clever king had listened to those who argued that an industrialized country which did not have both its own private source of raw materials and a privileged market was bound to be at a disadvantage. He had seriously considered, at one time, buying the Philip-pines, or Sarawak, or even a province in the Argentine. But when the news reached him that H. M. Stanley, launched on his way by Tipu Tib, had succeeded after a desperate journey of 999 days in tracing the course of the River Congo, Leopold saw and grasped his chance. Suppose that vast, blank space on the map which Stanley had just sketched in might somehow become his own property? Stanley was on his way to England: Leopold sent a messenger to intercept him at Marseilles. The explorer accepted £1000 a year from the king, and by 1877 was back in the Congo, as his agent.

In Europe, Leopold made uplifting speeches about the need to civilize the Congo and abolish slavery there, while Stanley worked his way up the great river, entertaining the chiefs on either bank with a clockwork mouse and a dancing doll until he had them sufficiently bemused to put their mark on a piece of paper which was in fact a treaty, yielding up their rights of sovereignty and property. By the time 450 such treaties had been quietly filed away, King Leopold felt that he had a colourable legal argument for laying claim to the Congo – not on his own selfish account, of course, but from philanthropical motives.

David Livingstone's recipe for extinguishing slavery had been 'Commerce and Christianity'. And now the world was made aware that a benevolent monarch intended to apply on a huge scale a solution very much the same as Livingstone's, if not quite. 'I insist upon the completely charitable, completely scientific and philanthropic nature of the aim to be achieved,' Leopold told the International Conference which he convened in Brussels in 1876, to consider the Congo. 'It is not a question of a business proposition.'

The society which Leopold set up had a scientific bias – 'a large proportion of its members were professed freethinkers', it announced, yet even so it liberally 'extended its protection to the missionary, without recognizing the claim of religion to hold a place in its counsels'. When religion might serve him, Leopold was willing to make use of it. Cardinal Lavigerie was just then preaching powerfully in the capitals of Europe, in the hope of uniting European governments against the Arab slave-traders. 'I will try to get him to say,' remarked Leopold, when he saw how popular the cardinal's appeal was becoming, 'that the Congo State must and can undertake this crusade.'

Leopold needed particularly to influence opinion in Britain and the United States. Manoeuvring the great powers one against another, entangling them with each other so that in the end they might allow him a free hand in the Congo, would be easier if he could appeal to the peoples over the heads of their governments. Therefore, enlightened businessmen, missionaries, and philanthropists on both sides of the Atlantic should be roused up to do his work for him – block political opposition, and even raise capital. He particularly addressed himself, therefore, to 'men of goodwill, who are horrified by the barbarities of the slave trade, to religious and believing men, who suffer to see the unfortunate blacks held in the ignorance of fetish worship'. The rhetoric was so impressive that in the early days almost no one doubted Leopold's good intentions. But he was making the mistake of trying to fool all the people all the time. Harry Johnston, the old West Africa hand who was, later, to finish off the Arab slavers in Nyasaland, wrote to warn Anderson, the African expert at the Foreign Office, that Leopold's International Association was commercial, aiming at 'a gigantic monopoly'. And so it proved.

Stanley began the work of civilization in the Congo by pioneering a road to bypass the falls which hitherto had blocked access by ship to the interior. On the broad stretch of water inland, where the river began to be navigable, Stanley came across a Baptist missionary called George Grenfell, who was trying to put together Arthington's prefabricated boat. *Peace* had been shipped out in 800 separate packages, weighing in all six tons. Grenfell was no engineer – their qualified man had died of fever – but once in his past life he had bought machinery on commission, and now, with marvellous patience, he was sorting out the jigsaw puzzle. Stanley had little use for religion – the Baptists privately thought him 'wicked' – but his orders were to help, because Leopold had reason to think that the Baptists might soon be politically useful.

King Leopold was already working the dapper and enthusiastic little shipping magnate, Sir William Mackinnon, for all he was worth. The pair of them had cooperated earlier, in East Africa, on the Royal Belgian Elephant Expedition. Leopold had wondered at the time if trained Indian elephants might solve the problem of transport in tsetse fly country. Mackinnon arranged for some Indian elephants to be shipped in, but the wise beasts refused to go ashore, walking back time after time to the ship, and even towing back into deeper sea the boats which tried to lead them up through the shallow water to dry land. Soon after landing, the elephants began to die.

Leopold was now encouraging Mackinnon and his partner in the Imperial East Africa Company, James Hutton, MP, to raise capital among their friends in Britain for his Congo railway. H. M. Stanley had already assured Manchester men that 'the Congo trade in cottons could be made to yield more than India' – journalistic hyperbole, no doubt, but there were 20,000,000 Congolese, and once civilized they would all want cotton clothes. But the British syndicate were too greedy for Leopold's liking – they demanded 10,000 acres of adjacent land for every mile of track laid (the cost per mile of track being £3000) and a tax situation which might soon have given them a stranglehold on all the trade flowing out of the Congo. What Leopold had in mind was a railway – and for that matter, a large colony – under his personal control, so he let Mackinnon and his cronies take up only a fifth of the shareholding, for an investment of £200,000.

The British government, too, did its best to cramp Leopold's style by pressing Portugal's claim to the mouth of the Congo – which in fact was as good as anyone else's and better than most. Now Leopold knew that if he had no access to the sea on his own terms, the more he civilized the interior, the more others, sitting there snugly at the river mouth, would squeeze the profit. By appealing to Britain's philanthropists, who by now had begun to think of him as one of themselves, Leopold managed to provoke a roar of indignation against Portugal which made the British government think twice.

The Portuguese had a bad name – they had officially ended their own slave trade only in 1878 – and could easily be given a worse one. They shipped out 'indentured black labour' and winked at the smuggling of slaves to Cuba, so that in Britain, the anti-slavery lobby could easily be whipped up into a fury against them. Then Bismarck, who had plans of his own in Africa, saw that the time had come to disoblige Britain by opposing the treaty with Portugal, and that was the end of it. Leopold's access to the sea was assured.

H. M. Stanley's reputation in the United States as an explorer and journalist was immense, so that men of goodwill there had no hesitation in believing him when he predicted that in the Congo, 'the European merchant shall go hand in hand with the dark African trader. Murder and lawlessness and the cruel barter of slaves shall for ever cease.' Lincoln's abolition of slavery was still in every American's mind, so Stanley found it not difficult to create a belief that Leopold wanted the Congo to become 'a republican confederation of free negroes'. The campaign succeeded: the United States was the first power to recognize the lone-star flag Stanley had designed for King Leopold – a gold star on a blue ground – and to acknowledge his sovereignty in the Congo. Once the United States had conceded recognition, Leopold's European rivals had little option but to follow suit. On 1 July 1885, *l'État Indépendant du Congo* was proclaimed. That same day, Mr A. H. Baynes, Secretary of the Baptist Missionary Society, presented an address of congratulation to King Leopold in his palace at Ostend.

At home, Leopold was a constitutional monarch, under the restraint of law, and with the critical eye of civilized Europe always upon him. But ever since the Belgian government had decided that the million square miles of the Congo – eighty times the size of Belgium – should be their king's personal responsibility, in Africa King Leopold was an autocrat. His will was supreme there; he could act in secret. He was powerful, well-connected, rich, and the supreme master in his day of public relations. Those who dared criticize him could easily be dealt with.

One indication of the success with which Leopold had passed off his 'gigantic monopoly' in the United States as a philanthropic enterprise is given by the sad fate of the American Methodist Mission. Talked into believing that the Congo was henceforth to be a model republic for liberated slaves, Bishop Taylor of the Methodist Episcopal Church, having in mind recent experience in the American South, launched a foreign mission to the Congo on new lines. Instead of living on money sent by the church back home, this mission, by standing on its own feet, would teach the liberated blacks the frontier virtues of self-reliance. There would be no carpet-bagging, no condescension. The watchword was 'Self-Support'.

In 1886, nearly forty of Bishop Taylor's supporters, high-minded but totally misled, came ashore at Matadi, which was as far up the Congo as a ship would go, 'trusting in the Lord' for accommodation. They were lucky enough to find a deserted government station at Vivi, where they camped. Their death-roll was high, for among Congo missionaries too there was the usual mortality – of forty-seven male Baptist missionaries, for example, who came out from Britain between 1879 and 1889, twenty-four died.

The local Africans, as the Americans soon discovered, liked gifts but despised work, but the Self-Support Mission had nothing to give away. After their centuries of contact with the transatlantic slave trade, their black neighbours were used to buying and selling, but as potential frontiersmen they were poor material.

A few of the American Methodists who still had money saw that the situation was ludicrous – indeed, desperate – and headed for home. Others bought goods from passing ships and became petty traders, which brought them into competition with African traders, and made them unpopular. A few started vegetable gardens; eventually, they had ten acres under cultivation. The American missionaries never managed to get their own sectional steamer up past the rapids, though for a while they used her as a freighter in the estuary, until undercut and driven out of business by the sea-going ships which came upriver to Matadi; in the end, their little steam-boat 'scarcely earned her paint and oil'.

The few tenacious souls who stuck it out went back, in the frontier tradition, to hunting, and lived by shooting hippos, selling the meat 'at absurdly low prices'. Not one of them ever managed to master a native tongue. By 1899 there was but one heroic American Methodist left, a lady called Miss Kildare, who lived in a shanty up a creek, near the port of Banana. Miss Kildare held out, not thanks to Self-Support – the Congo was not the American frontier, it was not even Liberia – but because she could finance her own small private mission from her own small private income.

The Baptists, both American and British, did better. The features of the British missionaries who set to work on Arthington's boat gaze out at us from a sepia photograph of the time: confident, self-reliant, plebeian faces, a remarkable number of them wearing steel-rimmed spectacles. They eked out a ration of tinned meat, sardines and condensed milk, which they had brought with them, by fried bananas. George Grenfell, then thirty-five, and self-taught both as mechanic and geographer, having managed to fit *Peace* together and launch her, set out on 13 June 1884 – a year before the Congo State was proclaimed – on a five-month voyage of exploration up the river.

He found that, for nine hundred miles from the lake where *Peace* took the water, the Congo was a navigable river. Then came sixty miles of cataracts – the Stanley Falls – which only canoes could cross. If the Congo's many tributaries were included, there were altogether 5000 miles of navigable waterway, fingering like liquid roads into the otherwise impenetrable wilderness.

After Stanley Falls came the upper Congo, also navigable but not safe, because Arab slavers living at Nyangwe and in Tipu Tib's little capital city of Kasongo were the power in the land. Kasongo, a flourishing community of 30,000 inhabitants, a peaceable-looking township of flat-roofed, white-washed houses, was set amid fertile irrigated fields. They were worked for Tipu Tib by the slave labour he systematically kidnapped downriver.

Grenfell, as *Peace* chugged up the Congo at her average eight miles an hour, was more than once ambushed from the banks. His riposte was to come in close, and from the cover of his arrow-proof netting throw gifts of beads and cloth to those firing at him, as proof of his peaceful intentions. Some of the more amiable natives begged Grenfell to sell them a few of his steamer-hands. The flesh of men from the coast, so they said, had the salty flavour which here, in the heart of the Congo (if not in New Zealand), was esteemed a delicacy. They offered Grenfell two or three of their women for one man from the coast. These inland Congo Africans, Grenfell discovered, kept slaves of their own. Some were being fattened, like cattle, for the pot. Others were their savings-bank account – valuable objects, to exchange against ivory. There was also a thriving traffic in sun-dried human meat.

In this part of the Congo, domestic slavery and ritual cannibalism had been traditional, though human meat was formerly used only for solemn feasts. The Baptists were not shocked by cannibalism for long: 'a bad habit, but it does not necessarily mark out the natives who observe it as being of a lower type'. The human flesh eaten ritually had hitherto been consumed with a certain uneasiness because 'the dead do not really die': your meal might come back and haunt you. But since civilization in its Islamic form crept closer, slaves were becoming of increasing significance, as articles of trade.

Fines extorted by a chief were frequently paid in human beings. Taxes might be met by parting with a member of the family. But though slaves were valuable, ivory (which could be exported to buy guns, whereas nowadays slaves could not) was better still. The Arabs had hit upon a particularly efficient technique for extracting it. They would raid a village, kidnap and enslave the children, and then trade them back to the parents against a ransom of elephant tusks. On the Congo, ever since the outside world intruded, human beings had in a most literal sense become things.

Having digested and made the best of some of these hard truths, the missionaries were obliged to stomach soon after an action which threw the first doubt on Leopold's sincerity as an anti-slavery crusader. Rich man though he was, Leopold had by this time over-reached himself financially. To extract all the wealth the Congo might have to offer, he must not only build a million-pound railway, and that with less help than he had been led to expect from international finance. He must also pay for the material means of enforcing his will – put gunboats on the river, import rifles, create a private army, a gendarmerie called *la Force publique*. He knew himself not yet strong enough to govern the upper Congo, where Tipu Tib and his like ruled the roost, for if the Arabs all got together they could put thousands of armed men against him in the field. So, with bland cynicism, Leopold accepted H. M. Stanley's suggestion and promoted Tipu Tib, the notorious slaver, to be his governor at Stanley Falls – besides offering to buy what ivory Tipu Tib could extort.

When the poacher was invited to turn gamekeeper, philanthropists were shocked, but for Leopold, philanthropists had already served their turn. On the upper Congo, under Tipu Tib, the name was changed but not the thing. Old-fashioned slave-raiding upriver of Stanley Falls diminished. Instead, the governor would send out his 'recruiters', armed with rifles, paying them a hundred francs a head to 'recruit Bantu labour'. As late as 1891, Tipu Tib made a contract to furnish 2600 such 'recruits' to work on the Lower Congo Railway.

Flattered by the attention he had so far paid them, Grenfell and his fellow missionaries still had a great deal of faith in Leopold – they tended, at first, to blame not the king, but his subordinates, and they continued to picture themselves as helping King Leopold in the good work of advancing civilization. To natives who increasingly complained of bullying by the black gendarmes of *la Force publique*, the Baptists in those early days would reply sedately that 'God had permitted the State authorities to take possession of their country, because they could not rule themselves. They were always fighting and killing one another.'

Encouraged by the king, George Grenfell set off in *Peace*, slowly and patiently to chart the entire Congo. When he reached Tipu Tib's country, Grenfell discovered that the repression of slavery was a fiction. Natives on the river bank slept in canoes, so that if Arab raiders came in the night they might have a chance of escape. Grenfell collected 1500 words for W. Holman Bentley, another Baptist, who was compiling an English-Kongo dictionary, and for his survey Grenfell was awarded the Founder's Medal of the Royal Geographical Society. On a scale of about a mile to an inch, his chart filled a roll of paper 125 feet long – and was, of course, of immense value to King Leopold.

Grenfell took a young African called Bungudi back with him, to Thorneycrofts at Chiswick, and there ordered a prefabricated boat of twenty tons called *Goodwill*, small enough to be taken, in pieces, over the cataracts of Stanley Falls, and assembled in the river above. On the upper Congo, *Goodwill* was put together entirely by Congolese labour, with Bungudi in charge – a measure of how fast Africans could master technique. The upper river was at last open to mission work. But King Leopold persuaded Grenfell himself to quit the mission, and travel 1000 miles on ox-back as his boundary commissioner, tracing the undefined southern frontier of the Congo state. The cleavage was beginning to show – the doubt as to which king the missionaries thought they had gone to the Congo to serve.

Peace had done so much government work that to commandeer her for taking troops and munitions upriver during a skirmish with the Arabs seemed nothing out of the way; a telegram from Brussels was necessary, to release her. The name of the mission ship had been discredited, and the men on the spot were hearing ugly rumours and having second thoughts, even though the Baptist Missionary Society's headquarters had been so flattered by Leopold's gracious patronage that they took much longer to disillusion.

Leopold was well aware that, once their propaganda usefulness for him was over, Protestant missionaries in the Congo might become awkward witnesses. Therefore he brought to bear considerable pressure to have them replaced by Catholics – best of all, by Belgian Catholics – who as members of a highly disciplined church which in those days was well-disposed towards royalty might be all the more under his thumb. In 1888 – by which time the Baptists had six stations, 500 miles up the great river – the Administrator-General of the Congo was reporting cheerfully to the Belgian Minister at the Vatican that there was 'no more interference from foreign missionaries; the new state is becoming Belgian from the religious point of view'. He was wrong.

Leopold had, so far, been spending his own money, and not recouping; by 1890 he was feeling the pinch. He created in that year an ivory monopoly for his private benefit. Anyone else dealing in ivory, except at the river mouth, was to be regarded as receiving stolen goods. Leopold also imposed a ten per cent import and export tax, *ad valorem*, 'so as to fight slavery'. The free trade he had promised Manchester men and agreed to by treaty was a luxury he could no longer afford. On the coast, foreign traders managed to keep their foothold, but by 1892 they had been squeezed out of half the state – *la domaine privée*.

As the demand increased for bicycle tyres and waterproof coats, rubber was becoming for Leopold an increasingly valuable export, and the boom had only just begun. In 1891, eighty-two tons of wild rubber were exported from the Congo. Ten years later, the export has risen to 6000 tons – motor cars were beginning to need rubber tyres, and the price was still rising. Money was pouring in at last, and Leopold intended to keep it for himself: in 1896, a secret decree designated as his personal property 112,000 square miles of the forest where wild rubber trees grew, between the Kasai and Ruki rivers.

The hardened old slaver, Tipu Tib, had been allowed to govern the upper Congo for five years. Leopold had used this breathing space to ring the Arabs' little dominion with forts, and to build up his own private army. The time for action approached. Leopold's ban on the sale of arms irked the Arabs, as did his tax on the export of their ivory: they let themselves be provoked.

The first bloody clash came in 1892, when news came to Commandant Dhanis of *la Force publique* that an ivory dealer called Hodister, trading in the upper Congo in competition with the Arabs, had been gruesomely killed on the Lomami river with all his party, including three Belgians. Not waiting for orders, Dhanis marched off, taking with him some cannibal irregulars. He crossed the Lomami, and his reprisal was a pure massacre. Three thousand were killed out of hand, and a participant, Henri Michaud, remarked, 'I doubt whether any demon Sabbath could be compared with this Christian vengeance. The Arab losses were terrifying.' After the massacres, the cannibal auxiliaries ate the slain. 'I knew it was horrible,' observed Michaud 'but still, for the moment, we had to pretend not to see it.'

In the last decade of the nineteenth century, a little Islamic principality, based on slavery and surrounded by hostile European powers, could hardly hope to survive. Leopold intended to crush it, and thereby both establish his own authority at last on the upper Congo, and refurbish his sullied halo. Early in 1893, Dhanis got orders to move, once more, against the Arabs. But since the entire *Force publique* did not amount to more than four thousand men, spread out thin across a million square miles, Dhanis placed reliance, this time, too, in his cannibal auxiliaries.

He captured Nyangwe in March 1893, Kasongo in April. The slaughter was immense, and the loot well worth having. Sidney Hinde, MD, serving as captain under Dhanis, described how 'the common soldiers slept on silk and satin mattresses in carved beds with silk mosquito curtains. The gardens were very luxurious and well-planted. I was constantly astonished by the splendid work which had been done in the neighbourhood by the Arabs.' But the ground outside was 'comparable to a cemetery of bones'. A thousand people had been killed in a few hours. Happily, Dhanis's cannibals 'ate them up at the same rate. It's horrible, but exceedingly useful and hygienic.' For his victories, Dhanis was ennobled, becoming Baron Dhanis, and as soon as Leopold had studied the account of the action, his brusque order came from Brussels by telegraph; 'Conserve the gardens, and turn them into a source of revenue for the State.'

The war dragged on, until Charlie Stokes, too, fell victim. When gun-running to the Arabs in 1896, the bearded and trusting ex-missionary was tricked by a Belgian officer, Major Lothaire, into entering his tent as a guest, only to be seized, handcuffed, and hanged after a mock trial. By that time, the doubts which British public opinion might have had about King Leopold were turning to mistrust. Charlie Stokes, as a British victim of his regime, if not perhaps a wholly respectable one, enjoyed a little flutter of posthumous fame.

On 18 November 1895, Reverend J. B. Murphy, of the American Baptist Union, reported a curious incident to *The Times* from Equatorville. He had observed a commissary counting severed hands, to verify that his soldiers had not wasted cartridges. Readers were sceptical; almost no one was yet inclined to blame King Leopold.

In the spring of 1897, at a meeting of the Aborigines' Protection Society, called under the auspices of John Morley, MP, and Sir Charles Dilke, MP, a Swedish missionary called Sjomblom asserted that soldiers in the Congo were cutting off the right hand of natives collecting rubber who failed to deliver their quota. A soldier and his woman had passed Sjomblom's mission station, carrying a basket full of hands. 'We counted eighteen hands. They belonged to men, women and children.' This atrocity story, though widely reported, was a storm in a teacup. Leopold's position appeared unshaken.

The American Presbyterians were running a mission up the Kasai river, actually in the rubber country. A black American among them, W. H. Sheppard, got a royal welcome from the Bakuba people on his arrival, since they thought his body must contain the spirit of some member of their own tribe come back from the dead. (In a roundabout sense, they were right.) For these Presbyterian missionaries, literacy and conversion went together, and the ex-cannibals living nearby soon became passionately keen to learn.

In 1898, as spokesman for the American Presbyterians on the Kasai, Reverend William Morrison announced publicly that a state official concerned in rubber collection there had let his soldiers pillage at will, and taken away several thousand local people as forced labour, against the protests of the missionaries working there.

As his enforcers, this local official used practising cannibals, and their methods of intimidation were horrifying; they engaged, moreover, in 'slave-raiding for the state'. Believing that Leopold himself could know nothing of this, and would put a stop to it if he knew, Morrison had written first to the king, but his letter had been ignored.

Leopold's reply to this warning rumble of criticism was ingenious. In September 1896, he set up a Commission for the Protection of the Natives, comprising three Protestant and three Roman Catholic missionaries, who were to report abuses to the Governor-General. But they had been hand-picked. They all lived a long way distant from each other – up to 1000 miles. They were paid no travelling expenses, nor were they granted the right to take evidence, and none of them happened to dwell in the rubber-collecting areas. There was, of course, something to hide in the Kasai.

Not only had Leopold introduced a Trojan Horse – the mission-aries – into his private domain. Some of the mercenaries of many nationalities whom he had recruited for his service were in the end to bear witness against him.

In 1889, a British master-mariner of Polish extraction called Korzeniowski, then thirty-two, landed at Boma to take up his promised command of a riverboat on the Congo. On the voyage out he had learned from a shipmate that sixty per cent of the men recruited for Leopold's service went back to Europe within six months; 'others were sent back so as not to spoil the death statistics.' Only seven per cent stayed as long as three years.

At Boma, he met the British consul, a young Irishman of twenty-six called Roger Casement: 'Thinks, speaks well, most intelligent and very sympathetic,' noted Korzeniowski in his journal. For a while he was kept 'busy packing ivory in casks: idiotic employment.' Then, after a nine-hundred-mile voyage upriver in the little fifteen-ton steamboat *Roi de Belges* – he had fever four times in three months – he reached the cataracts of Stanley Falls, 'in the heart of an immense darkness'.

Korzeniowski carried among his dunnage, wrapped in a brown paper parcel, the first seven chapters of a novel which he was eventually to publish as *Almayer's Folly*, signing the book Joseph Conrad. Now he stood there, as far up the Congo almost as a ship could go, having accidentally fulfilled a boyhood dream of travelling to the centre of Africa. 'Ten miles away, the yet unbroken power of the Congo Arabs slumbered uneasily,' he wrote. 'Their day was over. A great melancholy descended upon me, the unholy recollection of a prosaic newspaper "stunt" and the distasteful knowledge of the vilest scramble for loot that ever disfigured the human conscience and geographical exploration.'

Making use of the journal written during that journey in Leopold's service, up the Congo, Conrad was eventually to publish *The Heart of Darkness*, a story over which broods the evil atmosphere of a society based solely on greed and brute force. Joseph Conrad, by upbringing a Roman Catholic, had but one good word to say for what he saw in the Congo: the Baptist Mission where he passed a night was 'eminently civil-ized and very refreshing to see'.

King Leopold, having set aside as his personal property those 112,000 square miles in the Kasai basin where rubber trees grew wild, had gone on to devise a way of motivating his officials there so as to get out all the rubber that could possibly be collected while the price continued to boom. State officials in the Kasai were paid salaries, not in fixed amounts, but as a commission on the rubber they collected and despatched. The soldiers placed under their command were types who would stick at nothing – often men who in wartime had been allowed to practise canni- balism in lieu of being issued with rations. On the unlucky natives a heavy labour tax was imposed – payable in rubber. So long as rubber was shipped out, the Congo paid its way. Any witnesses of what might perhaps be going on in his faraway private estate could easily be discredited, so what had Leopold to fear?

The contrast between the 'charitable, scientific and philan- thropic' methods which Leopold was employing to extract wealth from the Congo, and the methods used by the missionaries there in their everyday work, distinguishes and indeed separates imperialism from religion. They are at last utterly at odds; the difference has been defined.

The Baptists took a more tolerant view of polygamy than the Anglicans or the Roman Catholics. An African who had several wives already might become a member of a Baptist church, though he must limit himself to the wives he had already married. The democratic structure of the Baptist church gave Congolese Christians their first hint of rational self-government. Baptist moral teaching, narrow though some might find it now, was intended, though often it failed, to train the Congolese in self- control – for which, in a tribal society ruled at every point by tradition and taboo, there had hitherto been no need. No African Baptist might hold slaves, or trade in them, or buy himself another wife. The Baptists were uncompromising opponents of the ritual murder which the tribal society around them had always taken for granted.

Slowly and patiently, if clumsily, the essential conviction was implanted at Baptist mission stations that an individual human being was, by nature, something more than a piece of merchandise to be bought and sold, or a piece of livestock, to be fattened up and eaten. Many converts lapsed, because what was asked of them was so immense, but the church struck root.

In the Congo as in Uganda, the Roman Catholics collected society's human debris – of which there was plenty, for as early as 1905 the tribal system there, under the simultaneous impact of tax collectors, cash crop, conscription and the gendarme, was near collapse. To stiffen it, Leopold was obliged to appoint brutal ex-soldiers all over the country as 'chiefs'. Catholics took up stray orphans, they paid dealers the purchase-price of their unhappy child-slaves, they gave sanctuary to fugitives. All these victims were brought together into a self-supporting agricultural colony where, while gaining a livelihood and learning a trade, they might slowly come under the influence of Christian modes of behaviour.

Hitherto in the Congo there had been a contrast between the social roles of men – destructive, cannibalistic, idle except in wartime – and those of women, who both mothered the children and grew the crops, yet were the first victims in man-made times of violence. In the fields around a Catholic mission, men and women were expected to set to with their hoes, as equals. Though the *chrétientés* of the Congo were never ideal utopias – their critics spoke of the preaching of submissiveness, and even of thrashings, though by 1902 such corporal punishment was forbidden by the hierarchy – yet they undoubtedly began to transform the unequal lives of African women, and they saved the lives of many children. In one of them alone, 1600 orphans were looked after.

The Catholic system was more paternalistic, and the Protestant may in a rudimentary way have been more democratic, but in the grim everyday world of Leopold's Congo neither could survive, except by removing the convert almost bodily from the disintegrating pagan world around him into a more serene private world. In going halfway to meet the hard facts of native life, the Jesuits had the greatest success. They would start a farm with a church upon it – *une ferme-chapelle* – near an African village, so that their crops were planted, their orphans looked after and their mass celebrated under the critically observant eyes of the villagers, thus providing them day after day with a living object-lesson.

Many of these priests and ministers made no public protest at the evil being done around them, even when they had the chance – though others opposed Leopold vociferously, and even at great risk. Yet the living example of their everyday life was itself seditious, even in trifles. A visiting French Catholic bishop was discovered one day, on the Leopoldville-Matadi railway, cheerfully travelling fourth class, among the Congolese. In great embarrassment the authorities insisted that he travel by special train.

Edmund Dene Morel was born in Paris in 1873. His father, a Frenchman, was a clerk at the Ministry of Finance; his mother was an Englishwoman of East Anglian Quaker extraction, so Morel grew up bilingual. When Morel was fifteen his father died, and the boy took a job in Paris at the Drexel Morgan bank. At seventeen, Morel moved with his mother to Liverpool, where he became a clerk, at £60 a year, in the West African department of the Elder Dempster shipping line.

Morel would very much have liked to ship out to the Congo, as purser, but his mother's brother-in-law, Major Phillips, had served King Leopold in the Congo in the early days, and died there, so to please his mother the young clerk stayed on shore, in Liverpool.

In the evenings, Morel began reading up everything available on West Africa, in both English and French – geography, history, fauna, flora – so as to augment his meagre income by journalism. By the time he was twenty, though still a shipping clerk at Elder Dempster, he had made himself known in the newspaper world as a recognized expert on West Africa. He wrote particularly for the intelligent liberal press: Scott's *Manchester Guardian*, Massingham's *Chronicle*.

In 1890, Elder Dempster had been awarded a contract by King Leopold to run a steamer line from Antwerp to the Congo. Morel was put in charge of their Congo department, and from 1895, when he was twenty-two years old, he began visiting

Belgium for business discussions with Congo Free State officials.

In *la domaine privée*, Leopold had introduced the system of concessions. To a company in which he was given a share, he would grant a monopoly of anything produceable on or under the soil of a great tract of land. The concessionaires were allowed, virtually, to get out what wealth they could, as fast as they liked, by whatever method they chose. By 1898, the Congo was divided up between forty-four concession companies, the African villager having by this time lost all rights in the land, not even being allowed to leave his village without a written permit. Once land was allocated to a concessionaire, all private trade there ceased.

Morel, from his studies of West Africa, was in favour of 'native rights' – the system of land ownership by independent African farmers which some far-sighted businessmen trading there, particularly Quakers with cocoa interests, held to be the best, in the long run, for everyone. British businessmen trading to West Africa who supported 'native rights' were often the lineal descendants of those who began trading to West Africa from philanthropic as well as business motives in the old anti-slavery days. They detested the concession system. Though it might at first be immensely profitable, in the long run it impoverished the African, even pauperized him, and he was the potential customer. If only the African farmer could sell his tropical cash crop – cocoa, palm oil, ground-nuts – not to a price-fixing monopoly, but in a competitive market at a fair price, then, they argued, he would buy more imported goods, and thus improve his standard of living.

Taking this simple piece of old-fashioned economic common-sense as his point of departure, the young Liverpool shipping clerk, having in mind the commercial gossip he heard every day and the ship's manifests he handled, began to ask himself quite what could be happening in the Congo. There was an inordinate gap between Leopold's talk of his civilizing mission, and the economic reality.

As he got older, Leopold could not resist flaunting the fact that the Congo was his personal property; he went so far as to claim 'absolute ownership, uncontested, of the Congo and its riches'. But since he was a self-proclaimed autocrat, any crimes committed in the Congo must be the fault – so the outside world could believe if it wished – of that one man, rather than of any method of government, or of the colonial system as such. Leopold therefore, for those who felt uneasy, was a perfect scapegoat.

The first missionary stories of atrocities in the Congo had been expertly fobbed off. What the case now called for was what young Morel dealt in: hard facts. The young Liverpool shipping clerk calmly decided to take on, with stone and sling, the Goliath of his day – one of the cleverest, best-connected, richest and most powerful men in Europe: King Leopold II of the Belgians.

Leopold's claim was that, with the willing consent of the other European powers, he was raising the Congo to the level of civilization, but the statistics, Morel found, did not bear him out. The population, for example, was falling dramatically – from over 20,000,000 in 1881 to 8,500,000 in 1911. And the trade figures, if expertly scrutinized, told an odd story.

Morel knew well enough, from his everyday experience, that in West African colonies where heavy costs for administration and armed forces had to be met, imports were always in excess of exports. In the Congo, however, he found that the disproportion was immense. From 1899 to 1902, in Leopold's private empire, £7,360,130 of exports had been 'paid for' – leaving military and administrative needs out of account – by only £893,317 of imports. Wealth was flooding outwards, but only trickling inwards; the African therefore, was being systematically robbed.

Morel went on to discover that Elder Dempster were taking cargoes of ivory and rubber out of the Congo which were not accounted for in the official returns. To balance the account, they were shipping to Africa large quantities of rifles and ball-cartridge: the means of coercion. 'Firstly,' concluded Morel, 'the natives were being robbed. Secondly, as they certainly couldn't be expected to work for nothing voluntarily, they were being enslaved.'

When in Antwerp on business, Morel began to hear boastful hints from men on leave from the Congo of even more sickening atrocities than those missionary disclosures which people had earlier found so hard to believe. Leopold was paying his administrators an income based on the rubber they collected, and to augment it they had devised a new technique of intimidation. Sjomblom was right. Africans not meeting their rubber quota had a hand cut off. But the facts admitted to Morel by those who had actually committed such deeds in King Leopold's name were even more sadistically lurid.

Half the stock in the Société Anversoise du Commerce au Congo was held by King Leopold himself, and in March 1900 his shareholding in the company was worth 23,000,000 francs, or nearly a million pounds. In the same year, two of the company's agents confessed 'to killing, by order, 150 natives, cutting off 60 hands, crucifying women and children, and impaling the sexual remains of slaughtered males on the stockades of villages whose inhabitants were slow in gathering rubber'. So it went on, until horror became monotonous.

Morel's documented articles in the *Speaker* on such Congo atrocities as these, factually irrefutable, came like a clap of thunder. The articles were unsigned – but Leopold had his own sources of information. He sniffed Morel out, and in no time was bullying Sir Alfred Jones, who ran Elder Dempster, into getting rid of this inconvenient clerk, by threatening that otherwise he would withdraw his profitable shipping contract. Meanwhile, as man to man, the king pleaded ignorance of the reported atrocities, and gave Sir Alfred his personal promise that there would be reforms. (The promise was never kept.) Eased out of his job, E. D. Morel entered upon the precarious life of a freelance, but he had found his purpose: to bring down King Leopold.

The spirit of the time was on Morel's side. To get and keep his footing in the Congo, Leopold had cynically manipulated too many tender consciences, and his dupes were now turning against him. Most men were still glowing with the sentiment which, seventy years before, had outlawed slavery. Now as then, they might reasonably hope to create a political alliance with those merchants and manufacturers who thought that their business interests would best be served by 'native rights' – African land-ownership and free trade. Imperialism, in its most modern, scientific and ruthless form, was making enlightened men in Europe and America uneasy, and if they were handled right, their concern, their twinges of guilt, could all be projected upon King Leopold.

E. D. Morel's *The Congo Slave State* was aimed at intelligent opinion in the United States. To counteract its damning facts and figures while putting his own view across, Leopold sent over a personal representative on a lecture tour. But skilful political publicist though the king had always been, in E. D. Morel he met his match, because Leopold depended on appeals to sentiment or cupidity, but Morel dealt in fact. Occurrences he wrote about were meticulously vouched for, arguments he used were impeccably documented, no one could contradict his figures. He lived with his wife and children in a country cottage near Hawarden, earning a living by journalism, staying in the background, but supplying public men in England, France and Belgium with deadly accurate information.

European governments which, twenty years before, had granted Leopold his sovereignty in the Congo began to stir uneasily. But they were curiously slow to act, and Morel was hard put, at first, to divine the reason. Belgium was, as it happened, a key link in a chain of understandings and alliances to which the rival great powers in Europe were committing themselves – a network of secret obligations which, a few years later, was to lead to world war. No Foreign Minister anywhere in Europe wanted to offend Leopold. But governments became aware that something must be done to tranquillize men's minds. If the facts had been exaggerated by the newspapers, as doubtless they were, then a sober inquiry might discredit the agitation.

Roger Casement, the British consul in Boma whom Conrad had known and liked, was sent off into the Congolese jungle to investigate the truth of what Morel had been alleging about the rubber trade. His official report, published in February 1904, was scarifying. The real situation was even worse than the agitators had implied. From then on, a tidal wave of protest began to roll.

Already in 1903, at the urging of Congo missionaries, the Free Church Council in Britain had passed a resolution condemning Leopold's methods. In 1906, in Belgium itself under Leopold's very nose, the Jesuit theologian Arthur Vermeersch, demanding reform, had written acidly in his *La question congolaise*, "A few tons of rubber are enough to deaden their consciences, to show them as grasping for profit and coldly cruel" – that is what people are saying of us.'

Leopold decided that he, too, had better appease public opinion. He would send out to the Congo his own commission of inquiry. Most members of the commission were his own subjects, or officials, but to make it look more impartial he added two Swiss jurists. Missionary evidence was certain to be given in English, but Leopold managed (surprisingly enough) to discover two eminent Swiss who spoke hardly any English, and so would find it hard to grasp what the missionaries were telling them. He refused to add a British representative.

Morel outflanked him by circularizing the missionaries in the Congo and inviting them to smuggle out to him a copy of the evidence they may have given, or tried to give. He would speak out for them. Morel soon discovered that once the commissioners had turned their backs and gone elsewhere, native witnesses were maltreated or imprisoned, sometimes killed. Attempts were made to intimidate missionaries who might give evidence; sometimes their lives were threatened.

Leopold's government did its best to suppress the words of the most damning witnesses, and to postpone the official report. But Morel had the missionaries' sworn words under his hand; he could satisfy Europe's curiosity. He translated the missionary depositions into French, and sent copies to the deputies of the Belgian parliament, not all of whom were Leopold's admirers.

In 1904, the year Casement presented his sensational report, E. D. Morel was sent cross the Atlantic by his British supporters, to present a memorial on the Congo to President Theodore Roosevelt. This was a shrewd blow at Leopold. In the old days, when the Congo was seeking recognition, he had always been particularly clever at playing the United States off against Europe. Leopold sent over large funds for a lobbying campaign against E. D. Morel in Washington. He spent extravagantly to get newspaper coverage for his own point of view and, in Washington, the Belgian minister was caught out trying to lever favourable articles into the press.

Leopold tried to put a better complexion on his personal monopoly by offering a stake in it to American investors. In October 1906 he launched the American Congo Company. He flattered influential millionaires, on their trips to Europe, by entertaining them royally in his Belgian palace. He used all the devices of modern public relations. But he reckoned without Mark Twain who, in his savagely witty *King Leopold's Soliloquy*, took Morel's dry statistics and made them unforgettably dramatic: 'If the innocent blood shed in the Congo State by King Leopold were put in buckets side by side, the line would stretch two thousand miles; if the skeletons of his ten millions of starved and butchered dead could rise up and march in single file, it would take them seven months and four days to pass a single point.' Stung to action, the Senate formally resolved to support any steps the President might take for ameliorating conditions in the Congo. An American consul-general was sent there with a watching brief, and thus the mysterious inertia of the European powers was overcome.

In 1906, a shame-faced weariness with the long-drawn-out Boer War, as well as alarm at what might be happening in the Congo, had been political factors in Britain helping to sweep a Liberal government to power with a programme of reform. That year there were resolutions condemning the Congo from the Anglican Convocation, the Free Church Council, and from meetings convened by the mayors of many British cities. An 'Appeal to the Nation' was signed by the Archbishop of Canterbury and (among others) the Church Missionary Society, no doubt glad that attention was at last being directed away from Uganda. By 1907, the pressure on Leopold to give up his one-man rule in the Congo, and transfer his rights there to a democratically elected Belgian government – the minimum compromise uniting most people, since it would at least put an end to the excesses of cruelty – became irresistible and overwhelming.

But E. D. Morel, at the height of his fame, had found another cause. While burrowing in London, Paris and Brussels for information about the Congo, and analysing the reticences and evasions of the Foreign Office, he had come across clues to the

existence of diplomatic understandings and secret military agree-
ments tending towards world war, of which the man in the
street knew next to nothing. Morel began to lead a campaign,
no less cogent but much less popular, against secret diplomacy:
for 'effective national control over our foreign policy'.

'Europe after 2000 years of Christianity', he declared in 1912
at Birkenhead, where he had been invited to stand as Liberal
candidate, 'is spending annually £400,000,000 and training
five millions of the flower of her manhood, not to improve society,
not to ensure a more equitable distribution of socially earned
wealth, not to fight poverty and preventable diseases, but to
kill men, and to break the hearts of women.'

Standing at Morel's side later in Birkenhead, Walter Runciman,
then a Minister, made this solemn declaration on behalf of the
British Cabinet: 'Let me say in a most categorical way, we have
no secret understanding with any Foreign Powers, which would
involve us in a European war.' E. D. Morel, an honest man
himself, accepted this assurance. For the time being, he too was
duped. In August 1914, war was declared on Germany.

Morel did not like being lied to. While most of his contemporaries were at once swept away into a wild patriotic enthusiasm,
he chose his ground carefully. 'The sole responsibility for the
war', he declared publicly, 'cannot in justice be wholly imputed
to Germany.' Morel had two motives for making this point,
and sticking to it. First, and characteristically, it was true. But
secondly, and with uncanny foresight, Morel saw, and had said
so as early as 1915, that a general belief in German war guilt
would lead to such hard peace terms being imposed as to make
inevitable yet another world war, later on.

For his obstinate refusal to let all the blame for the war be
heaped on Germany, E. D. Morel was turned into a newspaper
bogey. His foreign birth was itself suspicious. He was 'in German
pay' and 'the tool of the Kaiser'.

Morel was keeping in touch with wartime Africa, and the
conclusion he drew in 1917, in his *Africa and the Peace of Europe*,
makes all the previous century's talk of civilizing or Christianizing
Africa ring hollow: 'Native tribes have been dragooned or
suborned into taking sides with this or that belligerent, inter-tribal

warfare, with all its crude horrors, has been revived, on a far more comprehensive scale. Devastation, massacre and ruin have characterized the importation of European animosities into primitive Africa.'

On 21 August 1917, for a technical breach of censorship regulations which had only been in force eight days – he had sent an autographed copy of *Africa and the Peace of Europe* to the French writer Romain Rolland, then in Switzerland – E. D. Morel was arrested and refused bail. His solicitor, threatened with the loss of 'considerable and legitimate business interests', threw up the case. Morel was given six months in Pentonville ('on my right was a thief,' he wrote, 'on my left a man who had raped a child of tender years'). 'The prosecution not only wanted to suppress opinion,' explained Lord Courtney, 'but to lock up in silence anyone who could form an opinion they would like to suppress.'

Other good men besides E. D. Morel were in gaol that year.

11 Ethics Are Pity

'It is my belief, O Christ! that the conquest of the Holy
Land should be attempted in no other way than as Thou
and Thy Apostles undertook to accomplish it – by prayer
and love.' *Ramon Lull (d. 1315)*

'We were so happy before the whites arrived.
We would like to kill the white man who has made us
   work,
But the whites have a more powerful fetish than ours.'
*Bearers' song, noted by a Roman Catholic missionary in
the Congo, 1888*

'Civilization does not begin with reading and writing,
but with manual labour.' *Albert Schweitzer*

'Manual work does not mean time taken from prayer,
but time given to prayer.' *Charles De Foucauld*

During 1901, an anti-clerical government in France
suppressed the religious orders there, and confiscated their
property. In 1917, a conveniently large and empty monastery
in the French Pyrenees, called Garaison (a name derived from
guérison = healing) was put to use as an internment camp. The
place was cold, since the monks' cells were not designed to be
heated, but the best was made of the rations provided, since the
cooks interned in the camp had previously worked in Paris
hotels. Internment was used for aliens and suspects – for all who
might not be wholehearted in the war. In 1917 – the year of the
French mutinies on the western front, and of the anti-war
upsurge on the Russian front – anyone whatever, as the government saw it, who had the misfortune not to be French, might
well be a danger.

One day a crowd of new prisoners arrived from the Sahara,
men wearing a white burnous and a red skull-cap: they were
those White Fathers who were not born French. Some internees

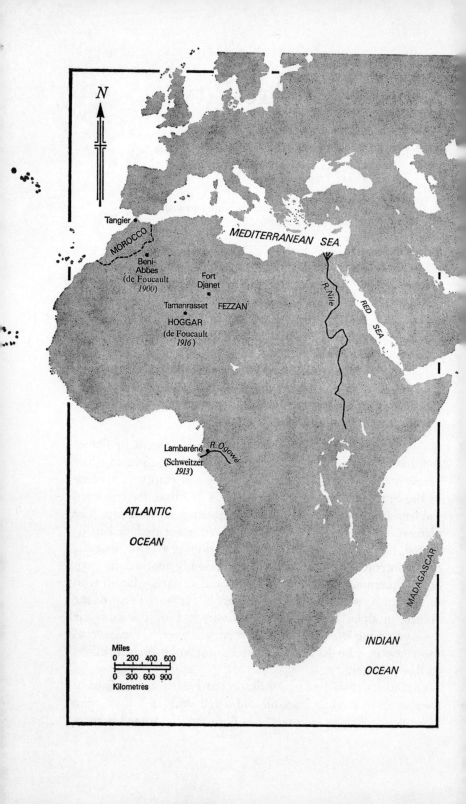

had married French wives. Their children, who had grown up speaking nothing but French, were also interned.

The monastery of Garaison soon became a microcosm of that authentic European civilization which the war – said to be waged in defence of civilization – was so rapidly smashing to pieces. There were men learned in every discipline of scholarship, and practitioners in every art. Musicians had brought their instruments. 'One needed no books in the camp. For everything, there were men with specialized knowledge.' The men least disturbed by the fact of imprisonment turned out to be the sailors: 'Life on board ship had taught them how to pass the time together.' But craftsmen with no tools of trade to hand were ill-at-ease; 'the worst sufferers were the artisans, thus condemned to idleness.'

Late in that year arrived a heavily built man with a square, strongly marked face, tired eyes, a heavy moustache, a shock of hair, spectacles. The order for his imprisonment had been given at the same time as the others, but he had come a long way: from the French Congo. He had broad, muscular hands, marked by manual labour. He was a fourfold doctor, in medicine, philosophy music and theology. On the voyage up from the Congo he had not been allowed to write, so he had kept tedium at bay by learning by heart some of Bach's Fugues. As he came into the camp, the sergeant of the guard tried to confiscate the copy he was carrying of Aristotle's *Politics*. It was forbidden to bring political books into Garaison.

Albert Schweitzer kept busy in his imprisonment. He was allowed to look after the sick prisoners. He drew out an organ keyboard on a table-top, and practised Bach. Quietly, almost furtively, he contrived in holes and corners to work on his *Philosophy of Civilization*. He had begun to think about this book on 5 August 1914, when first arrested in the hospital he ran at Lambaréné in the Congo.

Unluckily for him, Schweitzer had been born in Alsace, a French province which since France's defeat in the Franco-Prussian War had been forcibly incorporated in Germany: this made him technically an enemy alien. He had been a student of music in Paris, of philosophy in Berlin, and the principal of a theological college in Strasburg, which in those days was not only a midway point between France and Germany geographically, but a place where Latin and Teutonic cultures met and mingled.

Schweitzer wrote with equal ease in French and German, and had published original works in both languages, though he was willing enough to admit that in the privacy of his own mind, he counted numbers and dreamed in the dialect of Alsace.

In 1916, in Alsace, his mother had been 'knocked down and killed by cavalry horses on the road'. Günsbach, the village where his father had long been pastor, was near the front line, and often shelled. Schweitzer, when he mentions this, makes no great point of particularizing whether the horses and guns were German or French.

Here then, kept prisoner in Garaison, was a man who bore, personally and at every moment, the full burden of this war. He was a minister of religion; his faith was in crisis, too. 'Religion is not a force,' he wrote afterwards. 'The proof? The war. When war had broken out, religion capitulated. It became mobilized. In the war, religion lost its purity, and lost its authority. The one victim of defeat was religion.'

Albert Schweitzer had become a Protestant theologian after a century in which modernists and textual critics, most of them German, had managed to reduce not only the divinity or the historical existence but even the literary character of Jesus, vivid in the gospels, to a paper-thin shadow. To move his own thought a step or two onwards from this travesty of belief, Schweitzer had been obliged to hack a way through a thorn-forest of arid but enormously thorough erudition. The thesis for his medical doctorate, for instance, after he had qualified as a physician, had been to disprove, medically, that Jesus (let us assume he existed) had not in fact been what the cleverest modern psychologists were beginning with an almost audible snigger to argue: a paranoiac.

In March 1918 – to the annoyance of the commandant at Garaison, who very much wanted to keep the services of his conscientious and hard-working camp doctor – Albert Schweitzer was transferred to another internment camp, at St-Rémy, in Provence, for Alsatians only. Here, at last, he was allowed to hold Sunday services. The camp had previously been a lunatic asylum.

When Schweitzer went into the room where he was to bunk, it occurred to him that the stove in the corner looked strangely familiar. He had seen that iron stove before, in a painting. This was van Gogh's old room.

Albert Schweitzer had begun to play the organ at eight, as soon as his legs could reach the pedals. His passion for Bach and his professional study of theology went on thereafter side by side, each in turn attacked with a passionate thoroughness which would have worn out any ordinary man. As a conscript in 1894, Schweitzer carried his Greek Testament with him on manoeuvres, so that while soldiering he could work towards a scholarship on the Synoptic Gospels which would give him freedom for study: £60 for six years.

In a dumb, implacable way – hardly seeing at times, one feels, where he was going – with the brain of a scholar but the tenacious perseverance of a craftsman or a peasant, he proceeded to organize in his own mind his hostility to those men of vast scholarship but less heart than himself, who – like the followers of the *philosophes* and the Darwinists – had tried their best in the nineteenth century to disintegrate religion.

Schweitzer tracked the men he mistrusted back to their philosophical origins: to Kant who, when the ideas of the French Revolution were in the air, postulated a moral law, but, in the philosophical fashion of the time, avoided drawing a religious conclusion. And to Hegel, Prussia's officially esteemed philosopher, who saw the State as Reason incarnate, and whose principle, 'All that is real is rational; all that is rational is real,' has served to justify the denial of scope to man's free will, and as a convenient argument for those state structures which in our own time have made use of extermination camp and gulag. 'On the night of 25 June 1820,' Schweitzer was to observe of Hegel's epigram, 'when that sentence was written, our age began, the age which moved on to the world war – and which perhaps some day will end civilization.'

Schweitzer's own religious beliefs, what remained of them – in the end his religious view was defined by a severe critic as 'a peculiar mixture of agnosticism and animistic pantheism' – had

K

been thought unorthodox even when he taught theology. There were always men on the other side of the table who regarded him as scarcely Christian. In 1905 he had thrown up his brilliant career as Bach scholar, organist and theologian, to start again at the bottom of the ladder as a medical student. His plan was to go out to the Congo as a medical missionary.

The Paris Evangelical Missionary Society, which had appealed for men, was so taken aback by Schweitzer's unconventional beliefs that they accepted him only on condition that he healed the sick but did not preach. Even so, one member of the committee felt obliged to resign. This ban quite suited Schweitzer. 'I wanted to be a doctor that I might be able to work without having to talk. For years I have been giving myself out in words.'

Schweitzer later formed a poor opinion of black intellectuals who, having achieved an education, were no longer willing to work with their hands. His first consulting room, at Lambaréné on the Ogowé river, had been in an old fowl-coop. A medical mission had been started there as long ago as 1876 by an American Dr Nassau, but the law now required that all instruction be given in French, so the Paris Society took charge.

Schweitzer was besieged by sick people even before the seventy packing cases of supplies which he and his wife had brought out with them were emptied. They had to start from scratch. In their first nine months, they treated two thousand patients. 'Pain is a more terrible lord of mankind than death,' Schweitzer declared, as he contemplated this morass of suffering into which he had landed. The local diseases were malaria, sleeping sickness, dysentery, elephantiasis, heart disease, hernia, ulcers, and the venereal diseases introduced by Europeans. There was, however, no cancer or appendicitis.

Most of the local Congolese were away cutting *okoumé* wood for the local concessionaire. The French in their part of the Congo were imitating Leopold's profitable concession system. When the villagers were taken off to cut wood, crops were neglected and there was a risk of famine. That autumn – the autumn of 1913 – Schweitzer managed to put up a corrugated-iron building twenty-six feet by thirteen feet, with a palm-leaf roof, which served for consulting room, operating theatre, and dispensary, with bamboo huts around for the patients. Schweitzer's wife had trained as a nurse, so as to go out with him, and she served as his anaesthetist, but the Congo wrecked her health. She shared his imprisonment but when Schweitzer went back to the Congo after the war – there was an embargo on the return of German missionaries until 1924 – he had to leave her behind.

The families of the sick paid in food when they had it to give – bananas, eggs, poultry, or the money to buy other patients rice. From the poor and old, Schweitzer took nothing. He found that here, in Africa, he must always tell his patients the truth, without reservation. For them, death was natural. 'They were far more interested in the elementary questions about the meaning of life and the nature of good and evil', he reported, 'than I had supposed.' He was able, in fact, to preach without speaking.

After Johann Sebastian Bach's death his music had been all but lost to sight for nearly a century, until Mendelssohn's enthusiasm restored it to the concert programme. Mendelssohn, leafing through the manuscripts in the Royal Library of Berlin when a musically precocious boy of twelve, had come across the score of the St Matthew Passion. The enormous thoroughness of German musical scholarship then recovered, edited and published those texts which had not been irredeemably lost. But when Schweitzer began studying the organ in Paris, Bach's music was played by orchestras more elaborate than he had written for, or were sung for mixed choirs when he had written for the male voice. His organ music was usually played too fast, on modern factory-made organs, where air at high pressure enabled larger pipes to be done away with, but at the expense of the tone.

Before he left for Africa, Schweitzer was the first man, both as scholar and as instrumentalist, to master Bach's art in its entirety. This, for him, had meant also mastering the art of organ-building. He remarked, characteristically, 'The struggle for the good organ is part of the struggle for the truth.'

'Music was an act of worship, with Bach,' he wrote. 'Bach's real religion was mysticism. His whole thought was transfigured by a wonderful serene longing for death.' Schweitzer's *Art of Organ Building*, like his advocacy of playing Bach's music in the way the composer had in mind, slowly, thoughtfully, simply, without modern bravura, had put Schweitzer even before he left for the Congo into a radical opposition, at least in this one profound respect, to the spirit of his time. He was already beginning to detach himself from its dominant and unquestioned values.

The decision, at the age of thirty, of this brilliant and already celebrated young man to study medicine and go out to the Congo was taken in October 1905, at the height of the campaign against King Leopold. Protestant missionaries were not by this time made enthusiastically welcome in the Belgian Congo. Schweitzer went to Gabon, in the French Congo, and after qualifying he raised money by giving concerts. He left in 1913, with enough money to keep Lambaréné going for a year. At a reception after his last concert in Paris, Schweitzer had overheard gossip from members of the Russian embassy. They were saying that war was certain, as soon as Russia had completed her strategic railways in Poland.

On 5 August 1914, Dr Schweitzer and his wife, at work in the rudimentary little corrugated-iron hospital they had built, were told by the colonial authorities that since Alsatians were legally Germans, they were now prisoners of war. They must therefore have nothing more to do with their patients. Instead, they must obey the black soldiers sent to guard them. The concessionaire's timber trade came abruptly to an end. The local Congolese were conscripted as bearers, and sent off to serve in the war against the Germans in the Cameroons, where they died like flies. 'Europeans kill each other out of cruelty,' one of them declared to Schweitzer, 'and because they don't want to eat the dead.' To them, the doctor's imprisonment was incomprehensible, and so was the war. 'Why don't they have a palaver, and stop it?'

Soon after his arrest, Schweitzer began work on his *Philosophy of Civilization* – 'thinking and writing with deepest emotion as I thought of those who were lying in the trenches'. He admitted to himself that as long ago as 1899 he had doubted the reality of progress, and mistrusted power politics. 'The catastrophe of civilization started from a catastrophe of *Weltanschauung* –

world-view,' he wrote, and laboriously, thoroughly, with appalling and bewildering erudition, he began to search for a world principle more valid than that which had dominated the life of his time, and issued in world war.

By the end of the year, since there was no other doctor for hundreds of miles around, the Schweitzers were allowed to go back to work in their hospital, his old music professor, Widor, having spoken up for him in Paris. In September 1915, Schweitzer was travelling in a riverboat to a patient 160 miles away, and sharing the native cooking-pot on deck. 'When at sunset we were making our way through a herd of hippopotamuses, there flashed through my mind, unforeseen and unsought, the phrase, "Reverence for life".'

Schweitzer – simple and self-evident as it might now appear – had found his thread in the labyrinth, leading him through the wilderness of philosophical and theological learning, much of it tending to paralyse belief and deaden faith, in which he and his German Protestant contemporaries had been lost. Schweitzer's simple principle was, thereafter, to accept 'as being good, to preserve life, and as being evil, to destroy life, to injure life, to repress life'. Of course, there were paradoxes: as a physician contending with tropical disease, Schweitzer was, as he wryly admitted, 'a mass murderer of bacteria', though maimed animals and birds were welcome at Lambaréné. In fact once his thought had become simplified under the stress of war, instead of explicating his compassion, he lived it.

Then in September 1917 came the order condemning the Schweitzers to internment in France. While waiting for their steamer, *Afrique*, to sail, Schweitzer to everyone's astonishment worked on the beach with the black longshoremen, helping them roll two-ton hardwood logs. The Father Superior of the Catholic Mission came on board *Afrique*, as they were about to sail for Bordeaux, brushing aside the soldiers when they tried to stop him, exclaiming to them, 'You shall not leave this country without my thanking you for all the good you have done it.'

Men shaken by the blood-letting of 1914–18 looked around between the wars for explanations, for remedies and for prophecies. But all such theories – Leninism, fascism, the economics of the welfare state – were in those pure and simple and bewildered days not so much ideas to weigh and appraise, the good against the bad, as causes to fight for with passion. In the same way, for those Protestants who in wartime had lost all but a remnant of their faith, Albert Schweitzer's voice, though more modest and less apocalyptic, was also significant. He had his vogue as a prophet of the times, though to many people, even then, the answers he was giving did not seem very useful or complete.

Yet when organized religion, after compromising itself in the war, was under a cloud, Albert Schweitzer gave reassurance. His immense culture, his unassailable reputation as a musician, his first-hand experience as a doctor in the jungle – all these were taken into account by those who paid attention to the very simple answers this very complicated man now offered to a world which was becoming almost inexplicable. 'Ethics are pity. All life is suffering. The will-to-live which has attained to knowledge is therefore seized with deep pity for all creatures.' By actively doing good, therefore, one might 'step for a moment out of the incomprehensible horror of existence'.

When in Europe, Albert Schweitzer raised money for Lambaréné by writing books and by organ recitals. The hospital there became larger and more efficient, very well known and, as it were, a place, for others, of mental pilgrimage. For many good people, Lambaréné functioned in their imaginations as a material reassurance – a place where the common perplexities about science and religion, war and peace might be reconciled in simple action. Albert Schweitzer himself at last became what he can hardly have willed: the lay saint of the welfare worker, or of the kind of idealist who in our own day is found running a programme of aid in a developing country – people, that is, whose personal decision has been to do good effectively in an organized way. After the arguments, disappointments and shocks which have pulled apart their faith, this for many people is all they have left of religion, and the good they do, of course, is not to be despised.

But in opting for the life he appeared to advocate, of practical usefulness, such admirers perhaps did not always recognize in

Albert Schweitzer a dimension of thought which he shared with some of the French and most of the German peasants of his time – whom, emotionally, he often resembles. Individual compassion is always essential, but the state might help, too: the state, after all that had been said and done, was benevolent. Schweitzer was not one of those Christians, today in a minority, who look for little good from the state, or doubt if the good it sets out to do will ever have the result intended.

In his *The Relation of the White to the Coloured Races* (his title may now make the sensitive wince, fashions in phraseology having changed) Schweitzer lays down briefly and brilliantly a theme of this book: 'The independence of primitive or semi-primitive peoples is lost when the first white man's boat arrives with powder or rum, salt or fabrics. The chiefs begin to sell their subjects for goods.' Having put his finger on the origins of the problem, Schweitzer continues,' Independence has then already been lost, in the commercial advance of which the political colonization must be a corrective. I do not believe at all in the educative value of forced labour. The rights of man are a direct function of the normal organization of society. We have therefore to create a social organization and economic conditions in which the native can flourish face to face with Western Commerce . . . possessing houses, fields, orchards, workshops and the requisite capacity to create and use them.' This went little further than the familiar pre-war theory, shared by Morel and the Quakers, of 'native rights'. Schweitzer expected some state power or other to bring about these changes. Others – not the people themselves, those directly concerned – would create 'a social organization and economic conditions' for 'the native'.

The long and fatal association of Christian missionaries with the powers of this world betrayed even Albert Schweitzer as soon as he had to express himself in words instead of deeds. He tried to give credibility to the paternalism of the very state structures which he sensed in his profounder moments were neither rational nor real.

Charles Eugène de Foucauld was born in Strasburg, Alsace, seventeen years before Albert Schweitzer, when the province was still part of France, so his nationality was never in doubt. He was legally French and, moreover, a descendant of Bertrand de Foucauld, who died at the battle of Mansourah, on crusade with Saint Louis. Another forbear was Armand de Foucauld, a priest who at a crisis of the French Revolution had been taken hostage with many other aristocrats. After a mock trial, the unlucky ones were taken out and systematically chopped to pieces – piled up in a huge heap of gobbets of meat in the public square by the respectable and earnestly Jacobin members of the Paris Butchers' Guild: the September Massacres.

De Foucauld grew up as you might expect – patriotic, romantic, and mistrustful both of anti-clerical politicians and of the progress they claimed to represent. In his teens at Nancy, in the lycée, de Foucauld lost his religious faith. The Franco-Prussian war was not long over. Alsace had been forcibly incorporated into Germany, and his parents and only sister were recently dead. He was a lazy schoolboy, of less than average height, gluttonous and sceptical. In 1876 he just scraped into St Cyr near the bottom of the list, but almost failed the medical examination on account of 'premature corpulency'.

At the cavalry school at Saumur, where he went in 1878, de Foucauld played ducks and drakes with his fortune by giving extravagant dinners and playing cards for high stakes. He was often in trouble. As a young lieutenant of hussars, he was sent off to Sétif, in Algeria. He took his mistress with him, and passed her off as his wife. When ordered to send her away, de Foucauld refused, and resigned his commission. But the following year a marabout – a holy man – at Bu-Amama stirred the Algerians there to rise up yet again against the French. Charles de Foucauld rejoined his regiment and fought the campaign. His conduct as an officer was excellent. He even became studious, carrying a volume of Aristophanes in his pocket when he went into action. When the fighting ended, he was twenty-four.

Again de Foucauld resigned from the army, but this time stayed on in Algiers, studying Arabic. From Oscar Maccarthy, the keeper of Mustapha Pasha's library and the European who knew most about the Sultanate of Morocco, he learned all he could about this mysterious, forbidden country, with its ten million inhabitants. In those days, for a Frenchman to be found in the interior of Morocco would cost him his life.

Eccentric young officers of a romantically adventurous disposition are often nobbled as spies. A year later, disguised as Rabbi Joseph Aliman, a Jewish physician from Syria on his way to visit relatives in Morocco, Charles de Foucauld crossed the border, in company with another Jew, Mardochée, an alchemist and one-time Sahara trader who had been born in Morocco, and for pay – 600 francs for his family, another 600 if he got back alive – would act as de Foucauld's guide, despite the huge risk.

De Foucauld wore a Turkish waistcoat, a jellabah, a red cap, a black silk turban; in Tangier, before moving into the dangerous interior, he grew lovelocks. But besides changing his outward appearance, he managed to empty himself of the French officer, with all his habitual gestures, and simulate so well the role of a travelling Syrian rabbi that he could talk with other alchemists and even, in Tlemcen, enter the synagogue, yet not give himself away.

De Foucauld's long journey could be described as exploration, but since France was then making plans for the eventual conquest of Morocco, the more exact word would be espionage. He tramped the inland roads with a two-inch-square notebook in his left hand, the stub of a pencil in his right, noting at turns the new compass bearing, estimating the rise and fall of altitude with a barometer hidden inside his cloak. At night, on the pretence of going out to pray, he would take stellar observations with a sextant. He made discreet contact with Moroccan notabilities discontented with the Sultan and sympathetic to France.

Yet he was in another and in some ways more attractive world than France – an older, more frugal and more honourable world, where all that he liked least in modern France had not yet entered. Muslim society impressed him. The men might care little for their wives, but they loved their children. They were loyal to their friends, and de Foucauld was struck by the dutiful earnestness of their daily prayers. After eleven months of loneliness, dissimulation and danger, the length of the roads in the Moroccan interior of which the French military authorities

L

possessed exact knowledge had been doubled. De Foucauld went back to Paris, a celebrity. He was given the gold medal of the Société de Géographie. His book, *La reconnaissance au Maroc*, made him at once a lion of fashionable society.

In Paris, de Foucauld underwent a spiritual crisis, brought on partly by the contrast between the traditional, almost mediaeval Islamic society into which, stripping away his own personality, he had so recently plunged, and this sudden notoriety in a pleasure-loving Paris society of which he already had misgivings. He would come back from salon or dinner-party to his fashionable apartment, change into Arab dress, and sleep on the floor in his burnous. He wondered if marriage might be a solution. He seriously considered turning Muslim, but on reflection decided that as a religion it was 'too material'. He read hard, wrestling with the philosophers.

At this crisis in his life, de Foucauld was so fortunate as to meet with an exceptional priest, a man of great intellect simply expressed, who, sitting in his study with his cat on his knees, crippled as he was with rheumatism, would answer de Foucauld with such apparently obvious remarks as, 'One does much less good by what one does or says than by what one is,' which went straight home to his listener's predicament. The priest spoke of 'gaining happiness by abstaining from pleasure', and de Foucauld, contrasting his previous experience as soldier and explorer with his present life in self-indulgent Paris, became convinced this was true. 'The moment I knew that God existed, I knew I could not do otherwise than live for him alone.'

'Chastity became my delight and my heart's desire,' he wrote later of this winter in which he recaptured his boyhood faith. 'The devil's power is too great in an unchaste soul for the truth to enter in.' De Foucauld left for the Holy Land, rode over Galilee on horseback, celebrated Christmas in Bethlehem. The country was in those days under Turkish rule, and in appearance had changed very little since antiquity.

De Foucauld was a man of vivid fancy – 'tormented', someone later described him, 'by an overflowing imagination'. The turn he took next, on 14 January 1890, would have been less surprising at the time of the Crusades than for a man in the late nineteenth century, with all fashionable Paris at his feet: he became a monk, choosing the severest order, the Trappists. De Foucauld's chief condemnation of the world he had turned his back upon was its treatment of the poor.

As a postulate at La Trappe, de Foucauld was given a broom and told to sweep out: he had to confess, ruefully, that he did not know how; but manual labour in silence soon delighted him. De Foucauld was described by his superiors as 'ready to help, but excessive in austerity'. Eventually he went as a monk to Akbes in Syria, where the Trappists had improvised a monastery – buildings of cob and thatch inside a thorn hedge – against the day when an anti-clerical government might drive them out of France. The monks worked silently in the fields, kept livestock, looked after orphans. They had no choice but to look on help-lessly in 1894, when the Sultan of Turkey winked his eye at an enormous massacre of Christian Armenians: in a few weeks, 140,000 of their Armenian neighbours were dead.

Life in Akbes was as severe as most men seeking austerity could have wished, but de Foucauld, though cheerfully accepting the penitential discipline, was not quite content. He had become preoccupied by the vision of founding a new religious order, which might correspond to the needs of the exploited in the modern world: 'To lead the life of Our Lord as closely as possible, living solely by the work of their hands, without accepting any gift, possessing nothing, giving to all who ask, claiming nothing, stinting themselves as much as possible, scattered above all through infidel and neglected lands.' A highly intelligent, observant and compassionate man, de Foucauld wanted to abstract himself from a society which worshipped money, possessions, profit and power, and by deliberate renunciation assimilate to the victims of society: the poor. The prior of the Trappists later described de Foucauld as one who 'can do every-thing but perhaps he cannot follow direction, if it is too narrow'. After stipulating two years theology for him in Rome, the Trappists when the time came for him to take his final vows were wise enough to let de Foucauld go: he wanted to live as a solitary. In Rome he took two vows on his own account, of perpetual chastity, and never to own more than the poorest workman.

He went eventually to Nazareth, and in 1897 became an outside servant for the Poor Clares there. He slept in a hut six feet long, on a board propped on trestles, with a stone for a pillow. He dug the garden, mended the wall, swept the chapel, served mass, all with 'no papers other than my passport'. During Lent he lived on two slices of bread a day: 'Blessed are the poor; that is the beatitude I want.'

In August 1900, de Foucauld left the Holy Land, with a breviary and a basket of food, travelling fourth class, having begun at last to see his own way ahead. In May 1901 he was ordained priest. He secured permission – not easily granted – from the French government and the army, as well as from his religious superiors, to go to North Africa. Anticlericalism was at its height. The religious orders were being expelled from France. 'The remembrance of my companions, who died without the sacrament and without a priest, in the expedition in which I took part against the Bu-Amamas, urges me strongly to set out for the Sahara.' There were then a dozen missionaries in the Sahara – White Fathers – in a territory seven or eight times the size of France.

The Superior-General of the White Fathers was now that same Father Livinhac who a quarter of a century before had led the first Catholic missionaries, on donkey-back, to the court of King Mtesa, in Uganda. De Foucauld's confessor wrote, re-assuringly to Livinhac, to say that he was 'a hard instrument for tough work'. A Trappist monk at Staouëli confidentially informed Commandant Lacroix, author of La pénétration Saharienne, sometime comrade-in-arms of de Foucauld's and now Governor of Algeria, 'You can rely on him as a perfect instrument of pacification and moralization. He will do yonder on a small scale what the great cardinal [Lavigerie] did in Tunis for French influence.'

Other men from La Trappe were not, however, to be sent to join de Foucauld – though Trappists engage in arduous missions – because in the words of their Abbot, who evidently knew his man, 'The intensity of mind he imposes on himself and wishes to impose on his disciple might drive his disciple mad before he had been killed with the excess of austerities.' Though the governor of Algeria was being semi-officially urged to look on him as an 'instrument of pacification', de Foucauld's own expressed intention was to help French soldiers perform their religious duty, by setting up a small oratory near some desert garrison, 'and *above all* to sanctify the infidel population by bringing into their midst Jesus, present in the most Blessed Sacrament.'

De Foucauld went south into the desert very modestly equipped, with cloth for a tent, the necessary furniture for celebrating mass, sacks for a carpet, a bucket and fifty metres of rope for a well. He began work at Beni Abbes, in an oasis of 8000 palm trees not far from the border between Algeria and Morocco where a small French garrison had been established. On average it rained there one day a year. De Foucauld built himself a chapel of sun-dried bricks with a palm-leaf roof, and the local Muslims were so impressed with the holy man that, though pilfering was rife in Beni Abbes, the enclosure where he lived was used as a sanctuary, where property could safely be left unwatched. In a corner of his garden de Foucauld, who always anticipated a violent end to his mission and looked death in the face like a soldier, had dug and blessed his own grave.

He slept six hours a night, divided by one hour of vigil. Religious observance in the army of an anticlerical French government was never made easy but, as one soldier serving in Sidi Abbes later wrote, 'He used to say Mass when it suited us. If you asked him to say it at four in the morning, or at noon, he would always say yes. And what a Mass! When he said the *Domine non sum dignus* it was in such a tone that you wanted to weep with him.'

There were many slaves in the oasis. De Foucauld borrowed money to redeem them. He visited the sick and fed the poor – on one day alone, seventy-five poor people came to his hermitage gate with one need or another. He lived on bread and water, at a cost of seven francs a month: in those days, a dollar. Hearing of this, his confessor wrote to him warningly, 'Possess your own soul; do not cut yourself down too much; eat a little.' He was given ten francs more, to spend on dates and fruit. A cask addressed to him arrived soon after. The soldiers optimistically took it to be sacramental wine, but it was a bell for his chapel belfry.

In 1903, de Foucauld began to think about moving away from Beni Abbes – a relatively easy place, as he judged these matters – and beginning again further south, in the mountainous, turbulent, dangerous Touareg country. The Hoggar Touareg, numbering 4500, had just submitted to France. To his confessor, de Foucauld had written, asking, 'Should I not glorify God more by worshipping him as a solitary?'

For an imaginative man of military breeding and ascetic temperament, with a love of the desert and a romantic passion for the epoch of the Crusades, there could hardly in the early twentieth century have been a closer identification possible anywhere than that of Charles de Foucauld with the Touareg. They were a dignified and talented warrior race, who from the high plateau of their mountain homeland had long dominated the caravan routes of the southern Sahara. Up in their mountains the temperature was cooler; there were trees in the ravines.

Touareg civilization was reminiscent of early feudal society in Europe, from the time of the *Chanson de Roland* to the first Provençal troubadours. A Touareg aristocracy, poor in material things and sometimes going hungry, but witty, intelligent, brave and intensely proud, lived off a surplus scratched for them in the dry valleys of their high terrain either by slaves or by *harradin* – black freedmen with no civil rights.

When not away raiding for plunder on their racing camels, the Touareg passed their time fencing with their long, cross-hilted swords, or inventing epigrams, or declaiming their own poetry, or in amusing conversation. Black slaves did all their domestic work. They would travel a hundred miles to hear a witty woman of their own class sit under the rock or tree which was a known venue for an *ahâl*, and there recite a new poem she had composed, or play on the *imzad*, a one-string fiddle, or engage with them in the formal pleasure of conversation. There were conventions about flirting with her – as there had been once for the troubadours – but their more immediate needs they satisfied with black concubines.

The Touareg are proud-looking, dignified, white-skinned, and have about them something of the air of ancient Egyptians. The men veil their faces up to the eyes with a blue bandage, and they did their fighting in those days with the lance, the long sword, and a shield covered with antelope-skin. Charles de Foucauld found when he got to know them that though they claimed to believe in Allah, they were neither conscientious about saying the five daily ritual prayers of Islam, nor did they celebrate Ramadan, the forty-day Islamic Lent. They were too poor to buy rifles and because of this, in 1904, three of the six independent Touareg clans had yielded to the modern weapons of the French.

Charles de Foucauld arrived among them in a caravan escorted by fifty soldiers, all mounted. He had been offered a horse but refused it, so as 'to save money belonging to Jesus and the poor'. The Touareg saw him for the first time as a small man, on foot, at the dusty tail end of the caravan, in a white robe with a red cross and heart on the breast, his face wrinkled, his eyes sunk with fatigue and penance. His hair and beard he cut for himself, without the aid of a mirror.

They identified him at once as 'a great marabout', though there was no solemnity about it. 'When you are with the Touareg,' de Foucauld explained, 'you must laugh.' Having in mind also the needs of the religious order he hoped some day to found, of Christians who renounced all possessions and worked with their hands, de Foucauld explained how to win over strangers. 'You must first gain their esteem by an exemplary and holy life, then obtain their friendship by kindness, patience and all sorts of little services, small alms, remedies and hospitality – go above all and first of all to the poor, according to the Gospel tradition.' Though slaves were much better treated here than at Beni Abbes, on the question of slavery he would make no concession: 'Their condition is worthy of pity, and their dignity as human beings totally unacknowledged.' The slaves redeemed at de Foucauld's urging were later settled by the French in new villages nearby.

Children born out of wedlock – about a third of all those born – had always been put to death. De Foucauld asked for White Sisters to come out to the Touareg country as nurses, and help save these children, but this was asking too much, even for the most self-sacrificial of nuns.

De Foucauld learned both Tamahak, the spoken Touareg tongue, and the literary language, Tifinar. He began a Touareg dictionary (which, from modesty, he published under a pseudonym), and by Christmas 1904 he had produced a version, in Tamahak, of the four gospels. In 1905 he settled at Tamanrasset, a village in the heart of the Hoggar, amid the Dag-Rali, the principal tribe. 'Tamanrasset with its forty hearths of poor husbandmen', he wrote, 'is very much what Nazareth and Bethlehem may have been, in the time of Our Lord.' He made friends with thirty-five-year-old Musa, chief of the Hoggar Touareg, who had signed a treaty with the French. 'Very intelligent, very open, a very pious Muslim, at the same time ambitious, and loving money, pleasure and honour, like Mahomet, in his eyes the most perfect of men.'

Having managed to dominate the anarchic Hoggar, Musa was beginning to organize life there more strictly, according to Muslim principles. At Tamanrasset he built a mosque. But as Islam took a firmer grip on the minds of the Touareg, they became more anti-French. They had legends about the French: that they ate children, and turned at night into animals. De Foucauld found himself the only Catholic priest in an area of the southern Sahara 1250 miles north and south by 625 miles east and west, with a population of 100,000. Though his presence among the Touareg at least affirmed the confrontation between Christianity and Islam, de Foucauld must have known that in the foreseeable future, anyway, Islam was certain to triumph. In all his time in the Sahara, speaking the language, revered by the people, Charles de Foucauld had so far made only one convert – an old and blind mulatto woman, at Sidi Abbes, whom he had christened Marie.

At Ain-Salah, 450 miles to the north, was stationed the French commander-in-chief of the Saharan Oases, Henri Laperrine, an old brother-in-arms of de Foucauld's. A man with a pale, lean face and a fan-shaped auburn beard, Laperrine too loved the desert way of life, and except on formal military occasions he would dress and eat as did the tribesmen. Laperrine was a pupil of the Dominicans, and the brother of a monsignor: he had as deep an insight as a professional soldier with his duty to perform was likely to have into the real nature of de Foucauld's self-imposed mission. Laperrine had encouraged him to settle in the Touareg country.

Hearing that, by excessive self-denial, the great marabout had made himself ill, Laperrine sent him down three camel-loads of provisions, including sugar and condensed milk. On the strengh of de Foucauld's assurance, he let Musa have some 1874-pattern French army rifles for self-defence. When Laperrine built a small fort, thirty miles off, he wanted to name it Fort de Foucauld, but the priest wisely refused; it was called, instead, Fort Motylinski.

As well as preparing a lexicon of the written language, de Foucauld was collecting an anthology of Touareg poetry ('everybody writes verses'). When Touareg went to war, the opposing poets competed in rivalry as the warriors fought; the greatest poet of the past fifty years had been a woman: Kema ult Amâstân.

Outside Tamanrasset, in the hills, de Foucauld built himself a house, six feet wide and twenty long, which served him both as dwelling and chapel. Across the plateau before him, stony ground diversified by tufts of grass, went a *wadi* – a dried-out river-bed. Behind his back towered the peak of Assekreme, nearly 10,000 feet high. Not far off were the rush huts of some black *harradin*, who in the bottom of the *wadi* managed to grow barley and red peppers. The Touareg had never learned to spin, so de Foucauld, one of whose jobs in the Syrian monastery had been to darn the linen, practised knitting and taught his neighbours.

But de Foucauld's devotion to the Touareg was incomplete – he had been caught on a baited hook. When his old friend Laperrine consulted with the Touareg, de Foucauld acted as his interpreter, squatting on the ground beside the commander-in-chief's stool. Soon, appraising the anti-French feeling which had begun to develop around him, de Foucauld was writing to warn Laperrine that 'if there is a European war, there would probably be risings in the whole South'. In 1910, Laperrine went home on leave, taking Musa and some of the Hoggar noblemen with him. To impress his Touareg guests with the power and scope of France, he showed them gunnery trials at Le Creusot, a thoroughbred stud farm, and the Moulin Rouge: missionary work of a more cynical kind.

In 1912 the French at last established their protectorate over the hitherto independent country, Morocco, which de Foucauld when a young man had spied out and surveyed. When the country was invaded he at first felt a flicker of his youthful enthusiasm: 'I told General Lyautey that he had only to telegraph for me, and I would come directly.' But soon, even amid his romantic mediaeval society in the mountainous heart of the desert, he was discerning more clearly what, in economic terms, a French occupation of Morocco would really signify.

Though for de Foucauld civilization 'consists of two things: education and gentleness', yet in Algiers between 1881 and 1889, French civilization had meant forced sales on harsh terms of fertile soil – later turned into plantations – in the course of which Algerians had lost forty-five per cent of their land. When the speculators also began to enter Morocco, de Foucauld warned, 'If we do not fulfil our duty, if we exploit instead of civilizing, we shall lose everything and our uniting these people will turn against ourselves.' As matters got worse, he reiterated, 'If these unfortunate Muslims see as self-styled Christians unjust and tyrannical speculators, how can they be converted? How can they but hate our holy religion?' All these doubts were to be clarified in war.

The border nearest to the Hoggar country was with Libya, then under Turkish rule, where Italy and Germany had lately begun to intrude as rivals. By 1912, the Italians had defeated the Turks and established a colony near the coast. Inland, however, the militant Islamic missionary sect of the Senussi, with help from Turks and Arabic-speaking Germans, were in revolt against them: the Senussi were preaching a *jehad*, or holy war.

De Foucauld saw clearly enough that pious Muslims who allowed themselves thus to be manipulated were dupes (though he did not apply the same judgement to himself). He was un-cannily accurate in his prediction of the course Arab nationalism would take. 'A national movement will come about, an élite which will have lost all the faith of Islam, but which will keep the label in order to be able to use it to influence the masses. The educated élite, at a time of France's difficulties at home and abroad, will make use of Islam as a lever to rouse the ignorant mass, and

seek to create an independent Muslim African empire. If we
have not been able to make these people French, they will drive
us out. The only means of making them French is for them to
become Christian.' But his solution, if true, was impossible. A
holy war against the French was already being preached. When
he wrote prophetically about the future of Arab nationalism,
August 1914 had already gone by, and the converts so far made
by de Foucauld could be counted on the fingers of one hand.

When war had broken out, what should a Christian do?

De Foucauld seems to have been in no doubt, at least, in his
more superficial reactions, that France was fighting a just war,
though increasingly there were signs of an undertow going in
the opposite direction. He saw Islam as a force which had united
Arabs against the French, not just in the time of modern empires,
but for over a thousand years. Islamic conquest, in its day, had
destroyed Christianity in North Africa – obliterated the heritage
of St Athanasius and St Augustine. The only hope he saw of
Christianity's again striking root in North Africa would be if
France maintained control there. Though the war was evidently
a crisis, for de Foucauld it was not a crisis of belief. He never
questioned that it had to be fought: the war was a crusade.

On 9 September 1914 de Foucauld received 1500 cartridges,
to be handed on to Musa for his 1874-pattern rifles, in case the
Senussi raided that far, or raised the Saharan tribesmen against the
French. The authorities wanted de Foucauld to leave his little
hermitage, and go for safety to Fort Motylinski. Though well
aware that the decision might finish him, de Foucauld decided,
if he were not needed on the Western Front, to stay alone among
the Touareg. His writings show how deliberately he meditated
the probability, if he stayed, of encountering a violent death.
('Remember that you are to die a martyr, despoiled of everything,
stretched out on the earth, naked, unrecognizable, covered with
blood and wounds, killed with violence, and in great pain.')

Laperrine, now a general in France, discouraged de Foucauld's
impulse to volunteer 'at the front, as a chaplain or stretcher bearer'.
Laperrine handled de Foucauld tactfully. Without perhaps his
being fully aware of it, the hermit was an indispensable source

of information, an advanced observation-post. From December 1914 to 16 November 1916, the two friends wrote each other by every mail.

On 21 October 1914, forgetting that the Prussian knights, too, had been a military order, and that Prussia was founded in crusades against the pagan Slavs, who had been reduced after conquest to the status of serfs, de Foucauld remarked, 'This is a war for Europe's independence of Germany. It shows by what barbarians Europe was half-enslaved.' To the Prioress of the Poor Clares he wrote, 'France, in spite of appearances, is still the France of Charlemagne, St Louis and Joan of Arc.'

On 19 November 1915, the hermit was informing General Laperrine that 'the Dehibat post of Tunis is attacked by the Senussi, commanded by officers in khaki uniforms with field-glasses and revolvers (Germans no doubt)'. In January 1916, in a letter to another old friend on the Western Front, General Mazel, he still has no doubts. 'There are many unhappy things in France, but in the present war she is defending the world and future generations against the moral barbarism of Germany. For the first time, I really understand the Crusades.' In April 1916, de Foucauld is warning Laperrine that a thousand Senussi, armed with a field gun and machine-guns, have crossed the Libyan border less than 300 miles away, and are besieging Fort Djanet, where fifty men under a French sergeant are trying to hold them up. At this news Musa prudently sent out patrols, and got ready to move his people into the hills, because these anti-French raiders were likely also to take their revenge on the Hoggar Touareg.

There were, by now, only a handful in Fort Motylinski – thirty native soldiers and four French NCOs, under a subaltern. De Foucauld advised them not to stay cooped up, as a sitting target, but to retreat in good time, as Musa had done, into the mountains, taking with them their munitions and stores. Meanwhile, he turned his hermitage into an ingenious little fort – twenty feet square and sixteen feet high, with bastions at the angles, a dry ditch round it, and a well inside. The walls at the base were bullet-proof: two metres thick. Access was by doors so low that they could only be passed by stooping. The fort was impregnable against rifle fire, and against a rush attack could be defended by one man, lobbing grenades. On the wall of his little fort, de Foucauld raised up a crucifix made of tamarisk branches.

To General Mazel, now commanding the Fifth Army in France, de Foucauld wrote on 1 September 1916, 'When I see my embrasures, I think of the fortified convents and churches of the tenth century. They have given me six cases of cartridges, and 30 Gras rifles, which remind me of our youth.' A fortnight later, he was writing in alarm. 'Our troops are falling back before the Senussi. This retreat before a few hundred rifles is lamentable. There must be (how far up I don't know) some serious error in the command.' Saint and soldier have overlapped and can hardly be distinguished; the confusion is total.

The Senussi had established their headquarters in the Fezzan, just across the Libyan border, where deserters from French native troops and anti-French Touareg warriors from the Azjer clan went to join them. Musa was already up in the mountains, with his flocks and herds. Charles de Foucauld had created for himself a situation in which he would be utterly alone, and in great danger; the undertow was dragging him to his death.

A band of Muslim guerrillas, twenty of them armed with captured Italian repeating-rifles, and including hostile Touareg, moved towards Tamanrasset. Their plan, apparently, was to seize the weapons they knew to be stored in de Foucauld's little fort, and then take the great marabout away with them, as a hostage. They had an active helper in a black ex-slave called El Madani, to whom de Foucauld had been particularly kind, and who had an exact knowledge of his ways.

About forty men altogether moved in to kidnap de Foucauld. They dismounted, hid their camels, and waited for the propitious moment, when the hermit would be expecting a rider from the fort with his mail. El Madani walked up to the low door and knocked, shouting out, 'The postman from Fort Motylinski!' When de Foucauld reached out through the doorway to take the letters, his hand was grasped. He was pulled out bodily, and his arms were tied up behind his back.

What happened next is known. He knelt down and prayed, then sat with his back to the wall, staring in front of him. The hostile Touareg were meanwhile heaping their blessings on

El Madani, the humble and subservient black *harradin*, foretelling the delights he would enjoy in paradise for having so cleverly entrapped 'the marabout of the Rumi'.

They looted the fort, then began to interrogate de Foucauld. They wanted to know about army patrols, they wanted details of an expected military convoy, but they got no answers. They offered to let him escape his doom by reciting the *shehada* – the brief Islamic formula which clinches conversion. De Foucauld refused.

Had de Foucauld left his hermitage unfortified and stayed there, playing no role whatever but that of a solitary monk, it is not altogether unimaginable that the Muslims, respecting him as a holy man, might have spared him; or had they not, his death would have been of another kind. But his known connection with Fort Motylinski, the weapons he had accepted on Musa's behalf, the letters he continually wrote, all were fatal to him. His self-imposed mission – the quixotic attempt to Christianize the hostile Sahara – was now quite clearly at an end for, as the commandant of the fort was to write in his official account, 'at the time, all hearts in the Hoggar had been won over to the cause of our enemies.'

Every wartime compromise that de Foucauld consented to had turned against him. The arms stored in his little fort made it a target that guerrillas were not likely to ignore. His eagerness to greet the postman from Fort Motylinski had trapped him. Now as he sat there, arms tied behind his back, obstinately refusing to answer, towards him on their camels plodded two soldiers, arriving to pay him a friendly visit and deliver his mail.

In an exchange of shots, these soldiers were killed. Amid the fusillade, at point blank range, a Touareg – but not a Hoggar Touareg – put a bullet through Charles de Foucauld's head from behind; the ball entered behind his right ear, and came out through his left eye. Then his body was stripped of its white robe with the red cross and heart, and thrown naked in the ditch.

Martyr, or war-victim? Saint, or spy?

The police of a fiercely independent Algerian Republic, examining with officious suspicion the passport of any European not a tourist, who wishes nowadays to visit the Sahara, will ask with a sudden smile, when hearing the name Tamanrasset, 'Ah – you wish to visit the tomb of your great marabout!' His manly death, though ambiguous in terms of Christian belief, earned Charles de Foucauld the respect of those whom he could never seriously have hoped to convert: the Muslims. Nor would they ever have expected him to side with them against his own countrymen – his co-religionists – or to remain neutral. There are two sides in any crusade, and theirs had always been the other. To this extent, Charles de Foucauld had also been their convert.

Out of the pathos of his strangely mingled thought and life, perhaps the best part has survived. The religious order de Foucauld always had in mind, though viewed by his superiors during his lifetime with a certain mistrust – 'the apparent singularity of the mission to which he believes himself called' – took form between the wars as the Little Brothers of Jesus. A group of five followers came together in France, another in the Sahara – 'living like Christ's poor among the poor of the world, loving all men like brothers' – and soon Little Sisters of Jesus joined in the work. The order was recognized by the Roman Catholic Church in 1936, and by October 1953, 190 brothers were living all over the world in twenty-five fraternities – nine of them in France and Belgium, six in North Africa, three in the Middle East, three in Latin America.

The rule when it began was observed by small groups, because for a small group the practice of poverty and living among the poor was easier. Their apostolate was eight hours' manual work a day – as factory hands, as deep-sea fishermen, in mines and slums. They never accepted alms, and they engaged in no ministry. The Little Brothers of Jesus proposed to evangelize chiefly by example, wherever they might find themselves at work. The rule of never showing racial or intellectual superiority was strict. After working hours, the group would live communally in a small apartment nearby, of which one room would be the chapel, with mass before going to work, vespers at return, and the priest also a wage-earner. They tried to follow Charles de Foucauld's injunction: 'The life of Nazareth can be led anywhere; you must lead it wherever you will be most helpful to your neighbour.' Some of their sayings became celebrated: 'Something we absolutely owe Our Lord is not to be afraid of anything,' or 'Jesus is the Master of the impossible.'

Inevitably, the Little Brothers of Jesus soon found themselves being ground between the upper and nether millstones. To the organized working-class movement – under an intellectual leadership which in the Latin countries of Europe and America has usually been materialist if not Marxist – the Little Brothers of Jesus were perplexing, and probably up to no good. Were they not trying to sanctify the exploitation of man by man? At the same time, some in the church hierarchy were nervous of the way Roman Catholics in France, Italy and Spain, particularly those active in the anti-fascist resistance, had come halfway to meet their non-believing comrades. To them, the Little Brothers of Jesus, and not least their worker-priests, might be dangerous radicals. But here, in our own day, is emerging another kind of missionary – concerned with the poor, the lonely and the exploited.

Methodism in its early origins bore traces of just such a mission-ary intention, though its unspoken objective – or perhaps it would be fairer to say, the actual outcome of its evangelizing – had been to enclose the newly emerging working class in an invisible scaffolding of middle-class values. Will a mission to poor people and wage-earners by those who are themselves poor and work for wages – a mission owing nothing to the state or to the benefactions of the rich – have any different outcome?

The story of missionary endeavour is the stuff of tragedy, of good men trapped in helpless situations, of actions well-meant which led to cruel consequences.

There are two ways of looking at what the missionaries tried to do. One is to say – as those who hold rival world-views commonly do – that their doctrine was hypocritical or unscientific or ineffective, that in so far as Christian missionaries sincerely believed in what they preached, they were wasting their time. But, on present showing, are the alternative world views – science, historical materialism, *Realpolitik* – any less the stuff of tragedy, and any less likely to end in helpless situations and cruel consequences?

Another possible view which may have emerged in the course of this study is that missionary work met a futile or tragic fate whenever it was patronized by those who were bent on ends incompatible with Christian belief – as merchants, colonists, power-hungry soldiers or politicians; that missionary hopes were poisoned by the dew from Caesar's laurel crown. Supposing this to be true, then with Caesarism in the ascendant everywhere across our world, one may reasonably surmise that the Christian church, though persecuted, could again find itself making common cause, as in the earliest days of its history, with Caesar's victims. And this may give it a second chance.

Bibliography

(Publications in London unless otherwise noted)

ANDERSON, C., *To the Golden Shore: The Life of Adoniram Judson* (Boston, 1956)

ANDERSSON, E., *Messianic Popular Movements in the Lower Congo* (Uppsala, 1958)

ANSTEY, R. *Britain in the Congo in the Nineteenth Century* (1962)

Anthropological Society of London (Journal of) (1866)

Anthropological Society of London (Memoirs read before, 1863–1864) (1865)

Anthropology (The Popular Magazine of) (1866)

ASHE, R. P., *Two Kings of Uganda* (1889)
   Chronicles of Uganda (1894)

ASPINALL, A. E., *The British West Indies* (1913)

BARBARY, J., *The Boer War* (1969)

BAZIN, H., *Charles de Foucauld: Hermit and Explorer* (1931)

BEDE: *A History of the English Church and People* (1977)

BENTLEY, W. HOLMAN, *Pioneering in the Congo* (2 vols., 1900)

BLABY, H., *Death Struggles Against Slavery* (1853)

BOUGAINVILLE, L. A. DE, *Viaje Alrededor del Mundo* (Buenos Aires, 1954)

BRIDGES, G. W., *The Annals of Jamaica* (1968)

BRUCE, H., *Life of General Oglethorpe* (New York, 1890)

CAILLOT, A. C. E., *Les Polynésians orientaux au contact de la civilisation* (Paris, 1909)

CANTON, W., *The History of the British and Foreign Bible Society* (5 vols., 1904–1910)

CAREY, W., *An Enquiry into the Obligations of Christians to Use Means for the Conversion of the Heathen* (1792)

CHADWICK, H., *The Early Church* (1967)

CHATEAUBRIAND, F. DE, *Génie du Christianisme* (Paris, 1965)

CLARKE, R. F., *Cardinal Lavigerie and the African Slave Trade* (1889)

CLARKE, W. K. L., *A History of the S.P.C.K.* (1959)

COCKS, F. S., *E. D. Morel: The Man and His Work* (1920)

COLERIDGE, S. T., *On the Constitution of the Church and State* (1972)

COUPLAND, R., *The British Anti-Slavery Movement* (1933)
  East Africa and Its Invaders (Oxford 1956)
  Wilberforce (1923)

CRAGG, G. R., *The Churches in the Age of Reason 1644–1789* (1963)

CRAWFORD, D., *Thinking Black* (1912)

CREIGHTON, L., *G. A. Selwyn, D.D.* (1923)

CRÈVECŒUR, J. H. ST-J. DE, *Letters from an American Farmer* (n.d.)

CUNNINGHAME GRAHAME, R. B., *A Vanished Arcadia* (1901)

CURTIN, P. D., *Two Jamaicas* (Harvard 1955)

DALLAS, R. C., *The History of the Maroons* (1803)

DAVIS, J. (Newbury, C. W., ed.), *The History of the Tahitian Mission 1799–1830* (Cambridge, 1961)

DELACROIX, S., *Histoire universelle des missions Catholiques* (Paris, 1956)

DIDEROT, D., *Le neveu de Rameau et autres textes* (Paris, 1972)

DUFF COOPER, A., *Talleyrand* (1964)

DU PLESSIS, J., *A History of Christian Missions in South Africa* (Cape Town, 1965)

EDWARDS, B., *History of the British Colonies in the West Indies* (2 vols., 1794)

ELDER, J. R. (ed.), *The Letters and Journals of Samuel Marsden 1765–1838* (Dunedin, 1932)

ELLIOT, J. H., *Imperial Spain 1469–1716* (1972)

FERNANDEZ, M. G., *Bartolomé de las Casas* (Seville, 1953)

FINDLAY, G. G., and HOLDSWORTH, W. W., *The History of the Wesleyan Methodist Missionary Society* (5 vols., 1921–1924)

GOODALL, N., *A History of the London Missionary Society 1895–1945* (Oxford, 1954)

GOODWIN, H., *Memoirs of Bishop Mackenzie* (1864)

HANKE, L., *Aristotle and the American Indians* (1959)
  Bartolomé de las Casas (The Hague, 1951)

HARLOW, V. T., *Christopher Codrington 1668–1710* (Oxford, 1928)

HARRISON, J. W., *The Story of the Life of Mackay of Uganda: Pioneer Missionary* (1898)

HERNANDEZ, P., *Misiones de Paraguay: organización social de las doctrinas guaraníes de la Compañía de Jesus* (2 vols., Barcelona, 1913)

HEWITT, G., *The Problems of Success: A History of the Church Missionary Society 1910–1942* (1971)

HINDE, S. L., *The Fall of the Congo Arabs* (1897)

HUONDER, A., 'Jesuit Missions in Paraguay', *Catholic Encyclopaedia* (1911 edn, vol. XII, pp. 688–700)

HUTTON, J. E., *A History of Moravian Missions* (1923)

JEAL, J., *Livingstone* (1973)

JEAN-AUBRY, G., *The Sea Dreamer: Joseph Conrad* (New York, 1957)

LANTERNARI, V., *The Religion of the Oppressed: A Study of Modern Messianic Cults* (1963)

LATOURETTE, K. S., *A History of the Expansion of Christianity* (7 vols., 1937–1945)

LAUNAY, A., *Histoire générale de la Société des Missions Etrangères* (3 vols., Paris, 1894)

LEA, H. C., *The Inquisition in the Spanish Dependencies* (New York, 1908)

LUNN, A., *John Wesley* (1929)

MARTIN, A. D., *Doctor Vanderkemp* (1933)

MATHER, C., *Life and Death of the Renowned Mr John Eliot* (1691)

Missionary Register 1813–1854 (the journal of the Church Missionary Society)

MOFFAT, R., *Missionary Labours* (1842)

MOISTER, W., *A History of the Wesleyan Missions* (1871)

MONTALEMBERT, COMTE DE, *The Monks of the West* (1896)

MOORHEAD, A., *The Fatal Impact* (1975)

MOORHOUSE, G., *The Missionaries* (1973)

MYERS, J. B., *Centenary Volume of the Baptist Missionary Society* (1892)

NEILL, S., *Christian Missions* (1964)

NEWMAN, J. H., *An Essay on the Development of Christian Doctrine* (1974)

NEWTON, J., *Life and Selections from Correspondence* (1855)
Olney Hymns (1872)

NORTHCOTT, C., *David Livingstone: His Triumph, Decline and Fall* (1973)

OLIVER, R., *The Missionary Factor in East Africa* (1952)

OLIVIER, LORD, *Jamaica: The Blessed Island* (1936)

PAGE, J., *The Black Bishop: Samuel Adjai Crowther* (1908)

PARKMAN, F., *The Jesuits in Canada* (1925)

PARRY, J. H., *The Spanish Seaborne Empire* (1973)

PASCOE, C. F., *Two Hundred Years of the S.P.G. 1701–1900* (1901)

PASTELLS, P., *Historia de la Compañía de Jesus en Paraguay* (4 vols., Madrid, 1912)

PATON, J. G., *An Autobiography* (1889)

PERHAM, M., *Lugard: The Years of Adventure 1858–1899* (1956)

PRITCHARD, W. T., *Polynesian Reminiscences* (1866)

PROUT, E., *Memoirs of the Life of the Rev. John Williams* (1843)

RAMSDEN, E., *Marsden and the Missions* (Sydney, 1936)

ROBINSON, C. H., *A History of Christian Missions* (1915)

RUDÉ, G., *Europe in the Eighteenth Century* (1972)

SCHWEITZER, A., *My Life and Thought* (1933)

SEAVER, G., *Albert Schweitzer: The Man and his Mind* (1955)

SLADE, R. M., *English-speaking Missions in the Congo Independent State 1878–1908* (Brussels, 1959)
   King Leopold's Congo: Aspects of the Development of Race Relations in the Congo (1962)

SMITH, W., *William Smith's History of the Province of New York* (Harvard, 1972)

STANLEY, D. (ed.), *The Autobiography of Sir Henry Morton Stanley* (1909)

STANLEY, H. M., *Through the Dark Continent* (2 vols., 1878)
   The Congo and the Founding of its Free State (2 vols., 1885)

STOCK, E., *History of the Church Missionary Society* (4 vols., 1899)

THOMPSON, H. P., *Into All Lands: The History of the Society for the Propagation of the Gospel in Foreign Parts 1701–1950* (1951)

TREVELYAN, G. O., *Life and Letters of Lord Macaulay* (1908)

TUCKER, H. W., *Life of Bishop George Augustus Selwyn* (2 vols., 1879)

TYERMAN, L., *The Life of the Reverend George Whitefield* (1877)

VOILLAUME, R., *Seeds of the Desert: The Legacy of Charles de Foucauld* (1955)

VOLTAIRE, *Romans et contes* (Paris, 1972)

WALKER, S. A., *The Church of England Mission in Sierra Leone* (1847)

WAYLAND, F., *Memoirs of the Life and Labours of the Rev. Adoniram Judson, D.D.* (2 vols., Boston, 1853)

WESLEY, J., *Journal* (vol. I, 1827)

WILLIAMS, E., *Capitalism and Slavery* (1964)

YATE, W., *An Account of New Zealand* (1834)

Index